LEAVING THE WILD

LEAVING THE WILD

THE UNNATURAL HISTORY OF
DOGS, CATS, COWS, AND HORSES

GAVIN EHRINGER

PEGASUS BOOKS
NEW YORK LONDON

LEAVING THE WILD

Pegasus Books Ltd.
148 W 37th Street, 13th Floor
New York, NY 10018

Copyright © 2017 by Gavin Ehringer

First Pegasus Books cloth edition December 2017

Interior design by Maria Fernandez

ISBN: 978-1-68177-556-2

10 9 8 7 6 5 4 3 2 1

Printed in the United States of America
Distributed by W. W. Norton & Company, Inc.
www.pegasusbooks.us

In memory of my mother, Alison, and her favorite dog, Tigger.

Thanks for taking care of everyone.

We miss you!

CONTENTS

INTRODUCTION

D ogs, cats, cows, and horses. Not a day of my adult life has passed when I wasn't either working with them or writing about them.

As a college student, I guided horseback rides on a Colorado guest ranch. Afterward, I became a cowboy and helped care for a herd of more than 350 cows and their calves. I've used stock dogs—Australian shepherds, mainly—in my work, but also competed with them in dog shows and canine Frisbee contests. Barn cats, well, they just came with the territory.

I would go on to become a journalist, writing several thousand magazine articles about domestic animals and the people who bred them, raised them, cared for them, bought them, sold them, raced them, rode them, trained them, and competed with them. Most, like me, adored them, too.

Despite all that, I never stopped to give much thought as to how and why these animals came to live in our homes and barnyards in the first place. Domestication, I assumed, was just something our stone-age ancestors brought about for their own benefit. But my thinking changed when I crossed paths with horse trainer Buck Brannaman.

I met Buck at the Denver National Western Stock Show, a place where domestic animals and people come together in staggering numbers. Over a sixteen-day span, more than 6,500 animals are exhibited there before more than 680,000 visitors.

As anyone who has seen the documentary *Buck* knows, Brannaman is a cowboy straight from central casting. He's a tall, weathered guy with a pale, narrow face shadowed by a flat-brimmed, sweat-stained cowboy hat. If that doesn't ring a bell, Buck was also the inspiration for the fictional character Tom Booker in the Robert Redford film *The Horse Whisperer*. Like Booker, Brannaman has hard, calloused hands, but a tender heart when it comes to horses.

When he's not at his ranch in Wyoming, Buck travels the country giving clinics and demonstrations on natural horsemanship, a Zen-like training philosophy that takes into account life from the horse's perspective. Personally, I think it's wrong to call him a horse whisperer. He's more a horse conversationalist. He pays attention to horses, responding to them in the language they understand—body language.

At Denver, I watched Buck work with a chestnut-colored horse in a small, round pen. It was a colt, just a few years old and fresh off the open range. The animal, which belonged to a mutual acquaintance, had not seen a human at close distance until the day he was rounded up and unloaded on the stock show grounds.

With calm patience, Brannaman walked around the pen, letting the colt run and snort as he moved about. Whenever the horse turned to face him, Buck would step back a foot or two, relieving the pressure and rewarding the animal. In less than ten minutes, the horse turned, faced Buck, and stood still. You could see the colt's body relax and his face soften. He took a tentative step toward the horseman. Buck referred to this as "joining up," but you and I might call it "bonding."

Before the seminar was over, Buck had led the colt around the pen with a loose rope, put a blanket and saddle on him, and even ridden the horse in circles without a bridle. He'd convinced the horse—or rather, the horse had convinced himself—to put trust in a human as his partner and guide. It was a real-time parable.

That day, Buck gave me a gift of wisdom that stuck in my head. He said, "These animals gave up their freedom and their fear of us when they left the wild and came to our campfire. They serve us in many ways. In return, we owe them our care and our understanding."

From that phrase, I conceived the idea for this book.

Leaving the Wild is a book about four common domesticated animals. Each left behind a wild existence in exchange for our care, provision, and protection. Each gives of itself in its own unique ways. I chose *Leaving the Wild* as a title because it implies willfulness on the animals' part. As Buck pointed out, domestication wasn't a one-way street in which people were the only drivers or the only ones who gained something.

Biologist and Pulitzer–prize winning author E. O. Wilson aptly said, "I know of no instance in which a species of plant or animal gives willing support to another without extracting some advantage in return."

Central to the book is this question: "In choosing domestication, what did animals give up, and what did they get?" To find out, I spent a year on the road visiting the places animals lived and the people who shared life with them.

My journey began on Thanksgiving Day at the home of a renowned Colorado dog breeder and lifelong friend. After an ethereal turkey dinner followed by homemade pies, I bid my friends goodbye and climbed up into the cab of my recently-bought motor home. I turned the key and it coughed to life.

As we pulled out onto the highway, my Australian shepherd, Onda, hopped up into the passenger seat and looked out at a vast expanse of farmland and the narrow ribbon of highway. On we drove to see America—from the animals' perspective.

A howling windstorm tried to blow us off the highway all the way to Oklahoma City. Arriving safely, we watched horses that cost more than luxury cars compete for prizes as valuable as houses. From the well-heeled breeders there, we got our first lesson in how human values literally shape animals' lives, for better and worse. Then the road took us west, following traces of historic Route 66.

In Amarillo, Texas, we stopped to pet cattle that had been cloned from steaks—the beginning of our education in animal reproduction technology. Next, we watched a stallion earn $160,000 in a single afternoon, just by donating sperm. In the deserts of New Mexico and Arizona, we passed by dairy barns the size of Costco stores.

In California, we stopped in Anaheim to visit Mickey Mouse— and learn some things about Disneyland's cats. In Carnation, Washington, we took selfies in front of a shrine to the World's Most Productive Milk Cow. Then, we drove back to Colorado for the Denver County Fair—whose motto is "fairly weird." (It was).

Along the way, we watched dog shows, horse shows, cattle shows, and cat shows. We visited pet breeders' homes where animals were born and public shelters where others were killed. We talked to people who fought dogs and people who fought for dogs (and cats, too). We did rounds with veterinarians and ride-alongs with animal control officers. We visited universities and feral cat colonies, and feral cat colonies at universities. And in our downtime, I read research while Onda slept at my feet under my dashboard desktop. He got lots of sleep. The result is the book that you're about to read.

The narrative of the four species in this book is a mixture of natural history, human history, personal experience, and science. Understanding how once-wild animals came to live in our barnyards and under our roofs helps us, I think, to better understand our own place in the world. Their stories are our stories, too.

In some small way, I hope that Leaving the Wild helps us honor our end of the bargain that was struck when these creatures stepped out of the wild to join us at our campfire. For all that they give to us, we owe them our care and, especially, our understanding.

DOGS

To sit with a dog on a hillside on a glorious after-noon is to be back in Eden, where doing nothing was not boring—it was peace.

—Author Milan Kundera

ONE

A WOLF AMONG MEN

Even after hundreds of years of selective breeding, it would be hard if not impossible to produce a chimpanzee who could live with humans and have anything like such a good relationship as we have with our dogs.

—Primatologist Jane Goodall

Wherever we've gone, our dogs came along. Sometimes, they got there first.

On November 3, 1957, the Soviet Union astonished the world with the announcement that a little street dog named Laika had become the first cosmonaut to orbit the Earth. Sadly, Laika never made it home, giving her life for the cause of manned space exploration.

Dogs were the first animals to trade their wild existence for our care, protection, and pet food bowls. And while that arrangement hasn't been great for every dog (Laika, for one), it's been a pretty good deal for dogs as a whole.

As a measure of dogs' success as a species, consider this: gray wolves, the dog's closest living relatives, number about 180,000 in the wild. But there are *half a billion* dogs roaming planet Earth.

Wolves now inhabit a small and ever-shrinking portion of their historic range, which once included nearly the entire Northern Hemisphere. But go to the most remote tribal village in the Amazon, visit a community of reindeer herders above the Arctic Circle, or stroll through New York's Central Park on a Sunday and you'll surely be greeted by panting, barking, slobbering dogs. And while dogs don't inhabit the Antarctic, the first explorer to arrive at the South Pole, Norwegian Roald Amundsen, couldn't have gotten there without sled dogs.

Dogs are synonymous with civilization and could well have been a driving force in our own cultural evolution. People who kept them gained a survival advantaged; their dogs warned them of predators, protected them from hostile neighbors, helped them find, hunt, and retrieve prey. They sometimes served as meals themselves—Hawaiians kept the chubby poi dog just for food. On a higher level of culture, dogs have inspired art and literature since the dawn of history.

In turn, we were a civilizing force too. Were it not for humans, *Canis lupus*, the wolf, would never have made the transition to *Canis familiaris*, the familiar family dog.

So, what is it that set dogs apart? The answer is simple: it's us. Dogs' ability to gain our affection, to understand our communication, and to act as our helpers has been the key to their extraordinary good fortune. These abilities are no mere coincidence. They're a survival strategy written in the dogs' DNA and passed down from generation to generation. We call that strategy "domestication."

Domestication comes from the Latin word "domesticus," which means "belonging to the house." Latin's ancient speakers, the Romans, were crazy for dogs, gathering and trading the different varieties they encountered all across their empire. They used dogs for hunting and herding, protecting their flocks and farms, in gladiatorial games and warfare. Roman rulers even prized dogs as royal lap warmers. (Emperor Claudius, who ruled from A.D. 41 to 54, was said to be particularly fond of white Maltese dogs, an ancient breed even then).

As for the dog's place in the Roman home, one need only look to the House of the Tragic Poet in Pompeii, Italy, which was buried under volcanic ash in the first century. In the doomed building's entryway, archaeologists unearthed a tile mosaic of a chained, snarling canine bearing this familiar inscription: *cave canem.* Beware of dog.

By the time of Pompeii's destruction, dogs had been warming themselves by the human hearth and catching table scraps for 10,000 years or more, making them the first domesticated animal. It's been no easy task to determine where dogs came from or how they came to live with us.

Zoologists today agree that the wolf is the dog's closest living relative and sole ancestor. But how did they ever arrive at that conclusion? Spend a day at a dog show or just visit a busy dog park, and you'll encounter dogs of every size, shape, color and coat texture, from the fashion-forward toy poodle to that slobbering but lovable oaf, the St. Bernard. Any reasonable person might conclude that animals with so much variety couldn't possibly share the same common ancestor.

Charles Darwin, the father of evolutionary theory, reasoned that dogs must have descended from a mixture of several different wild canine species, either living or extinct. Some fellow nineteenth century colleagues even suggested that there must have been a wild ancestor for each type of domestic dog, though Darwin thought that idea absurd.

"Who can believe that animals closely resembling the Italian greyhound, the bloodhound, the bull-dog, or Blenheim spaniel . . . ever existed freely in a state of nature?" he wrote dismissively.

However, many of his contemporaries believed that dogs must have descended from a single wild canine, though which one was under debate. Could it have come from one of several jackals, or wolves, or wild dogs, or instead from some wild canine, now extinct?

A century later, the debate was still on. In 1953, Nobel Prize winning zoologist Konrad Lorenz published his best seller, *Man Meets Dog*. There, he voiced his strongly held (but scientifically tenuous) view that dogs had descended from the golden jackal, *Canis aureus*, a coyote-like native of Eurasia and North Africa.

Regardless, by the late twentieth century, most biologists placed their bets exclusively on wolves, whose anatomy and behavior were the most similar to dogs'. Even Lorenz finally changed his tune when his own field studies showed that jackals sound nothing like dogs and wolves.

But drawing hard conclusions about dogs' early origins still seemed impossible. All of the ten species in the genus *Canis* share the same number of chromosomes and are capable of interbreeding. The fact that their DNA is nearly identical suggests that the canine tree branch split very recently and that all of its members—wolves, coyotes, domestic dogs, wild dogs and jackals—could be incestuous cousins.

However, in the last half of the twentieth century, a new field of biology emerged to resolve the debate. In 1997, a team of scientists set out to determine the dog's evolutionary beginnings with help from a relatively new tool—molecular biology.

Led by biologists Carles Vilà and Robert K. Wayne at UCLA, the research team collected hundreds of gene samples from dogs, wolves, coyotes and jackals. After mapping the genes, they discovered that the mitochondrial DNA in dogs and wolves is far more similar than it is among any of the other canine species, differing by less than a fraction of a percent. Coyotes, by comparison, differed from wolves by about 4 percent. They concluded that wolves and dogs were closely related, having likely shared a common ancestor during the last 100,000 years.

At some point during that chunk of time, at least one and possibly several groups of wolves broke from the wild and continued evolving alongside people. Through forces of both natural and artificial selection, the wolves morphed into new forms and adopted new behaviors until, today, one of their descendants is Lady Gaga's French bulldog, Miss Asia.

Vilà and Wayne's study proved that wolves were the ancestral forbears of today's domestic dogs. But over the thousands of years that we have lived together, the dog has become a species distinctly different. When and where did the chasm that separates the two species first open? Scientists believe humans first wandered onto the Eurasian continent between 40,000 and 50,000 years ago. There, they encountered their primate cousins, the Neanderthals.

Though we tend to think of them as dim-witted knuckle draggers, recent studies reveal that Neanderthals wore jewelry, created art and architecture, made complex tools, and developed sophisticated big-game hunting strategies. All this suggests that they were capable of symbolic thought and social coordination—qualities long thought to belong exclusively to humans. And for 300,000 years, these culturally astute Neanderthals walked among wolves—yet no evidence suggests they domesticated a single one.

For 30,000 or 40,000 years, it appears we did no better. Then, suddenly, 10,000 years ago, dogs began to show up everywhere, from East Asia to the British Isles, in Africa and the Americas, too. Something had to have occurred to create this radical change. But what was it?

The ice melted.

The single, biggest change in man's prehistoric lifestyle came about at the end of the last ice age. As ice that had covered much of the Northern hemisphere receded back toward the North Pole, humans did something they'd never done before. They began to settle into villages. And settlement, argued the late biologist Raymond Coppinger, created the environment necessary for wolves to become dogs.

Coppinger taught biology at Hampshire College in Massachusetts. For him and his wife, Lorna, dogs have been a lifelong professional and personal interest. In 2001, they published the best-selling book *Dogs: A Startling New Understanding of Canine Origin, Behavior and Evolution* that upended decades-old beliefs about dog domestication.

Prior to the Coppingers' book launch, the commonly held belief among scientists and laymen alike was that prehistoric cavemen found some wolf pups on the trail, adopted them, and transformed them, Pinocchio-like, into hunting companions. Then, they judiciously selected qualities over thousands of years in a process Charles Darwin named *artificial selection* that resulted in the widely varied creatures we call dogs.

The Coppingers envisioned an entirely different domestication story. It begins with the development of permanent villages, which first appear in the archaeological record 12,000 or so years ago. As people built and inhabited villages, they also created garbage piles which, naturally, attracted hungry wolves. When someone came to the dump to toss out a spoiled carcass or other food scraps, some of the wolves ran away. But those that were less stressed out around people stuck around and got the best morsels.

These chilled-out wolves gained a survival advantage in this new village niche. Scavenging required less energy than hunting, and people's presence protected the village wolves from aggression by other packs. Because the humans killed or chased off the overly aggressive individuals, tame behavior came to be the norm in the village wolf pack.

In this scenario, the village created an environment in which selection for tameness arose. Tameness wasn't taught, but rather an inherent requirement. Those that didn't have it didn't survive.

Those that did thrived. And dogs, which were at first just naturally tame wolves, domesticated themselves.

After the Coppingers' book came out, more and more scientists began embracing the village domestication hypothesis, which accords well with the principle known as Occam's Razor: The simplest explanation is usually the best.

"The artificial selection theory requires early people to embark intentionally on a long-term wolf-taming and breeding project, which is difficult to do," wrote the Coppingers. "The natural selection theory doesn't require people to do anything other than live in villages."

John Bradshaw, foundation director of the Anthrozoology Institute at the University of Bristol, in England, and author of *Dog Sense*, agrees:

"I'm firmly of the opinion that the pioneers of the long road to today's dogs were wolves that were simply exploiting a new niche," he explains, "a new concentration of food provided by man, as humans began to live in villages rather than be constantly on the move."

In time, the village wolves would have developed social habits or physical characteristics that created a reproductive barrier between them and other wolves. The unwillingness or inability to breed with related animals is one of the ways we decide if animals are separate species. Once this split occurred, the wolves were no longer wolves, but dogs.

Biologists define species in various ways, and choosing one is rather like choosing a weapon for battle. It affects the outcome of the dispute. One of the most common definitions of species is "a group of living organisms consisting of similar individuals capable of exchanging genes or interbreeding." In the case of the dog, it's not a very sharp knife.

All of the true canids—dogs, wolves, coyotes, jackals, dingoes, and wild dogs—fit this definition. All of them are capable of interbreeding with the others, and many are so similar in shape

9

and function that it can be difficult even for experts to tell their skeletons apart. As Raymond Coppinger told me, "bury an African side-striped jackal in New Mexico, and a biologist would probably describe it as a coyote."

Ecologists like the Coppingers define species differently. They consider an animal's relationship to his (or, to be non-sexist, her) environment. Northern gray wolves, for instance, evolved to hunt large herd animals like elk, deer, caribou and horses. That's one reason gray wolves form packs—because it's easier to gang up on big animals than to take one down alone.

This definition forges a nice weapon for an argument on canine species because all of the "true canids"—dogs, wolves, coyotes, jackals, dingoes, and wild dogs—fit into different niches. Black-backed jackals and side-striped jackals, for instance, hunt small- to medium-sized game in the grasslands of the Old World. Similarly, the coyote (sometimes called "the American jackal") evolved to hunt small- and medium-sized prey in North America.

Dogs, according to the Coppingers, are neither wolves nor a subspecies of the wolf simply because they don't fit the wolf's eco-logical niche. A domesticated dog, by its very definition, depends on humans for its daily meal. As the Romans would say, dogs belong to the house. This helps to explain why fossil evidence of dogs prior to 12,000 years ago is so scant and highly questionable. Before there was the dog—an entirely new species of the genus *Canis*—there had to be a niche for it. There had to be houses. In short, dog is where the home is . . . *cave canem*.

Not everyone is happy with the idea that dogs—which to many westerners are as dear as children—emerged from the wild to eat our trash. In my heart, I wanted to agree with many people who feel that our relationship began when a boy or girl encountered a wolf pup on the trail, and it was love at first sight. But in time, I became more and more convinced that the Coppingers had it right. Dogs wanted our trash. Affection came later.

Even today, most dogs in underdeveloped countries do not live a comfortable existence in human homes, sleeping on beds and eating kibble from stainless steel bowls. Instead they live semi-autonomously by scavenging, their diets consisting mainly of leftovers and rotting garbage. Dogs, as the Coppingers noted, evolved to fill this scavenging niche. And the Coppingers are not alone in believing that trash was the key to the dog's domestication.

"I think Ray Coppinger has a big part of it," biologist Ben Sacks told me. "His scenario about the garbage pile, the idea of a shorter flight distance . . . are insights that must be correct. I think that is the general picture of how you get from wolf to dog."

I'd called Sacks, who heads the Center for Canine Diversity at the veterinary genetics lab at University of California at Davis, to get his opinions on the whole dog domestication debate. Sacks is a young professor whose specialty is wild dog conservation. But he's always had a keen interest in domestic dog origins. And he's been keeping a close eye on the scientific debate about the origins of our first pets.

"Currently," he told me, "the two most hotly debated theories propose that dogs originated in Southeast Asia or the Middle East."

Many zoologists, he continued, believe that the likely ancestors of today's dogs were not the large northern wolves found in the cold-climate regions of Europe and North America. Instead, they were smaller, more dog-like southern wolves native to North Africa, South Asia, and the Arabian Peninsula. Compared to the northern gray wolf, these small Arabian and Asian wolves are scarcely bigger than coyotes and dingoes, and have correspondingly smaller heads and teeth.

Adding to this evidence are recent genetic studies which place the dog's origins in either the Middle East or the Far East. Rival camps of researchers using genetic data have attempted to pinpoint which of the two regions is the more likely origination place of the dog and have come to different conclusions.

One study performed by Robert Wayne and colleagues at UCLA asserted that the Middle East was the place with the greatest variability within the native dog population. This hypothesis supports the conventional wisdom that dogs evolved in the Fertile Crescent, where nearly all large domestic animals and many domesticated plants first came under our control.

"Wayne's group does this whole genome study, concluding that wolves in the Middle East are related to dogs everywhere," Sacks told me. "They show that dogs, in general, are more closely related to wolves in the Middle East than wolves anywhere else."

Archaeological evidence to support the Middle Eastern hypothesis exists among the remains of the very earliest settlers in the world, the Natufians. Among the most convincing was the skeleton of an elderly man buried with a puppy cradled in his hands.

However, the Middle East hypothesis stands in stark contrast to another study by Wayne's colleague, Sweden's Peter Savolainen. His study's conclusion was that dogs today could be stamped MADE IN CHINA. According to Savolainen's interpretation of the genetic evidence, dogs originated 16,300 years ago in China, south of the Yangtse River, from just a handful of female wolves.

In support of Savolainen's Asian hypothesis, Sacks pointed out to me that dogs have a hook on their lower jaw where it attaches to the skull. This hook is present only in Asian wolves, not gray wolves or Middle Eastern wolves. Furthermore, evidence suggests that farmers cultivated rice in China's Yangtse River Valley as many as 14,000 years ago, creating the preconditions for villages and, of course, dogs. This also would put dogs closer to the Beringia land bridge, over which the first North Americans are thought to have crossed from Siberia to Alaska—along with their dogs. That bridge closed 11,000 years ago, at the end of the last ice age.

Sifting through the science, we still haven't pinpointed with any certainty when and where the dog came to our campfire. And there is no reason to believe domestication could not have happened almost simultaneously in East Asia, the Middle East, and possibly

Europe, too, since all that was needed were villages, wolves, and trash heaps.

And, to throw even more combustible material on the fire, scientist Susan Crockford, a zoologist at the Royal British Columbia Museum, says there is evidence of a separate origin for Native American dogs, distinct from the domestic dogs of Eurasia. So, maybe they didn't need that land bridge after all.

"This corroborates the idea of at least two 'birthplaces,'" she said. "I think we need to think about dogs becoming dogs at different times in different places."

If the Coppinger's argument is correct, the transition from wolf to woof happened, not wherever and whenever Paleolithic cavemen met the wolf on the trail, but instead when humans settled down into villages and began to grow food rather than merely follow it. Like wheat and rice, the dog is a product of the agricultural revolution that occurred at the end of the last Ice Age, during the same period that would usher in nearly all the important domesticated crops and animals of use to us today.

Regardless of when and where dogs first appeared, humans must have placed great value on them. Because wherever humans went, their dogs came along.

TWO

THE GENERIC DOG

*The people had always feared the wolves, so the
dog decided that it would be good to show that he
himself was afraid of the humans. So he lowered
his tail and his head and looked up at the people
with his eyes wide to show that he was afraid of
them and crept over to the fire and lay down.*
—"How Dogs Came to Live With Humans,"
as told by Menominee Indian Chief Oshkosh

And what were the first dogs like? Probably a lot like Dog. Dog
is the companion of globe-traveling photographer and author
Lorraine Chittock. She came upon the dog while moving into
a new home in a village not far from Nairobi, Kenya. The flea-
covered freeloader was there in the yard, like a piece of abandoned

furniture. Chittock was looking for a hiking companion. Dog knew a gullible westerner when he saw one. The two bonded immediately.

Most North Americans and Europeans would take one look at Dog and call her a mixed-breed "mutt." We'd likely try to guess at the combination of purebred parents that contributed to her appearance. But Dog is not a mutt. She's just a dog.

According to American Kennel Club statistics, the Labrador retriever is the number one dog breed in America today. But village dogs like Dog are the most common "breed" the world over. Of the half-billion or so dogs on earth, the World Health Organization estimates, roughly two of every five are free-ranging domesticated dogs whose breeding is not under human control. A large proportion of these dogs live in rural villages which they seldom, if ever, leave. Hence, the name "village dog."

Many village dogs descend from native dogs whose roots go back hundreds and even thousands of years. Recent studies suggest that at least some trace their bloodlines to the earliest domesticated dogs, untainted by the "pure" blood of modern breeds.

Village dogs also make up a subset of the huge urban populations of street dogs found in developing countries, as well as in Eastern Europe and the Balkans. These street dogs roam the cities like juvenile youth gangs, congregating in parks, sleeping in alleys, tearing into garbage cans, and scavenging at city dumps. (Moscow's street dogs are known to also ride the metro lines).

Lorraine's dog, Dog, likely traces back to indigenous dogs that have lived in Africa for thousands of years. A genetic study of African dogs conducted by Cornell researchers showed that village dogs from most regions of Africa are genetically distinct from non-native breeds and mixed-breed dogs. Their origins reach back as far as the first dogs to populate sub-Saharan African 4,500 years ago. The study confirmed something Lorraine Chittock already knew in her heart.

"If we were to step back 10,000 years to sit by the fires of our ancestors, we'd see a dog similar in appearance to the village dog of today," she says.

Dog is typical of the African village dog or "Africanis." She's skinny, weighs about thirty pounds, and is roughly the size of a border collie. Her ears are triangle-shaped and stand up (although floppy ear tips are also common among village dogs) and they flick back-and-forth like radar antennae to catch the sounds of nature, vehicle traffic, or Lorraine's voice.

Color varies a great deal among African village dogs, just as it does among wolves and dog breeds. Dog happens to be pale yellow, like a golden lab. She has a narrow, wedge-shaped head, a moderately long and tapered muzzle, and almond-shaped brown eyes rimmed with black, like eyeliner. Her bushy tail curves over her back in a quarter-moon arc. When she sits, her back legs splay out to the sides like those of a yogi patiently meditating on a mat.

Lorraine has traveled with Dog and her other village dog companion, Bruiser, throughout Africa, Egypt, and parts of North, Central, and South America. It used to surprise Chittock how frequently she encountered dogs like her own, though she now comes to expect it. Such encounters are as likely in the village enclaves of the Central American rainforest as they are throughout the villages of the Kenyan grasslands.

Village dogs can be found in underdeveloped and developing countries throughout the world, scratching out livings by scavenging, begging, and snatching food on the margins of human communities. They've even been discovered in isolated pockets of the United States. It's believed that the Carolina Dog, discovered in the 1970s living in the piney woods and cypress swamps of the Southeast, is an ancient indigenous dog. However, according to the World Health Organization, the largest concentrations of native village dogs live in India, Asia, and Africa.

Most village dogs exist in a netherworld somewhere between modern house dogs and truly wild dogs such as dingoes. On the one hand, they are dependent upon humans as their main source of food. On the other hand, they socialize and breed freely, without direct human intervention, and so are not generally subject to artificial selection. Because there are no restrictions imposed upon the dogs' breeding choices, village dogs' physical and behavioral traits are almost entirely the product of the environment in which they're born.

If we were to travel back 10,000 years in time, we might begin to see how natural forces shaped the wolf into the generic village dog. Relative to wolves, dogs have proportionally smaller brains—about 20 percent smaller. Big brains, like ours, use a huge amount of energy—about 25 percent of the calories we consume each day go to feeding our brains. (Hunger is your brain telling you it wants more sugar!) Dogs scavenging in the village don't require the brainpower of wolves hunting large game. During early domestication, village life gave a selective advantage to dogs with smaller brains.

Similarly, wolves need large teeth and powerful jaws to grab, hold, and bring down the hoofed animals upon which they feed, to tear apart and devour their prey, and to crush large bones to get at marrow. Evolving in the village niche, dogs' teeth downsized to smaller, more gracile forms and jaw strength diminished to a degree better suited to the easy demands of scavenging. Today, even a large dog such as a Rottweiler that matches a wolf in size cannot equal that wolf in biting strength.

Moderate size best suited the earliest village dogs, just as it does their modern counterparts. Too large a body and a dog's daily calorie requirement might not be met in the village; too small, and the dog would find himself having to fight other larger, stronger dogs for a share of the daily take.

However, the more northern village dogs are larger than their southern cousins—an adaptation to cold environments where larger mass means greater warmth. Also as one travels north, village dogs transition from smooth, single coats without underfur to heavier double coats, like those my Australian shepherds are constantly shedding on the carpet and my clothing. Sled dogs of the arctic are extreme examples of village dogs well adapted to a particular niche—in this case, the featureless arctic ice fields and tundra.

In short, the adaptations required to fit into the village niche explain how we get from a large, powerful apex carnivore, the wolf, which preys on hoofed mammals many times its own size, to the moderately sized generalist scavenger, the village dog. And the variations among them also explain many of the traits found in modern breeds.

In the hot desert of Arabia, for instance, village dogs evolved among nomadic Bedouin tribesmen into lithe runners with short coats (think of greyhounds) capable of chasing down small game. In the Arctic, they became thick-coated, stocky dogs (think of the spitz breeds), which the Inuits used for thousands of years to pull sleds.

Besides the lessened energetic demands of village life and climate differences, other pressures were at work transforming the wolves into dogs, and the dogs into different varieties. Principle among them was how they interacted with people.

Ray Coppinger's domestication hypothesis proposes that a crucial characteristic of tameness is a short "flight distance," the point at which an animal chooses to run from an antagonistic predator that might injure or eat it. Those with shorter flight distances are, by nature, the least fearful and the more tame.

But how does tameness play a part in the transformation from wolf to dog? By the late 1950s, most scientists had come to accept the idea that dogs originated from wolves, but the mechanism by which that transformation had taken place remained a puzzle. Most believed that through thousands of years of conscious selection for desirable traits, humans transformed the wolf into the dog. But in Russia, a scientific experiment was underway that would provide an entirely new solution to the puzzle.

In the 1950s, a Russian biologist named Dmitri Belyaev began breeding commercial foxes for tameness. The result proved to be one of the most significant experiments in evolutionary biology conducted in the twentieth century.

Belyaev was the very archetype of a Stalinist-era Communist bureaucrat. He was a thick, broad-shouldered man with a ruddy face and heavy, brooding eyebrows. During the post-war period, many of his scientific colleagues were imprisoned or banned from conducting experiments. Belyaev's own brother was killed by the Stalinists. With guile, Dmitri flew under the radar of the repressive communists, who strongly opposed Darwinism and Mendelian genetics. He managed to get a post in Siberia, where he worked in obscurity to improve commercial fur breeding.

In 1959, Belyaev quietly began an experiment designed to re-create the conditions by which a wild animal might become domesticated. He was convinced that if he selected animals for one trait and one trait alone—tameness—a whole suite of biological changes might occur. Drawing on his background in fur-bearing animals, he chose as his test subject the Russian silver fox.

Belyaev designed a rigorous selective-breeding program, choosing only the most tame foxes from each generation for breeding. Over the more than forty-year course of the experiments, 45,000 tame foxes were produced. As the experiment progressed, the researchers began to see radical changes in the animals. The first were changes in the foxes' coat colors—mainly the appearance of white spots from a loss of pigmentation. Some individuals developed star-shaped patterns on their faces, a trait not seen in wild species but not uncommon among domestic animals such as horses, dogs, and cows.

Next came traits such as floppy ears and curled or curving tails, another characteristic of many domesticated species, particularly dogs and pigs. After 15 generations, the experimenters began to see foxes with shorter tails and legs. Today, Belyaev's domesticated foxes bear a striking resemblance to border collies.

After many generations, the tamest foxes were dog-like not only in appearance, but also in some of their behaviors. They not only tolerated humans, they sought their attention. In short, Belyaev's experiment showed that tameness alone could result in the vast physiological and behavioral changes associated with domestication.

But how do we explain this? On a biological level, as generations of foxes were selected solely for tameness, their bodies began producing different levels of hormones. Hormones, as we know, are chemicals secreted by cells or glands which send messages to other cells of an organism. Hormones can stimulate or inhibit growth, affect the mental state, stimulate sexual arousal and control the reproductive cycle, and prepare the body for mating, fighting, fleeing, eating, and other activities.

As the amounts and the timing of hormones were affected by selection for tameness, they set off a cascade of changes in the foxes—changes that would come to characterize many of our domestic breeds, but especially our dogs.

Were he still alive, Charles Darwin would have been dumbfounded but also probably delighted by Belyaev's results. In his books, the father of evolutionary theory argued that speciation and domestication were processes of incremental change taking place over many thousands of years. But Belyaev generated proof that domestication and speciation could occur in a very short time: in the case of the silver fox, less than a half a human lifetime.

Darwin had said that evolution did not happen in leaps. Belyaev proved him wrong. As the farmed fox experiment showed, the transformation from wolf to dog could have happened in an evolutionary blink of an eye. Coyotes are believed to have shared a common ancestor with wolves between one and two million years ago; by comparison, the dog's emergence between 10,000 and 15,000 years ago makes it a late-shining star within the canine constellation.

However, after their initial and likely rapid transformation, dogs remained little changed for thousands of years. The specialized dogs that we might identify as breeds today did not enter the story until about 3,200 years ago. Only with the dawn of human civilization does the fossil record begin to yield wide variation in dog sizes and shapes, the first steps toward distinct breeds. It's likely that, up until this time, humans exerted very little control over dog breeding.

As westerners, we seldom think about how humans and dogs related to one another in the past, nor do we know much about how they continue to relate in places where PetSmart, specialty dog food, and even leashes and collars are unknown. Lorraine Chittock, who has spent a lot of time among Third World villagers and their dogs, believes that they provide a window that allows us to see how village dogs might have lived 3,000 years ago or more . . .

On a visit to the desert village of Maikona in Northern Kenya, Chittock spent time watching villagers and their dogs. The dogs there have never heard the Kenyan words for "sit," "down," or "stay," nor have they ever felt the tug of a leash. There is no traffic to threaten their lives. They come and go as they please. Without demands placed upon them by humans, the dogs spend most of their time sleeping, socializing, and searching for food. Chittock compares the village to one big dog park—but quickly pulls the rug out from under that quaint notion.

For a Maikona village dog, life is tough. Most have never felt the prick of a vaccine needle. Mange, parasitic worms, and insect infestations are endemic to nearly all village dogs. Consequently, their lives tend to be short. Attachment inevitably brings heartache to those humans who bother to befriend the dogs. For this as well as other cultural reasons, the villagers in Maikona are seldom affectionate toward "their" dogs in the way that westerners tend to be.

Observing the humans and the dogs of Maikona, we might characterize them as indifferent to one another's presence. Both go about their business in their own ways, on their own schedules. But nearly every villager owns a dog (or at least, has a dog that claims the vicinity of that home as its territory). At the end of the day, the dogs return to their homes to stand guard and perhaps receive some scraps and the rare pat on the head from their keepers—generally out of sight of other villagers.

But even among the indifferent Maikonans, Chittock managed to find affection and attachment toward dogs. One woman dressed in brilliant red seemed to be constantly accompanied by a pack of four dogs. Chittock decided to follow the woman into the modestly stocked shop she owned and learn more.

"Other people in Maikona have dogs," said Lorraine to the woman, named Waatu, "but their dogs just guard their homes. Why do your dogs follow you?"

"They know I care for them," said the African woman thoughtfully. "They get lonely without me and I get lonely without them. Also, I try and treat them well and give them special food and meat sometimes. Other people treat their dogs meanly. Dogs don't like that."

When Chittock explained that people where she comes from often touch and stroke their dogs, Waatu told the westerner she'd never seen this in her village. Although, she confided, she did like to pet her own dogs.

To us, the Maikonans may seem cold. But there are good reasons people can be standoffish when it comes to village dogs. In areas with heavy concentrations of free-living dogs, the animals often carry and transmit diseases. Every year, fifty-five thousand people worldwide die from rabies, while another fifteen million receive post-exposure rabies treatment. Dogs cause 99 percent of rabies fatalities in developing countries.

The majority of rabies deaths occur in India, Asia, and Africa— places where village dogs are most prevalent. Even those not bitten by feral dogs face the possibility of contracting disease from the ticks and fleas the dogs carry, or from the feces that litter the ground in large cities such as Bangkok, where animal control agencies estimate that two hundred loose dogs roam each square kilometer.

India, in particular, suffers from a feral dog epidemic; no country has as many stray dogs. As a consequence, until very recently Indians suffered about one-third of the world's rabies deaths. And it's probable that rabies has plagued Indian society for a very long time. According to Dr. Charles Rupprecht, chief of the rabies program at the Centers for Disease Control in Atlanta,

Georgia, rabies originated on the Indian subcontinent thousands of years ago.

However, in 1997, the Animal Welfare Board of India began a birth control and anti-rabies program. Funded by the Indian federal government, it has had spectacular success in eliminating the country's "rabies menace" and could serve as an example across the underdeveloped world.

In the nineteenth and early twentieth centuries, rabies outbreaks and street dog overpopulation existed nearly everywhere, including in America. Only in the last forty years or so have Europeans, Americans, and Canadians created adequate shelters and animal control solutions (such as the widespread surgical sterilization of pets) that got dogs off the streets.

In Third World countries, eradication through mass killing remains the favored approach for solving the street dog problem. But not everyone feels eradication is the best solution to the free-living dog problems. Lorraine Chittock, for one, worries that the injudicious killing of stray dogs in many parts of the world endangers village dogs worth saving.

Village dogs which have resided in their natural state for centuries or even millennia are also threatened by the arrival of purebred dogs, which often become strays from neglect. When the dogs are rounded up, the purebreds are typically spared and placed in rescues while the village dogs are killed. In most cases, Lorraine observed, villagers and city people alike admire the high-status "breed" dogs at the expense of indigenous native dogs. And that doesn't bode well for the future of indigenous village dogs, like Dog.

"Humans love variety. We love being able to name our dog's breed, just as people love saying 'I own a Toyota,' or a BMW," Lorraine told me. "If you put aside the long-haired (village dogs) from cold regions like the Arctic, there are probably only five different basic 'looks' among all village dogs—floppy ears as opposed to ears sticking straight up, certain muzzle structures, and varying differences in body type. Villagers who've been seeing these 'brands' all their lives are naturally entranced when seeing a Pekingese."

What she'd like would be greater resources dedicated to trapping, spaying, vaccinating, and releasing village dogs back into their native environments, a practice gaining widespread acceptance for feral cats. But for many Third World countries struggling to control their human populations and vaccinate their own citizens against disease, such solutions for dogs will likely remain a low priority.

And this is a shame not only for the dogs' sake, but because village dogs may yet answer many of the questions about just how dogs "came to the campfire" in the first place. Their ability to transform from semi-wild living to sharing life with someone like Lorraine shows just how adaptively predisposed these dogs are to living with, rather than just among, people.

Village dogs are hardy. Thousands of years of adaptation under challenging conditions have made them less susceptible to the genetic diseases which plague virtually all of our closely related purebred dogs and even our mutts. Village dogs have a higher degree of resistance to tropical and sub-tropical diseases and better natural defenses against skin diseases and other ailments than do purebred dogs.

In the struggle to stay alive, the village dog has, through natural selection, managed to adapt to a huge variety of local conditions and climates. It can thrive on nutritionally spare food. Reproductive fitness is high. There are no humans to bottle feed the weaklings, causing offspring to have strong constitutions and the will to survive.

Only the most well-adapted and resourceful village dogs pass along their genes to the next generation. They were and remain the pool of dogs from which all our other dogs came, and as such deserve our protection and respect. And yet, across the globe, the effort continues to wipe them out and replace them with purebreds.

Before we end our discussion, Chittock tells me a poignant tale. She was camped on Lake Titicaca when a Bolivian girl of about ten approached her. A fluffy white lap dog appeared, probably the possession of another foreign camper. The girl, Lorraine says, "went a bit loopy, full of giggles and cooing." But when a four-month-old street puppy came up to the girl, she snarled at the puppy to stay away.

"Nothing I could say was going to change the way she saw this pup, who I thought had an endearing face. Clearly, she shared an opinion about the different types of dogs that came from her peers and her family."

Chittock would like to see greater efforts made in developing nations to control the entry and breeding of purebred dogs from the West that are displacing village dogs. Many people in rising developing countries like China, she says, are buying western dogs as a show of status or for the sheer novelty, just as people do in America and Europe.

"But the result is that these dogs and their offspring end up where they shouldn't—out in the streets. There's nothing sadder than to see a German shepherd, Maltese, or other breed of dog with long, thick hair living outside in hot, humid climates, or to see greyhounds with little hair living outdoors at elevations of 15,000 feet in the Andes," she says. Ultimately, the village dogs suffer less and live more happily, inhabiting the niches to which they are adapted, than the western dogs which threaten to replace them.

To summarize Chittock, we should let more dogs be Dog.

THREE

THE FIRST BREEDERS

*At its height, Rome was a veritable melting pot of
both domesticated animals and people.*
—Historian Mary Elizabeth Thurston

W hile on a visit years ago to Seattle, I went to see the King Tutankhamen exhibit. I was awestruck by this ancient Egyptian's
gold sarcophagus, beautifully formed alabaster jars made to hold
salves and oils, and jewelry of gold and lapis lazuli stones. But for
me, there was one particular item that made me feel closest to this
god-like child ruler: a dog collar. Made of leather and bronze, it was
covered with dog-shaped charms—representations of dogs whose
descendants can still be found 3,300 years later, lolling around in
the shade of the pyramids.

Thinking about his having had a dog made Tut seem more real and human. I could relate because, if there is an afterlife, I like to imagine that I will find my dog, Onda, waiting for me to put on his collar and throw a Frisbee.

From the outset of Egypt's greatness up to the civilization's decline under Roman rule, dogs played an important part in Egyptian daily life, in art, language, and religion. Nine-thousand-year-old cave drawings show that people living in the Nile River Valley already were hunting with dogs by their sides. In the millenniums to follow, the dog would become important not only in daily life, but in religion, art, war and trade.

It's often said that cats were the most highly regarded animals in ancient Egypt, but that was true only during the last 1,000 years of Egypt's greatness. Dogs held high status, too, and for a much longer time. Around 450 b.c., the Greek historian Herodotus wrote that when a family cat died of natural causes, Egyptians shaved their eyebrows in mourning. But when the family dog died, they shaved their entire bodies—just as they did to mourn a family member.

Egyptians also named their dogs—something they did with no other animals. In wealthy households, dogs wore broad, ornate collars like the one found in Tut's tomb. On the neckbands remain names like "Town Dog," "Reliable," "Blackie," "Good Herdsman," and one that I think many pet owners today can empathize with—"Useless."

The Egyptians' ancient neighbors did not share their adoration of dogs. The Old Testament of the Bible, the basis for the Hebrew, Muslim, and Christian religions, contains thirty-one references to dogs—all of them negative. But the authors had their reasons. During times of pestilence, the Middle Eastern *pariah* dogs (a derogatory name for village dogs) would feed on human corpses. So it's not surprising that cultures of the ancient Middle East considered the animals unclean and untouchable.

But to the ancient Egyptians, even the street dogs' odious work of dispatching the dead held spiritual meaning. The dogs' close association with death gave rise to one of ancient Egypt's most revered gods, Anubis, who had the body of a human and the head of a black dog. Black was symbolic of death but also of the fertility of the Nile and its soil. So, Anubis represented both death and rebirth, the cycle of life.

In 1897, while exploring a dark Egyptian crypt, French adventurer Jacques de Morgan heard much cracking and snapping underfoot. It turned out he was knee deep in dog bones, having literally stumbled upon the world's largest pet cemetery. It lies beneath the Temple of Anubis in Saqqara, a vast necropolis in the country's ancient capital of Memphis.

Studying Anubis's bones today are Paul Nicholson, a professor of archaeology at Cardiff University in Wales, and his research team, who hope to learn more about the dogs that lived in Egypt eight centuries before the birth of Christ.

"[Saqqara] would have been a busy place," says Nicholson, "a permanent community of people living there supported by the animal cults." Visitors to the temple would have strolled bazaars with merchants selling dog amulets, papyrus paintings of dogs on the hunt or herding, dog figurines made of bronze, ceramic, ivory and wood, and other mementos.

Clearly, pet dogs alone could not account for the eight *million* dog skeletons unearthed beneath the temple. Such a huge repository indicates that the Egyptians practiced ritualized canine sacrifice. Courting Anubis's favor, worshippers would have placed mummified dogs from the temple shops in small alcoves set along the tomb walls. In all likelihood, the Anubis temple holy men were among the earliest "puppy mill" breeders, churning out dogs for sacrifice. And they likely kept favored pups for purposes such as guarding the temples, which would also have made them practitioners of artificial selection, much like dog breeders of today.

They weren't the only ones, either. Though their canines would not likely meet today's strict definition of breeds, it is evident that the Egyptians practiced selective breeding, finding ways to "improve" dogs and other animals such as goats, sheep, and cattle and creating distinctive types to meet their needs and fancies.

Most of what we know of these animals comes not from bones, but from art. In wall paintings, sculptures, and reliefs, one sees among other animals a wide variety of canine types—dogs with spots like Dalmatians, dogs with stout bodies and curled tails reminiscent of spitz breeds, and short legged dogs similar to corgis. But the pride of Egyptian royalty was the long-legged and fleet dog that resembled modern-day sight hounds—breeds such as Salukis, Ibizan hounds, greyhounds, and the so-called pharaoh hounds (who, despite the name, are not of ancient origin, but recently bred—to look like the dogs in ancient Egyptian art!)

How did Egyptians get from generic village dogs to these distinctly shaped and varied types? By the time Egypt had begun to coalesce into a powerful nation, many civilizations in the ancient world were already practicing selective breeding of plants and animals. But of these groups, Egyptians valued animals most and went furthest in their efforts to tame, domesticate, and breed them.

Egyptian farmers attempted to domesticate many wild animals, including hyenas, gazelles, and cranes, but abandoned their efforts toward the end of the Old Kingdom, around 2,180 B.C. Afterward, their propensity to experiment with animals shifted to the intensive breeding of domesticated species, nearly all of them handed down from Neolithic times.

Knowing nothing about genes, the Egyptians nonetheless guided their efforts by the basic principle that like begets like: If you breed a dog with short legs to another dog with short legs, you're likely to get dogs with short legs. By selecting for certain behaviors and physical characteristics, they learned to exaggerate desirable traits. With this direct intervention in the breeding process, Egyptians invented new varieties of domestic animals. But the Egyptians did not forge these new breeds from scratch; what they cultivated and refined were already existing *landraces*.

A landrace is a variety of domestic plant or animal that is geographically or culturally defined. Unlike breeds, whose reproduction is controlled almost exclusively by human choice, a landrace is created mainly by natural processes, sometimes aided by intentional selection.

Shetland sheep provide an example. The poor grazing conditions of the remote Scottish Isles produced sheep that were slow to mature and smaller when compared with most other domestic types. From these, Shetland Islanders selected sheep with exceptionally fine wool that was commercially valuable, thus isolating a breed from within an existing landrace. Then, to care for the small sheep, the Shetlanders took a landrace herding dog of Scotland, the collie, and bred *it* down (probably with a toy breed, like the King Charles Cavalier Spaniel) to create a smaller collie, the Sheltie. It, too, is a landrace that became a breed.

In 1934, Jewish couple Rudolph and Rudolphina Menzel traveled the Middle East to study the native village dogs. In their exhaustive survey, they identified four different native landraces, plus dozens of sub-varieties. These Middle Eastern landraces included heavy sheep dogs used as flock protectors, mid-sized dogs similar in appearance to wild dingoes, and another mid-sized dog, slighter of build and more refined in its snout. The latter became the basis of the modern Canaan dog breed, now the national dog of Israel.

Also in the desert areas, the Menzels encountered slender, long-legged, short-haired dogs—the sight hounds. These thrived in arid environments where chasing prey over open terrain called for exceptional reactivity to movement, visual acuity, rapid acceleration and speed, plus agility. It was these lithe creatures that the Egyptian royals, like Tutankhamen, favored and selectively bred for their sport hunts.

Though we don't know for certain whether the Egyptian nobles tightly controlled and inbred dogs (as breeders do in modern times to set or "fix" a breed type), it's more than likely that they did— because that was exactly the way they reproduced themselves.

Among Egyptian royals, incest was more often the case than the exception. (Cleopatra, for instance, married two of her brothers).

In early tomb paintings, images of regal sight hounds appear more frequently than those of any other dog. The royal dogs stayed in mud-brick kennels. At the royalty's request, a hunt would be arranged and dogs brought out to pursue prey, which might consist of anything from a hare to a gazelle, or even an exotic animal imported just for sport.

During Egypt's Eighteenth Dynasty (1567–1320 B.C.), sight hounds and the native pariah dogs were joined by a wide variety of dog types. At that time, Egypt's empire was expanding north and east toward the Euphrates River and south up the Nile toward present-day Khartoum. With expansion came trade with cultures across the Mediterranean, Arabia, Africa, and Asia: Greeks, Hittites, Babylonians, Palestinians, Syrians, Nubians, and others.

Along with trade items such as gold and spices, exotic canines were sold, allowing traders to take advantage of the Egyptians' adoration of dogs. Among the most notable type were lap dogs from Nubia and Libya, initially given as a tribute to the pharaoh. Lap dogs have remained a royal favorite the world over up to the present day.

Large, mastiff-like dogs entered Egyptian life around 1600 B.C. with the invasion of the Hyksos, nomadic Asian warriors who also introduced horses, chariots, and the composite bow. (It's thought that the spiked dog collar was a Hyksos innovation). All would exert a profound impact on the conduct of war in the ancient world.

Military leaders incorporated the Hyksos war dogs into the Egyptian army. A single handler would be assigned to each dog so that the dog, trusting no other, would attack anyone else. In times of peace, handlers put the dogs to work protecting herds, hunting large game, and guarding royal estates. In modern dog show speak, these constituted the "working dog" group of their time.

At the bottom rung of Egyptian canine society, below the noble sight hounds and the lap dogs of the nobility, below the working dogs, below the temple dogs and even the temple's sacrificial puppies, were the pariah village dogs that roamed the streets. Pariah dogs slept on the edges of towns, roaming the streets and rummaging through garbage, just as they do today.

In times of contagion, pariah dogs spread disease by eating the flesh of the dead. Sometimes the dogs attacked pedestrians returning from the market. They also attacked livestock and leash-trained pets. According to canine historian Mary Elizabeth Thurston, the Egyptians rarely went out of their way to help these animals, afraid as they were of rabies and other diseases. Like the poorest members of Egyptian society, pariah dogs held no status. As a class, they stood in stark contrast to dogs of nobility, whose lavish care would rival that of a modern show dog.

Thurston makes the thought-worthy observation that the same canine social stratification still exists on a global level. One portion of today's dogs live pampered lives of leisure in which their every need is catered to, just like the pharaohs' pets. Another group constitutes a modern working class—dogs that perform police and military work, act as guide dogs, and continue to carry out herding and hunting duties. Then there are abandoned and homeless dogs given up to public shelters, of which close to a million are euthanized each year in the United States alone. Their bones would handily fill the tomb of Anubis. Lastly, are the village pariah dogs, social outcasts of the world.

Ancient Egypt's greatness began to ebb with the arrival of outside conquerors, most notably the Greeks and Romans. Like the Egyptians whom they conquered and subjugated, Romans maintained a deep and abiding interest in animals that went well beyond the confines of agriculture—though the results were sometimes exploitative and cruel. Watch Russell Crowe fighting wild animals in the film *The Gladiator*, and you'll see what I mean.

As the Roman Empire expanded throughout the entirety of the Mediterranean, on up into Central Europe and eventually as far as Britain, the Romans took a keen interest in the dogs they encountered along the way. At its height, Rome became a crucible of people from throughout the ancient world. And as always, with the people came their dogs.

Roman soldiers and traders encountered landrace varieties of dogs throughout the vast empire, bringing them back to Rome to serve as hunters, herders, soldiers, fighters, guardians, and pets. More than any other influence, the Romans, with their fondness for canine novelty and their drive to acquire as many different dog varieties as existed in ancient times, formed the basis for our modern dog breeds.

In her book, *The Lost History of the Canine Race*, Mary Elizabeth Thurston recounts the variety of dogs assembled by the Romans during their expansion.

> . . . "Exotic" dogs continued to arrive from Northern Europe, Africa, and the Middle East. Outcrossed with one another as well as with the more primitive, Neolithic canines still residing in the rural parts of Southern Europe, they gave rise to a plethora of new varieties: giant "Mastiffs," spitzes, chubby, Beagle-like canines, curly-coated "Poodles," pocket-sized lapdogs, and a large constituency of mild-mannered, midsized hounds with upright and drop ears, square muzzles, foreshortened faces, or coats of differing colors, lengths, and textures.

One could find several Roman dog breeds for each of the recognized groups seen in modern kennel club dog shows. But the dog most associated with Rome remains the Molosser, which came to them through the Greeks and may trace back to the massive dogs of war brought to Egypt by the Hyksos.

Large, muscular dogs weighing in excess of one hundred pounds, with square heads tightly coiled with powerful muscles that drove cruel mouths, the Molossers were aptly described as "death incarnate." Despite their size, these dogs were fast and agile, capable of knocking or dragging an armed horseman out of his saddle and literally tearing him apart limb by limb.

Molossers comprised a major military asset for the Romans and were treated to meals of ox meat in an era when common people went without such luxury. Legions of dogs were sent throughout the Roman realm, from North Africa to the Middle East, to terrorize Rome's adversaries and help the Roman conquerors to secure new territories.

Rome's enduring canine legacy stems from its nurturing of this fearsome fighting dog. Today, more than one hundred breeds can be traced to this ancient dog, including the "mountain breeds," such as the St. Bernard and the Bernese Mountain dog, pugilistic breeds such as boxers and bulldogs, large guarding dogs such as the Anatolian shepherd, the Rottweiler and the Great Dane, and finally dogs one might not expect, such as the golden retriever. Later, I will dedicate a chapter to one of the dogs that most exemplifies the Molosser's fierce nature: the pit bull.

By the fourth century, the empire had become geographically overextended and began to crumble. No longer able to support the huge military necessary to hold its territories, Rome began to fail under the onslaught of the Germanic tribes. The Empire ultimately divided into eastern and western territories under separate rule.

The proverbial last straw proved to be a common parasite: the flea. Hitching rides on black ship rats across the Mediterranean from Egypt in 540, fleas carrying the deadly bubonic plague spread rapidly throughout the Eastern Roman empire. Almost no one was spared the affliction; in some areas, mortality rates soared as high as 95 percent.

The once tightly knit society unraveled. Entire villages became ghost towns. Over a two-year span, about twenty-five million people died—roughly 13 percent of the world's population at that time. Dogs, though immune to the ravaging effect of the bubonic plague, were nonetheless its victims. Their immunity caused superstitious fear in the populace, encouraging the notion that dogs possessed evil spirits.

During the height of the contagion, legions of dogs became ownerless and homeless. At night, packs of these dogs roamed the villages, baying and barking like the hounds of hell. Or at least, so thought people already convinced that the apocalypse had come. Fear and ignorance plunged the world into the Dark Ages, establishing a new political system ruled by rapacious kings in uneasy relationship with the growing power of the Roman Catholic church.

As the empire collapsed, so did the Roman's role as the dog's cultivator. Breeding fell to those barbarian rulers endowed with the wealth to feed dogs in a time when food was scarce. Throughout the Dark Ages, the wealthy, land-owning nobility and clergy alone were positioned to foster and develop distinctive varieties of dogs as hunting companions, guardians, and treasured pets.

The British, who had always been keen on dogs for hunting and battle, would eventually become the most important contributors to the next chapter in the evolution of dogs, with Britain emerging as the epicenter for a type of dog heretofore little seen: the purebred.

FOUR

ENGLAND GOES TO THE DOGS

For a hound is a most reasonable beast, and best knowing of any beast that ever God made.
　　　　—Master of the Game, fifteenth century

Early in the summer of 1859, British gun maker W. R. Pape and a few of his well-off hunting pals got together to put on a dog show in Newcastle upon Tyne. Only pointers and setters competed, as these were the only dogs the men owned. In lieu of blue ribbons, the winners received Pape shotguns—and doubtless were happier for it.

It was a low-key start to what soon became a fanatical Victorian pastime.

In short order, dog fanciers throughout England began creating shows of their own. The early provincial shows were casual affairs, often held in pubs. Women lifted their skirts above the sawdust-covered floors to avoid urine spots. At one Manchester show, chickens shared top billing.

These gatherings earned the scorn of urbane critics, one of who characterized the upper class participants with their sporting dogs as "toffs" and lower class exhibitors with their terriers as "ruffians"—with both as likely to kick their dogs as pet them, said canine historian Mary Elizabeth Thurston.

But that soon changed. By 1863, interest in dog shows had grown so much that 100,000 people came out for a weeklong contest at a hall adjacent to Cremorne Gardens in Chelsea. Considered *the* social occasion among Londoners that summer, the event included among its participants the Prince of Wales. The newly esteemed "dog fancy," as the Brits referred to it, had come of age.

As competition for exhibitors and audiences grew, show officials clamored for aristocrats to add panache to their events. Coverage of a particularly well-attended show reflects this elitism, as a correspondent wrote, "Yesterday, at the Botanic Gardens, half the Peerage seemed to be present at the Ladies' Kennel Show, and the list of prize winners reads like a report of a Queen's drawing room."

The biggest prize of all was England's beloved Queen Victoria.

Throughout her long life, Queen Victoria reveled in her dogs. It's said that on the day of her coronation, she left the festivities to go bathe her favorite childhood pet, a Spaniel named Dash. Though she was a woman who had everything, Victoria's favor could still be earned with the gift of a cute puppy.

Her magnificent and spotless kennel at Windsor Palace included Skye terriers, Scottish terriers, Irish terriers, spitz breeds, Pomeranians, Tibetan mastiffs, chows, Saint Bernards, Great Pyrenees, Chinese Spaniels, greyhounds and Pekingese, a breed she helped rescue from extinction. Her favorites, though, were Scottish herding dogs. She especially favored her border collies Noble and

Sharp, the latter a sometimes unpleasant character known to nip at members of the Queen's entourage.

Her Majesty whole-heartedly joined the "show fancy," exhibiting dogs at the highest levels. She filled entire rooms of Windsor Castle with trophies, ribbons and portraits of favorite dogs.

Needless to say, Victoria's dog show involvement sometimes led to conflicts of interest among those courting royal favor. Charles Lane, an in-demand show judge, reportedly took offense when members of show committees leaned on him to place the Queen's dogs. The unbendable Lane stood on principle rather than giving preference to Her Royal Majesty. Show dogs were to be "judged on their merits," he said, a policy he maintained would "have been approved by Her Majesty . . . if the circumstances came to be known at the palace."

Shows were one of the few occasions when commoners competed alongside the upper crust on a (mostly) level sporting field. This represented a huge crack in a dam that for a millennium had kept well-bred dogs out of the hands of run-of-the-mill Europeans. Literally from the fall of Rome to the early nineteenth century, dogs of the best quality and uniform in type had been a privilege almost exclusively of the privileged.

Following Rome's decline and breakup, barbarian warlords seized control of Europe. For eight centuries, the feudal system the barbarian kings put in place profoundly impacted Europeans and their dogs.

Throughout the Middle Ages, Christian-ruled lands, in principle, belonged "to God." But following the dictates of a claimed "Divine Right," the kings as well as the Catholic Church pretty much did with them whatever they pleased. Aristocrats claimed vast swaths of the countryside as private lands for their personal enjoyment. If a lord chose to, he could evict an entire peasant community—and still demand that the people pay him taxes.

This is precisely what happened to Nuneman Park in Oxfordshire, when the first Earl Harcourt removed an ancient village to provide a more picturesque view for his enormous home. Perhaps it was divine justice (or karma) that, as Earl Harcourt strolled his newly landscaped grounds, he forgot where the old village well had been, fell down the hole, and drowned.

Along with lands, the peasants lost ancient rights to whatever lived on them. Beginning in the fourteenth century, game laws turned rural people's enjoyment of hunting and fishing into a crime. Peasants imagined a special place in hell for game wardens, who not only enforced the laws but also extorted money and goods for petty violations such as gathering firewood.

It's no coincidence that the story of Robin Hood, who according to legend poached in the King's forests, likely dates from the time when the game laws were operative. Robin Hood's nemesis, the Sheriff of Nottingham Forest, was none other than a game warden.

Intent, it would seem, on making life for the peasantry as miserable as possible, the gentry placed heavy restrictions on dog ownership. From the fourteenth to sixteenth centuries, English and Scottish commoners were banned from owning sight hounds useful for hunting, such as Irish wolfhounds, Scottish deerhounds, and greyhounds. Peasants tried to get around this prohibition by breeding sight hounds to working sheepdogs as a way to disguise their looks, producing highly-intelligent, speedy hunting dogs known as "lurchers."

But the would-be poacher had to be careful. A peasant dog of hunting size could be confiscated or exterminated for being too large to pass through a looping "dog gage." Peasants were also obliged to cut off three toes of dogs used for pulling carts, guarding livestock, or performing other useful work. The word "curtailed" has its origins in medieval laws which dictated that commoners cut off their dogs' tails so they could be easily distinguished from the aristocrats' animals. The practice eventually led to calling common, nondescript dogs "curs."

A nobleman's entitled existence extended to his dogs, which were generally better off than the peasants—Britain's King

Henry VIII fed his dogs a diet of bread, milk, and meat, the last a luxury peasants seldom tasted. Naturally, a commoner would resent a nobleman's well-fed dog whose collar was rendered in embroidered silk and attached to a leash studded with jewels worth more than he'd earn in a lifetime.

Mimicking their own rigid class structure, the English distinguished between the selectively bred dogs of nobles and the common dogs of the masses. In the sixteenth century, Johannes Caiuss, physician to Queen Elizabeth I, wrote a book about dogs in which he broke down all the existing breeds of his day, classifying the noble hunting breeds as "the gentle kind" and those of the peasantry as the "homely kind." This distinction still survives at modern dog shows, where dogs may be of the "sporting" variety (high-class bird dogs, hounds, and gun dogs) or the non-sporting type (lower-class herding dogs, working, and utility breeds).

As keepers of the canine aristocracy, nobles, the landed gentry and clerics were responsible for the creation of many of the European dog breeds such as the King Charles Cavalier Spaniel and the (Reverend) Jack Russell terrier. The pattern also held in Asia, where people were forbidden to own sacred or royal dogs such as the Pekingese in China, the chin in Japan, and the temple dog Lhasa Apso in Tibet.

By the late Middle Ages, hunts had become lavish, ritualized affairs. Noblemen competed among themselves to provide the fastest, keenest, and most talented hunting dogs. It was each nobleman's goal to create a line of dogs unique to his family or estate, much like a vintage wine.

Virtually all nobles maintained kennels. Tudor King Edward III established a royal kennel on the Thames, which Londoners simply referred to as "Dog Island." Henry VIII later used it for his packs of greyhounds and hunting dogs. The corpulent king also kept mastiffs for baiting, a popular blood sport in which the dogs attacked captive bears or bulls. Fierce attack dogs also protected noble manors.

Dog breeding reached its first golden age during the Renaissance, dating from the mid-fourteenth century. Noblemen nurtured good natured retrievers, which had been brought from the Far East during the Crusades, as well as dogs that had first arrived in Spain with the Moors around 800 A.D., naturally known as Spaniels. From Spaniels, hunters developed the barbet, a curly-haired water dog and ancestor to the French poodle.

When it came to canines, though, what most set the nobility apart from the rabble were their pets. Rare was the commoner who could afford to keep a dog of no useful purpose, so pets supplied another means for the wealthy to flaunt their privilege.

Aristocratic women favored lap dogs, typically miniaturized versions of hounds, terriers, or Spaniels. The ladies' attendants brushed and perfumed the dogs daily, and rubbed their coats with haircloths to remove stray fur that might adhere to their mistresses' fine gowns. It was also said that the dogs drew fleas off one's person—nearly everybody was infested with the biting pests.

The ancient Maltese breed, thought to have been brought to the island of Malta by Phoenician traders, captured many a fair lady's heart. The Bichon Frise arrived in Europe from the Canary Islands in the fourteenth century and gained popularity in the French Court during the sixteenth. The Papillon, one of the oldest European toy breeds and likewise a favorite of French royalty and nobles, served as pets of Marie Antoinette, Henry II, and Madame de Pompadour. These tiny dogs with ears like the wings of butterflies appear in Renaissance portraits by Rembrandt and Rubens.

Among the most famed of dog fanciers was England's King Charles II. He seldom went anywhere without his pack of Blenheim Spaniels, named for Blenheim, the estate of breeders the Duke and Duchess of Marlborough. The King valued the dogs' company so much that he decreed that this breed be permitted in all public spaces, including the House of Parliament, where they were reviled for defecating on the floor.

Charles' small dogs became so famous that people began kid-napping them, which caused the King to post grumpy advertise-ments in newspapers demanding their return. Because of their close identification with the King, the dogs became known as King Charles Cavalier Spaniels. ("Blenheim" is still sometimes used for the red-and-white variety).

Children of royals were likewise surrounded by pets, which often served as their sole playmates. Raised in social isolation, royals often grew up to care more for the animals than they did for other human beings, even their own children. Historian Katharine MacDonogh explains this in her book *Reigning Cats & Dogs*.

> Most monarchs were raised with pets from birth and, in the loneliness of their privileged childhoods, formed a lifelong bond. [Pets] helped reduce the strains of office and fill the vacuum at the heart of monarchy. They countered the ennui and artificiality of court life with its insistence on etiquette and protocol.
>
> For men, and more especially women, pets frequently acted as surrogate children, receiving the parental affec-tion denied their biological issue. Pets were not merely humanized; they were superior to man.

Given the aristocracy's affection for their pets, it's no surprise that dogs appear everywhere in Renaissance art, just as they did in Roman and Egyptian art. By the late Renaissance, the elite so valued their animals that dogs and cats were often made to sit for their own portraits (thus giving us a means to identify the various breeds of the day).

Italian ducal families especially loved dog portraits; many of Italy's finest portrait artists filled their pockets painting these family pets. Marquis Francesco Gonzaga commissioned one such painting from artist Francisco Bonsignori. It's said the painting was so lifelike, one of the Marquis' dogs tried to attack it.

The Age of Enlightenment and subsequent Industrial Revolution brought about economic and political changes that undermined royal authority and loosened the aristocrats' hold on their dogs' bejeweled leashes. Resentment of the gentry's pampered pets was especially strong in France, where in 1770, the ministers of the French Crown had levied a heavy tax against dogs—not those of the elite, of course, but of the commoners.

The people's anger at centuries of injustice finally boiled over during the French Revolution. As monarchs and lords fled from the ire of revolutionaries, life became perilous for their blue-blooded dogs. When revolutionaries captured and imprisoned Queen Marie Antoinette in 1793, her loyal dog, Thisbe, followed her to the guillotine.

> The Queens head fell—there was a moment's dead silence, then the loud, agonizing howl of a dog. In an instant, a soldier's bayonet pierced its heart. "So perish all that mourn an aristocrat," he cried; and mourning indeed, an aristocrat died.

In the wake of the French Revolution, monarchs fearful of losing their heads began enacting social reforms. As the last vestiges of feudalism and absolute monarchy collapsed, so did hunting and fishing regulations which had endured for centuries. Restrictions on dog ownership and taxes were discreetly withdrawn too, or at least no longer enforced.

It had always been the case that royal kennel keepers smuggled puppies out of the castles to sell to commoners rather than give the inferior ones the blade or bludgeon. With the reforms, dogs of quality could finally be displayed and traded in public.

By the late eighteenth century, dogs of noble breeding were becoming more common in the countryside. Commoners valued greyhounds especially, long considered the epitome of aristocratic entitlement. Once comfortably kept in the royal kennels, some at last appeared brazenly tethered in villagers' yards. Also popular were hunting dogs adapted to men on foot, as only the wealthy could afford horses. It's said that the French created the plodding, short-legged basset hound for this purpose. In cities, those who could afford them began keeping dogs as pets—a novel phenomenon.

By Queen Victoria's time, the Industrial Revolution and the global expansion of the British Empire had brought wealth to non-aristocratic merchants, traders, factory owners, and high-ranking military officers. Queen Victoria's interest in dogs melded with their social aspirations, igniting demand for "purebred" pets. With these dogs, people who could not claim blue blood themselves could at least take pride knowing their dogs possessed it.

Now ubiquitous in any discussion of dogs, "purebred" denotes a variety of animal (a "breed") with unique, easily recognizable characteristics setting it apart from others—like the heavy-set body and jowly, pushed-in face of the British national symbol, the English bulldog. Breeders achieve such characteristics through generations of selective breeding, almost entirely exclusive of any mixing with other breeds. (When the ancestry is recorded, the animal is known as a "pedigreed purebred.")

The purebred practice, if not the term itself, owes its genesis to a British country gentleman named Robert Bakewell. Born in 1725 in Leicester, England, Bakewell inherited a family estate near Dishley, about one hundred miles from London. While still a young man, he took many long, rambling horseback trips in the countryside searching for quality animals with which to stock his farm.

In Bakewell's youth, the livestock kingdom was a conglomeration of local landraces and nondescripts, with breeding taking place haphazardly in fields. Cows were primarily raised for milk and sheep for wool, with meat as an end product only when the animals had served their main purposes. Bakewell, however, saw a future in big, meaty livestock bound for Londoners' dinner tables. On his journeys, he sought out and bought animals with this end in mind.

Over the years, Bakewell melded together the various animals he'd acquired and closely bred the ones whose bulkiness he preferred to create boxcar shaped meat producers—Leicester long-horn cattle and Leicester sheep, in addition to the early ancestors of the black Shire draft horse. Bakewell understood that traits tend to run in families—which is why brothers and sisters, even cousins, often look so much alike.

The same holds true in domestic animals, so Bakewell made it his practice to breed closely-related individuals (fathers to daughters, brothers to sisters, etc.) to achieve uniformity. He was meticulous in measuring the results, breeding only the animals whose offspring proved to be big producers.

Bakewell was so successful, his wooly sheep were said to be as wide as they were long. At one point his ewes' legs became too short for their lambs to nurse, causing him to reverse the course of his breeding experiments. With a marketing man's flair, he called his sheep "machines . . . for turning herbage into money." In short order, the Leicester sheep replaced other breeds throughout the Midland counties, with the provision that Bakewell be able to buy back the best of their offspring for breeding.

As the eighteenth century progressed, breeders recognized and began to use Bakewell's almost magical formula for improving stock. Between 1700 and 1800, the weight of British bulls sold for slaughter rose from just 370 pounds to more than 840. Like the fat stock on his farm, Bakewell's selective breeding method spread ever wider.

Bakewell's animals became a subject of intellectual curiosity for Charles Darwin, as they ably demonstrated just how quickly variation within a species could be magnified into large differences in just a few generations. Even King George III took notice of Bakewell's innovations, honoring the "wizard" with an inquiry about his "new discovery in stock breeding."

The dog world was slower to warm to Bakewell's methods. In the first decades of the nineteenth century, people by and large still categorized dogs not by breed, but by purpose—coach dog, hound, beast dog, butcher dog, and vermin dog were terms applied to a variety of types. A dog that hunted foxes, naturally, would be called a foxhound. A herding dog from the Scottish borderlands was a border collie.

Outside the aristocracy, dog breeders remained blissfully unconcerned with the purity of their animals' bloodlines. They simply mated dogs according to how well they performed the task for which they were needed. But as the nineteenth century progressed, Bakewell's highly efficient selective breeding techniques combined with the dog fancy to render uniformity of breed the new gold standard.

The so-called "improvement" of the show dogs began with good intentions. Certainly, many working and hunting dogs of the day were poor specimens. They might have had bowed legs and swayed backs which caused them to fail in their work. But beyond improving obvious physical weaknesses, breeders became more and more obsessed with how the dogs looked, which was all that really mattered in the show arena and to prospective pet owners with no intentions of riding to the hounds, herding sheep in the mountains, or hunting birds in the field.

By mid-century, dog breeders were applying to canines the same principles used to make sheep meatier and bulls larger. Their goals, however, were almost purely aesthetic. For instance, basset hound breeders in England sought to make their dogs heavier, to make herding dogs' noses longer (rough collies), and to develop a variety of distinctive color and coat varieties among the retrievers. These variations made the dogs no more functional and, in fact, began to hold some breeds back from their intended uses. But they accomplished one thing: they made the dogs unique, distinctive—and therefore desired.

"The majority of breeds . . ." writes author Kim Kavin, "were developed like today's Louis Vuitton scarves or Jimmy Choo shoes or Fendi clutches that visually announce a person's economic status."

Because dogs were becoming status symbols, breeds with good stories, such as long-established histories or aristocratic associations, proved highly desirable. These included poodles, Pomeranians, Spaniels, and exotic specimens such as the Japanese chin, a breed popularized by Danish Princess Alexandra, who upon marrying England's Prince Edward received one of the dogs from the British Royal Family.

The public came to view purebred dogs much as they did the royals themselves: as refined, elegant, and morally superior. Writing in *Our Domesticated Animals*, author Charles Burkett acknowledges that these aristocratic canines "may very well be the product of inbreeding," but that "a dog which has no blood cannot be noble. We baptize him with the name 'street cur.'"

For the bourgeoisie with upper class aspirations, dog ownership began and ended with purebreds. As the Victorian era journalist Gordon Stables noted, "Nobody who is anybody can afford to be followed around by a mongrel dog."

Charles Darwin's wealthy cousin, Sir Francis Galton, took the idea of breed purity to a logical but very dark conclusion. Since people can breed domestic animals for desirable behaviors and looks, why shouldn't we do the same with ourselves?

Galton's writings launched a social philosophy called "eugenics," based on the principle that societies had a moral obligation to encourage breeding for desirable qualities and sterilization of those with undesired traits, such as habitual criminals or the mentally ill. Ultimately, eugenics played a role in the Nazi government's extermination of Jews, Poles, gypsies, and homosexuals during the Holocaust.

In the canine world, the desire to "breed pure" led to the creation of breed associations, breed books, and breed pedigrees. Clubs responsible for keeping the records began refusing to register dogs resulting from the mixture of two different breeds. This resulted in closed gene pools, a precursor to genetic problems little understood at the time.

Demand for documented ancestries in the animal breeding world arose first in the Thoroughbred racing industry. In 1791, a scandal erupted in Britain's horse racing community. Unscrupulous owners had been falsifying race entries to rig the betting system. To restore confidence, James Weatherby, with the blessing of the British Jockey Club, began compiling a public "studbook" that traced ancestry and markings to help identify racehorses.

By the early 1800s, much of the livestock community had adopted studbooks and herd books. Proven parentage added value to animals, especially when that parentage traced to race winners and show champions. It's not coincidental that in 1826, John Burke began publishing *Burke's Peerage,* which traced the ancestral backgrounds of England's aristocrats—essentially creating a studbook for the United Kingdom's upper class.

Almost eighty years after the racehorse industry reformed and created a horse registry, the Victorian dog show world underwent its own corruption scandals. With pride and prize money at stake, show dog owners began finding ingenious ways to outwit judges. Some used dyes, shears, and even cosmetic surgery, such as ear trimming on their dogs to deceive the officials. Others simply bribed the judges to gain their favor.

It was not above competitors to sabotage their fellow ring mates. A determined competitor might take shears to a rival's unattended bitch to damage her coat and ruin her blue ribbon chances. Rumors circulated of competitors poisoning others' dogs. At the shows, exhibitors kept locks on their kennel cage doors to protect the animals from being stolen.

Another ruse was to put an inferior dog in the place of one that had gained favor among judges at previous shows. In this way, the celebrated dog could miraculously appear at two widely separated shows on the same weekend. And even the best breeders sold inferior dogs, claiming them to be ring champions, to inflate the prices while keeping the actual winners at the home kennel for breeding.

Just a dozen years after the first modern dog show in Newcastle, poor sportsmanship and corruption threatened to destroy the enterprise. So, in 1873, a group of prominent dog men met in London to discuss the future of dog exhibiting. Their goal was to found an organization that would establish fair rules for dog shows and field trials, and to see to it that shows were run cleanly under established rules for the welfare of the animals. They called their organization, simply, the Kennel Club.

Within the year, Britain's Kennel Club created a studbook to record the performances of show winners and to register dogs so that they could be identified properly. Soon, any show that hoped to attract a large pool of entrants had to adopt the rules of the Kennel Club and employ its judges. Likewise, exhibitors were forced to show only pedigreed dogs. Within a decade, the Kennel Club would exert an iron fist on the Victorian dog show world in England, and the pedigrees it generated solidified the idea of registered purebred dogs.

The gentlemen who started the Kennel Club doubtless had no idea of the impact they'd have on the canine world. In Europe and across the British Empire, kennel clubs spread like poppies in a field. In order to participate, enthusiasts formed specialty clubs to support their breed interests and register their dogs. Then, the clubs would petition to join the national kennel club, or cause a national kennel club to be formed.

But English dogs held the day. Prior to 1900, nearly all the dogs exhibited in kennel club shows in Europe, Canada, and the United States were either imports from the United Kingdom or their descendants. Despite inroads made by others, the English still led in the creation and promotion of national breeds.

In the span of just fifty years, a variety of long-existing British landraces and working dog types were picked over by British breeders and streamlined to form uniform breeds, such as the old English sheepdog, the rough collie and the English bulldog. New breeds were created by crossbreeding existing varieties to form new combinations, such as the whippet, a downsized variety of greyhound resulting from outcrossing to English white terriers.

In the years preceding the turn of the twentieth century, the English exported tens of thousands of purebred terriers, Spaniels, pointers, setters, collies, corgis, greyhounds, whippets and other breeds. Meanwhile, British military and government officials stationed in distant countries scoured the empire, looking for new breeds to develop and exploit.

Plucking dogs from regional landraces and loosely defined breeds, the Brits would return to England and engage in selective breeding programs along the lines established by Bakewell. They gave each "found" breed a formal name, created a written description against which the dogs of the breed could be judged, and sold the "improved" varieties to the public at prices far above what the native animals could bring. They even exported them back to their original countries, where people would pay more for the refined versions of breeds already available in their backyards.

From East Asia, the British brought the chow chow, the Chinese crested, the pug, the Pekingnese, the Japanese chin, and the Sharpei; from Africa, the Basenji; from the Middle East, the Afghan, Saluki and Canaan dog; from Malta, the pharaoh hound; and from Tibet, the Tibetan mastiff, Tibetan Spaniel, Tibetan terrier, the Lhasa Apso, and the shih-tzu.

Breeds were also formed by isolating individuals of a similar type by color, coat, size or other criteria—much the same way the monk Gregor Mendel isolated different varieties of pea plants by selectively breeding them for height, seed color, and pod shape. Examples of this practice are the various setter breeds, including the English, the Irish, the Gordon, and the Irish Red and White. Another was poodles, which breeders divided into toy, miniature, and standard breeds.

Fanciers also resuscitated ancient breeds, such as the already-mentioned Pekingese, nearly wiped out during the Great China War of 1860. When the invaders looted the Summer Palace, they found five little "lion dogs of Peking" in the emperor's quarters. Enchanted with these diminutive beings, they took them back to England. Queen Victoria received one, whom she named Lootie. As for those remaining in China, their royal masters so worried that they'd fall into the hands of common people that they had them all killed. So, the Pekingese owes its modern existence to just those five that escaped that fate and were smuggled to England.

With England setting the example, the other western countries followed suit, selectively breeding land races and regionally known hunting, herding, and utility dogs into specific breeds with registries and written breed standards. Particularly active were the Belgians, French, Germans, Austrians, and the Dutch, who would eventually band together to counter the British dog-dealing juggernaut. In what today would be called "building a brand," breeders began using place-of-origin for naming breeds, such as the German shepherd, the Belgian tervuren, the Swiss mountain dog, the Afghan hound, and Swedish vallhund.

Today, the names of roughly 70 percent of recognized dog breeds refer to a country, region, or a town where they presumably originated. Many of these evolved as "natural" breeds—landraces—used by local people to herd, hunt, protect property, or carry out some other useful purpose. Most flourished in limited geographical areas, performing tasks that determined both their bodies and behaviors. Then the dog fancy swept them up and gave them names, created breed clubs, registries, and standards.

On the other side of the pond, the Yanks' interest in dog shows lagged behind the Brits due to the intrusion of the Civil War. But once hostilities ended, Americans embraced the fancy with great fervor. History records that the Westminster Kennel Club held its first dog show in 1877, making it America's second oldest annual sporting event, right behind the Kentucky Derby.

Just as in England, this first Westminster show featured setters and pointers owned by hunters. Early prizes included pearl-handled pistols useful to the bird hunters and terrier men who worked their dogs in the field. Held at Gilmore's Gardens (soon to be renamed Madison Square Garden), the show attracted 1,200 dogs and proved so popular it had to be extended from three days to four.

In America, too, dog shows began as high-society affairs because of their association with hunting. America's most prominent families all maintained kennels on their estates, and their kennel keepers labored to create blue-ribbon dogs. Show catalogs from the late nineteenth and early twentieth centuries brim with names of America's most prominent families, including the Astors, Rockefellers, Morgans, Whitneys, Belmonts, and Goulds.

A strong market in North America meant that a British breeder could earn considerable money exporting dogs from champion bloodlines. In some cases, small fortunes changed hands. For example, author Mark Derr, in his book *A Dog's History of America*, notes that around the turn of the twentieth century "the most desirable purebred dogs routinely started at $1,000 and ran to $5,000." And more. To help us gauge the amounts Americans were willing to spend, consider that Henry Ford's Model T debuted in 1909 at a cost of $825.

In 1906, wealthy financier J. P. Morgan got into a bidding war with Samuel Utermyer for a highly-regarded rough collie named Squire of Trytton. Ultimately, Utermeyer paid $6,500 for the dog. In 1908, Californian William Ellery purchased the famed Collie Anfield Model for $10,000—about $239,000 in today's dollars.

The Victorian-era show ring has exerted a lasting impact on dogs. Beginning with the formation of the Kennel Club in 1873, the desire to produce dogs which closely resembled their parents and bred true to type became intense, leading to the production of purebreds maintained in closed gene pools. This practice would later lead to health problems, which plagued canine and royal bloodlines alike.

The dog show age represented a significant turning point in the history of dogdom. Most of the breed types that exist today were already defined by the Roman period. But the actual breeds, possessing distinctive and reliably reproducible characteristics, were mostly beyond the ancients.

In his book *Show Dog*, Josh Dean cites an often-made statement, that of the four hundred or so breeds that exist today, a majority were created by humans in only the past two hundred years. The most explosive period in dog breed diversity happened during the Victorian era, a period that UCLA's Dr. Robert Wayne calls "The Age of Novelty." Wayne estimates that "70 to 80 percent of the modern breeds were born in this period of parasols and bowler hats."

Beginning with that first show in Newcastle upon Tyne, the Victorians forever changed the rules of the dog breeding game. They established that it was no longer enough to simply breed good dogs to good dogs, or to breed for a specific task or purpose. Now, a dog's parents had to be of indisputable purebred ancestry and their offspring judged on conformity to breed standards. Pedigrees had to be recorded in breed registries, where outcrossing was at best frowned upon and generally forbidden.

For good and for bad, the legacy of the nineteenth century Victorian dog fancy and the importance it placed on pedigreed, purebred canines continues to shape dogs well into the twenty-first century.

FIVE

A BREED IS BORN

When a man's best friend is his dog, that dog's got a problem.

—Author Edward Abbey

My dog, Onda, is currently resting his head on my feet. He sleeps under my writing desk inside the RV while I tap-tap-tap on the keys. When I get up to go somewhere, he rouses himself and follows me. Stickiness is so common in Australian shepherds that breed aficionados often refer to them as "Velcro dogs."

Aussies, as they are also nicknamed, offer a good example of how dogs become breeds and how breed recognition affects them, for good and for bad. I've been involved with the breed for thirty years, witnessing the changes.

I first saw Aussies with my father at Windansea Beach in La Jolla, California, back in the late 1970s. Two, sometimes three, medium sized bob-tailed dogs would loll around on the beach, waiting for their masters to paddle into shore. I was intrigued by their marbled coat colors—a swirling mix of black, bluish gray, white, and gold. Each dog seemed customized, like the surfers' brightly painted boards.

Our guess was that one of the surfers bred the dogs and sold them among the tight-knit surfing community. (A dog breed's popularity tends to spread, like waves, among like-minded groups of people). My dad and I didn't know what this then-rare breed of dogs was, so we just called them "blue surf dogs."

Name confusion, it turns out, went with the breed. First off, Australian shepherds did not originate in Australia. In fact, their ancestors were developed as landrace herding dogs by Basques in the Pyrenees Mountains of Spain. The little bob-tailed dogs accompanied their owners in places all over the world, shepherding their fine-wooled Merino sheep.

Before the turn of the twentieth century, Merino sheep began arriving in the western United States in large numbers. Since nobody there spoke Basque, a language unrelated to any other, and since the sheep came mostly from Australia, Americans just assumed the dogs did, too.

I got my first Aussie in 1986 while working on a 6,500-acre horse ranch in Colorado. At that time, two Aussies, one named Hyper Hank and the other Bouncing Boo, were winning championships in the new sport of canine disc. My dog, whom I named "Hobie," an homage to the surfer and boatmaker Hobie Alter, proved as adept at rounding up Frisbees as he was with horses and cattle.

One day, we'd gone to the United States Air Force Academy in Colorado Springs to compete in a freestyle dog disc contest where we finished second. We were celebrating on the grass afterward when a slender blonde in her mid twenties walked up. She had an air of confidence and a smile that could sell toothpaste.

"Excuse me," she said, and offered congratulations. "I'm curious to know your dog's bloodlines."

"I don't know," I replied. "He's not papered. But I believe he's a half Hartnagle dog."

"Well, I am a full Hartnagle. I'm Carol Ann Hartnagle."

I felt like I'd met royalty. No family had played as big a role in fostering the Australian shepherd breed in its early decades than the Hartnagles of Boulder, Colorado. Carol's parents had been instrumental in the formation of the breed's official registry, the Australian Shepherd Club of America, and her older sister, Jeanne Joy, literally wrote the book on the breed. It was called *All About Aussies*, and I had a dog-eared copy in my cabin at the ranch.

Today, the Australian shepherd ranks among the twenty most popular breeds in America, according to the American Kennel Club. It's also the AKC's most popular show dog, with the most canine contestants and human exhibitors. And all of them have the Hartnagles largely to thank.

When family patriarch Ernest Hartnagle returned from the Pacific following the Second World War, he found that, with his father deceased, he had his mother, two younger brothers, and a sister to support. Besides running the family farm, he helped out on his uncle's cattle ranch in the Gore Range, on the steep slopes that would later become Vail Winter Resort.

When summer came, "Ernie," as friends call him, would take a horse and three shepherd dogs so he could herd the cattle down into the valley to graze. In the afternoons, they'd climb back up 3,500 feet in elevation on what are now black diamond ski runs. When the weather got hot and the cattle balked, the two Scottish border collies would sometimes quit on him. But one dog named (I'm not making this up) Rover would haze the cattle up and down hills, running, barking and nipping at their heels all the while. Ernie admired the dog's stamina and grit.

Come wintertime, ranching families like the Hartnagles looked forward to the National Western Stock Show and Rodeo, Denver's annual livestock extravaganza. One of the often-featured acts was an Idaho cowboy named Jay Sisler and his dogs, Shorty, Queenie, and Stub. Ernie watched in amused astonishment as the dogs danced on their hind legs, walked on their front ones, played leapfrog over one another, climbed a ladder, played see-saw, and even skipped rope with Jay. For the finale, Jay had Shorty and Stub sit on the ends of a broomstick. Then, he lifted up the stick and put it in his mouth, with the two dogs balanced on either end. And the crowd went wild.

Ernie didn't know what the dogs were, but they looked a lot like Rover. When Ernie befriended Jay, the cowboy told him the dogs were called Australian shepherds.

"I'd never heard the name before, but I decided I was gonna get some of those dogs!" said Ernie.

Not long after the stock show, Ernie met and fell in love with a pretty A&W Root Beer Stand carhop named Elaine Gibson. She'd grown up on a Wyoming ranch and, coincidentally, her family had owned Aussies since the 1920s. They'd called them "bobtail shepherds."

In 1953, the couple acquired their first Aussie, Snipper. Very pleased with her, they went searching for more. Sisler had none to sell, so they reached out to a feisty widow in Lakewood, Colorado, named Juanita Ely. The ranch woman had gotten her original dogs from Basque shepherds in Idaho.

The dogs Ely sold them, Goodie and Badger, laid the groundwork, or what's known as the "foundation stock," of the Hartnagle family's Las Rocosa Australian Shepherds, established in 1955. Concurrent with raising pups, the Hartnagles also started their line of five children, Jeanne Joy, Christine, Joseph, Jim, and the youngest, Carol Ann.

If there were an official birthday for the Aussie, it would be May 5, 1957, when Ely and seven other aficionados got together in Tucson, Arizona, to form the Australian Shepherd Club of America (ASCA). Savvy stock woman that she was, Ely knew that registered pedigrees ("papers," in the dog world) would add value to her dogs, so she and the fledgling club worked with the National Stock Dog Registry to add Aussies to its breed registry.

As a club, ASCA was familial and friendly, its shows less like the formal American Kennel Club events and more like Sunday picnics. People often entered the show ring dressed in cowboy hats and boots.

Although growth in the breed registry was slow, Sisler's dog act, plus the appearance of his Aussies in a few short Disney films, fueled interest in Aussies among livestock owners and horsemen. Many of them came to Denver for the livestock show and left with a pup from the Hartnagles, Ely, rodeo ringmaster Fletcher Wood, or one of a handful of other Colorado breeders.

Chief among them was Denver veterinarian Weldon Heard. Whereas Ely, Wood, and the Hartnagles strived to produce dogs built for the rigors of ranch work, Heard pursued a different ideal based on structure and appearance—qualities that produced show ring success for his "Flintridge" line of dogs.

Visiting Colorado in 1969, a California man named Philip Wildhagen bought a dog from Heard, borrowing Ernie Hartnagle's pickup to fetch the pup. Dutchman of Flintridge, as Wildhagen named him, was a flashy blue merle with a spectacular white bib, perfect for his owner's show ring ambitions.

Wildhagen showed the dog extensively on the West Coast, and Dutchman became ASCA's first champion of record. Mating Dutchman with Thistle, another of Wildhagen's Aussies, achieved what breeders call a "golden cross," meaning that the offspring were of consistently superior quality. Soon West Coast breeders began replacing their large, coarse ranch Aussies with the smaller, more attractive descendants of the Flintridge dogs.

In 1973, Wildhagen moved back east, where Aussies were virtually unknown, and began building enthusiasm for the breed there. Meanwhile, some of the Hartnagle dogs ended up with breeders on Martha's Vineyard, who in turn placed puppies with the Kennedy clan.

"That made Phil [Wildhagen] so jealous," remembers Jeanne Joy Hartnagle.

But the Wildhagen dogs, and by extension, those of Dr. Heard's Flintridge Kennel, had an outsized impact on the breed on both coasts.

"Of all the foundation bloodlines," wrote Ernie in the book *The Total Australian Shepherd*, co-authored with daughter Carol Ann, "the Flintridge line exhibited the greatest influence on the modern Australian shepherd."

Wildhagen's Dutchman came along at a time of transition for ASCA. A leadership crisis in the early 1970s had nearly disintegrated the club. When Ernie stepped in to right the ship, he discovered that ASCA had just $15 dollars in its treasury. With the Hartnagles' guidance, ASCA initiated a more robust activities program, giving people more opportunities to exhibit their dogs.

Concurrently, it was decided that the vague breed standard that had served the association for nearly two decades needed a makeover. In 1975, ASCA's board elected the Colorado chapter headed by Ernie and Elaine to tackle the job, with help from their five children.

The process proved contentious. Judges use breed standards to evaluate dogs in conformation shows, so if your aim is to win those, you lobby for a standard that accords well with the dogs you've got in your kennel. With a stake in the outcome, everyone wanted to bend the new standard to favor their own dogs. Debates got pretty heated, recalls Jeanne Joy.

"At one meeting, there was a lady who tried to trip mom. And then, she and mom got into a fistfight! People got very passionate . . . ! They wanted it their own way."

To its credit, the committee did everything possible to make the process fair and objective, evaluating movement, temperament, structure, and appearance with an objective eye. Their work included measuring the heights of hundreds of dogs across the country. A statistician from the Coors Brewing Company compiled the figures into a chart with a bell curve—with the majority falling between eighteen inches (for a female) and twenty-three inches (for a male).

"That's how we arrived at a size range for the standard," said Jeanne Joy, acknowledged as the breed's most authoritative historian. "It wasn't arbitrary."

One debate centered around coat color. Some argued that red coated Aussies, for which the Hartnagles were known, were not traditional in the breed. But Ernie countered that color had no impact on working ability. He got his way, and today, most red Aussies have Hartnagle ancestry somewhere in their past.

After two years of wrangling and refining, members approved the new standard. By then, the club was celebrating its twentieth Anniversary, and 3,000 dogs appeared in its registry book. But in Ernest Hartnagle's mind, and in the minds of many others, one thing was still missing: recognition by the American Kennel Club. By their way of thinking, a breed just wasn't a breed until the AKC said so.

As ASCA's president, Ernie wrote the AKC in 1976, letting them know the Australian Shepherd existed and requesting that it be added to the AKC studbook. The reply was a polite "No." The reason: there weren't enough dogs. It's not specified in the bylaws how many dogs are needed for the AKC to recognize a breed, but by someone's reckoning, ASCA didn't have enough.

A few years later, when the registry numbers had swelled to more than 5,000, ASCA tried again, and was again turned away. Like the proverbial woman scorned, members responded angrily. Many simply said, "To hell with the AKC!"

In 1984, ASCA's executive committee met in Las Vegas. On the agenda was the question of whether the club should apply for AKC recognition a third time. Heated arguments came from both sides, and in the end, the majority voted no. But after the meeting, the discussion continued and it seemed inevitable that they'd give it another try. Given the ever-growing number of Aussies, the AKC was bound to say yes.

The group never got the chance. A faction of ten breeders unhappy with ASCA's majority decided in secret to form their own club. All of them were show exhibitors impatient to attain AKC recognition so they could compete in its prestigious all-breed shows, such as the National Dog Show in Philadelphia and the Westminster Kennel Club Dog Show in Manhattan.

Calling themselves the United States Australian Shepherd Association (USASA), they wrote their own club bylaws and breed standard, which was subtly different from ASCA's and more favorable to the "show type" Aussie. Despite having only a small number of registered dogs, the breakaway USASA applied for AKC recognition—and got it.

That night, the acting ASCA president called long-time executive secretary Jo Kimes and told her in a pique, "We've lost the Aussie."

"For some reason, they broke a hundred years of tradition," said Kimes. "They thought it was best for the Australian Shepherd."

Jeanne Joy Hartnagle, who can still recall the face slap, put things bluntly. "It was a betrayal," she said. "Justifiably, it angered many. These people came in with a hidden agenda . . . to be part of the AKC. Some were handling other dog breeds. Their concern wasn't for the dogs, but for their own ambitions."

In her opinion, when the USASA chose to rewrite the ASCA breed standard, they were creating a new dog. "The show Australian shepherd is a golden retriever compared to the real working Aussie. You cannot breed to two different standards and pretend that the dogs are the same," she told me.

In ASCA, a dog's working ability had always been paramount. People like the Hartnagles might enter a dog in a sheep herding trial in the morning, then brush the mud from its coat and go into the show ring that afternoon. But the USASA members weren't interesting in the dirty work of herding; they wanted primped and preened Aussie show dogs that could go head-to-head with AKC dogs in prestigious all-breed shows.

When Dr. Heard began breeding dogs to his Platonic ideal for the breed, a small crack was formed between a "show type" and "working type" Aussie. The creation of the USASA and the breed's acceptance into the AKC drove a wedge into that crack.

"It's a dirty secret people don't like to share," said Kristin Tara Horowitz in a blog posted on her website, theaustralianshepherd.net. "There are two types of Australian Shepherd, conformation and working. Generally, the two don't mix."

Working dog supporters today criticize the extreme conformation show lines as "Bernese mountain dog types" with heavy coats, heavy bones, large heads and loose, drooly jowls—and worst of all, no inclination to herd. Show breeders likewise ridicule the working type Aussie as being spindly and inconsistent in appearance.

"AKC breeders breed for beauty and ASCA for herding," said Laurie Thompson, whose dog Tucker was the No. 1 Aussie in the USASA in 2010. "When you look at the herding dogs, a lot of them are really ugly."

Thompson, who lives on an island not far from Seattle, is typical of many people in the dog show hobby. A middle-class woman who has always loved dogs, she grew up watching the Westminster Kennel Club Dog Show and imagining herself taking part with a beautiful dog. She began showing Great Pyrenees in 1980, but later decided the dogs were simply too large. So, she downsized to German shepherds, then to Aussies.

She got her first Australian Shepherds around the time Barack Obama became president. It was a period when few professional handlers showed an interest in Aussies, which gave an amateur owner/handler like Laurie a greater chance for success.

Somehow, Laurie caught lightening in a bottle with her first dog, Whidbey's Moonlight Frost, whom she calls "Tucker." He was, she said, "my once in a lifetime dog," a handsome black tri-colored dog that looked, well, rather like a small Bernese Mountain dog.

Tucker quickly rose to the top, becoming the number one Australian Shepherd in the USASA in 2009, which earned Laurie an invitation to the 2010 Westminster Dog Show. By Laurie's estimate, she was spending $10,000 a year on entry fees, hotel rooms, flights, and grooming—more than $50,000 over Tucker's four-year career in the AKC. One of the biggest expenses was advertisements touting Tucker's show successes.

"Yes, you have to advertise to influence the judges," she told me candidly. "I can't tell you how many times I was at ringside, watching judges look at the [show magazine] ads."

And she got off cheap. In an article that appeared in *The New York Times* the same year Thompson competed in New York, the reporter noted that "a top-notch campaign can easily cost more than $300,000 a year, and because it takes time to build momentum and recognition, a typical campaign lasts for two or three years."

Laurie spoke glowingly of the highs—Tucker becoming one of the top ten Aussies in the AKC, then the number one Aussie in the nation; the invitation to Westminster and Tucker's turn in the ring at the famous Madison Square Garden; and best of all, the day at a regional AKC competition in the Pacific Northwest when Tucker defeated all the other "best of breed" dogs to win "best in show," a pinnacle of success for most show dogs.

These triumphs, she said, helped offset the snarky behavior shown to her by her ring competitors.

"When you get to the top, people become jealous. The rumors start. I've been accused of dying Tucker, that he is missing teeth. On and on . . . As soon as you have a dog that's winning, the bad comes out of people. Not all people, but some. Even people I consider friends."

To win USASA/AKC conformation shows, she observed, "you have to start with an exceptional dog." But, as in any show business, talent can only take you so far on the trajectory to stardom.

"I've been doing this for five years. And I've learned, *it's not about the dogs*. You need people to get anywhere," she said to me.

People in the AKC, that is. Laurie also showed in ASCA, but found it to be too "cliquish." As a newcomer, she felt the judges didn't give her or Tucker a fair chance. I asked whether Laurie knew Carol Ann Hartnagle, a much sought-after breeder/judge at ASCA shows.

"Not well," she said. "Carol Hartnagle is a name in ASCA but . . . (she shrugs) in the AKC? She's nobody."

When I related this story to Carol, now an executive vice president of an international data storage company, she laughed it off. Despite the heels and tailored suits, she's still a cowgirl as tough as the dogs she breeds. And still determined to have a say in their future.

In spite of the betrayal inflicted on her family by the USASA, Carol became an AKC herding judge and is currently bolstering her credentials as an AKC show judge. She is doing so, she says, "Because it's the way I can most influence the future of the breed."

In addition to judging dog shows all over the world, she leads seminars to educate judges about the Australian shepherd and the attributes that make it an exceptional *working* dog. In this way, she hopes, she can pull the dogs back from the excesses seen in nearly every show line in every breed recognized by dominant registries like the AKC and the British Kennel Club.

It's no secret that pedigreed, purebred dogs are in trouble. Nearly every breed of dog is afflicted with one or several genetic disorders, the result of generations of closed breeding pools mandated by the Victorian-era kennel club system, and by the distorted priorities of conformation dog shows. Aussies have not been immune.

In the 1990s, one of the wealthiest and most successful Australian shepherd show breeders, also one of the ten who formed the USASA, owned two prominent grand champion dogs. Both produced prodigious offspring, and as it turned out, a number of those descendants developed epilepsy. The effect was especially pronounced in England, where one of the dogs was sent, because importation restrictions and the relative newness of the breed there had left breeders with few studs from which to choose.

When word spread of an epilepsy epidemic in the breed, the initial reaction in the U.K. was "not constructive," according to C. A. Sharpe, a show exhibitor who would eventually found the Australian Shepherd Health and Genetics Institute to inform and educate Aussie breeders about genetic health problems and to support research into canine epilepsy.

Prominent show breeders in Great Britain adopted a defensive posture, resorting to threats and coercion to silence those who spoke out about the problem. But a core group of dedicated fanciers stood together to try to limit epilepsy's spread. They shared pedigrees of affected animals, collected DNA samples for research, and imported new dogs with "clean" bloodlines.

Breeders overseas remained blissfully unaware of or indifferent to the British breeders' problems until 1994, when a one-page in memoriam ad appeared in ASCA's *The Aussie Times*. It consisted of a photo of a beloved dog, the dates of his birth and death, and something usually not included in such tributes: the cause of death and a two-generation pedigree that implicated the dog's ancestors and their owners.

"That's when the manure hit the circulating cooling device," recalls Sharpe.

People with related dogs were furious. Breeders, and especially stud dog owners, denied that their dogs were affected, denied that epilepsy was the cause of the seizures, and denied that the genes could have come from their side of the pedigree.

"And the band played on as they continued their self-destructive waltz . . ." Sharpe wrote.

As things would turn out, I would become one of the victim owners. Following Hurricane Katrina, I decided to adopt a dog orphaned in the flood. As I web surfed dogs on the adoption site petfinder.com, I came across a striking Aussie girl named Kona being kept at Golden Retriever Rescue of the Rockies. Since she needed a home as much as the dogs down in New Orleans, I drove to Golden, Colorado, to see her. With her beautiful blue merle coat and her eyes—one blue, the other brown—Kona stood out from the uniformly blonde mates in the private adoption kennel. She was sweet and happy and . . . perfect. Or so I believed.

Within a few weeks of arriving home with me, Kona began having epileptic seizures. She would lie down and begin running in place. Her mouth would salivate so much that pools of sticky fluid would form on the floor. Her body convulsed so hard it shook the house, and I had to be careful to avoid her snapping teeth as I held her down to protect her from self-injury. When one of these grand mal seizures ended, Kona would weave around drunkenly, then drink her water bowl dry.

I controlled her seizures as best I could with costly medications. But a year later, I was vacationing with Kona in Mexico when she went into seizure. I rushed her by boat to a vet, but the seizures continued. There was nothing the doctors could do. After she had suffered six grand mal seizures in a single day, I made the decision to put Kona down. A veterinarian administered pentobarbital to Kona in the back of my Dodge Caravan, and the next day, I borrowed a shovel and buried her in a graveyard during a rainstorm. Tears poured from my eyes for the sweetest, happiest dog I'd ever known.

It's hard to imagine why anyone who professes to love dogs would continue to breed animals with known genetic disorders, causing untold pain to the dogs and heartbreak to their owners by hiding that fact. And yet, what I learned during my two-year stint in the dog show game was that it includes bad actors for whom a blue ribbon or a Westminster title is more important than any number of dogs' health and well-being. Their will to win blinds them to the harm they inflict on their dogs and on others' lives.

In 2008, a bombshell exploded amid the purebred dog world in the form of a BBC documentary called *Pedigree Dogs Exposed*. The hour-long documentary showed that inherited disorders and welfare issues related to tightly-restricted breeding affected millions of purebred dogs around the world. Most of the problems originated with Victorian-era breeding practices, including closed book registries (in which no animals outside an established breed can be registered) and the common practice of inbreeding to maintain desired physical characteristics and behaviors, collectively known as "traits."

Besides bringing on diseases like epilepsy, rare cancers, and congenital heart problems, overly selective breeding also cultivates exaggerated features; when carried to extremes, this practice has resulted in numerous breeds barely capable of functioning. While it's easy to cast blame on all-breed registries like the AKC or the Kennel Club, the problem actually begins with the judges in the show ring and the breeders who strive to please them.

In 2017, the Westminster Kennel Club Dog Show bestowed its highest honor, the Best in Show title, on Rumor (Grand Champion Lockenhaus' Rumor Has It V Kenlyn), a German shepherd from the herding group. It was the second time in Westminster history that the breed had won and a thrill for fans of the AKC's second most popular breed.

But even from the cheap seats high up near the rafters of Madison Square Garden, it was plain to see something was wrong with this dog breed.

Compared to the other herding dogs, the show German shepherd is a disaster. To do its job, a herding dog requires balance, strength, athleticism and agility. At Westminster, though the show-bred Aussies, border collies, and Shetland sheepdogs might not have been able to match the tireless enthusiasm for herding cows in the Rockies shown by Rover way back when, they at least *looked* like they could do the job. The same could not be said of Rumor.

As he circled the arena, his rear pasterns (the rough equivalent of our leg shins) nearly scraped the artificial turf, as though he was walking on his knees. His stride was so long, it would have been impossible for him to pivot away from a deadly cow kick or the butting head of a ram. And his back had such an acute sloping angle he appeared to be trotting up a steep hill.

Once an admired working breed used by police forces and the military the world over, during the last couple of decades, German shepherds have earned a reputation for being sickly and dimwitted. Even in Germany, the police have replaced them with Belgian malinois, which are healthier, more intelligent, and more aggressive. Likewise, when Seal Team Six raided the Bin Laden compound in Pakistan, they brought a malinois for the mission.

Despite its popularity, the German shepherd in America is the canine poster child for hip dysplasia, a genetic disorder characterized by a loose hip joint. An estimated one in five German shepherds has inherited this painful and potentially disabling disease.

But for reasons known only to those in the breed, the show version of the dog is far worse off than the pet variety. A typical show shepherd like Rumor hunches over like a canine Quasimodo, its back deformed into an arching "U" shape. The rear haunches are now at such an extreme angle that the typical show German shepherd resembles a frog on a lily pad.

The main reason breeders select dogs like this is to emphasize the breed's spectacular "flying trot," which gives them an almost floating movement. But the extremes to which the German shepherd has been bred for this gait results in a dog that is wobbly and easily knocked off balance. It's a fault that is detrimental to the dogs' original purpose—herding—as well as its function as a working police and military dog, but one that for some reason pleases exhibitors, owners, and judges.

Dog show judges often say they are not judging a beauty contest, but instead selecting dogs that adhere most closely to each breed club's written standard. But in the real world, beauty and excess often triumph in the show ring. Case in point, Rumor.

Of the 3,200 dogs in 200 breeds that went through the Westminster rings in 2017, Rumor was chosen for "Best in Show" as the individual who conformed most closely to his breed's standard. But a look at the German shepherd breed standard shows that Rumor deviated substantially from the description of a dog whose "withers (shoulders) are higher than and sloping into a *level* back [emphasis mine]."

Rumor's back could, by no stretch of the imagination, be described as level. In fact, it sloped like a table with two legs sawed in half.

In 2016, an even more afflicted German shepherd became the center of controversy at Cruft's Dog Show, the English equivalent of Westminster. The breed winner of the German shepherds, Crughaire Catoria, was shown on television crabbing around the ring, her sloping back hunched over and exhibiting "a painful looking, out of step gait," according to *The Daily Mail*. Cruft's television commentator, Clare Balding, described the dog as "distinctly unsettled," adding, "it did not look like a healthy, free-moving dog."

Hundreds of viewers wrote to Cruft's show directors, complaining that the owner, Susan Cuthbert, should be cited for animal cruelty. England's Royal Society for the Prevention of Cruelty to Animals released a statement that it was "shocked and appalled" to see the dog's condition. In response, show officials said they were considering eliminating the breed from future competitions. But once the media tempest had passed, Cruft's pulled back from banning the breed, instead choosing to implement a tepid roster of rule changes.

Caroline Kisko, the secretary of the Kennel Club, said: "The breed standard was changed in 2016 to emphasize the importance of GSDs being capable of standing comfortably and calmly, freely and unsupported in any way."

Being able to stand seems like a low bar to set for any dog breed, much less one celebrated for their heroism by both sides during the Second World War. As Caen Elegans wrote on his website, Science and Dogs, "there was a time when a GSD could clear an 8.5 foot wall; that time is gone."

"The German Shepherd Dog is . . . a breed that is routinely mentioned when people talk about ruined breeds; maybe because they used to be awesome," says Elegans, who is trying to educate people about the negative impact of dog show excess.

In a popular online photo essay, Elegans uses historical and contemporary images of dog show champions to demonstrate the extent to which judging that favors physiological extremes has made many of today's show dogs into mutant beings. Because of dog show aesthetics, breeders have stretched once moderate Dachshunds to such absurd lengths that they now suffer high rates of intervertebral disc disease.

Pugs, boxers, and bulldogs have, over the past century, become so flat faced that they have breathing problems; most airlines now ban them for fear of heat stress-induced asphyxiation. And the St. Bernard, once a noble working dog, has become so furry, loose-skinned, and heavy that it is now functionally unemployable; any exertion causes it to overheat.

Ultimately, Elegans lays the blame at the feet of judges, breeders, and breed clubs too set in their ways to revise standards and improve education in the interest of advancing breed health.

"No dog breed has ever been improved by the capricious and arbitrary decision that a shorter/longer/flatter/bigger/smaller/curlier 'whatever' is better. Condemning a dog to a lifetime of suffering for the sake of looks is not an improvement; it is torture," he concludes.

Ironically, the best hope for the future health of purebred dogs lies with the very breeders who caused all the problems in the first place. Kennel clubs have awoken to the fact that they need to be more responsible when it comes to the long-term health of the dogs they register.

Long ago, Sweden's national kennel club decided to make health-testing mandatory for registrations. In the early 1990s, it began requiring breeders to x-ray the hips of eighty breeds afflicted with dysplasia. A simple three score system enabled breeders to easily make breeding decisions; if the dog scored a two, it could not be bred. A dog with a score of one could be bred only to a dog with a score of zero. It was the organization's first step toward making registration a mark of quality rather than a mere record of parentage.

As more health tests became available, they were slotted into Sweden's existing system and made a condition of registration. As inbreeding became a greater area of concern, the Swedes forged new tools to help breeders better pair dogs to encourage healthy outcomes. Their pedigree database includes a calculation known as a "coefficient of inbreeding" which allows a breeder to create a theoretical "test breeding" that shows how closely related any offspring will be.

The Swedes also prevent highly inbred dogs from being brought into the country and registered. And they've added temperament and performance tests as requirements for awarding championships. Working abilities, likewise, may be tested. Border collies, for instance, must pass a herding test. To reduce the show ring excesses caused by fashion, the Swedish kennel club educates their judges about breed health—without having been provoked to do so by a scandalous national documentary exposé.

To protect dog buyers, the Swedish Kennel Club worked with government to create consumer protection laws: if anything goes wrong with the health of a pup in the first three years, the breeder is held financially responsible. This measure severely cuts down on lackadaisical puppy mill breeders, who must now think twice about creating litters without precautions such as health testing for disorders commonly found in the breeds. And woe betide the backyard breeder who chunks out a litter of poodles to fund a summer vacation, only to later find herself on the hook for her customers' veterinary bills.

In America, the AKC is aware of the need for greater accountability when it comes to dogs' health and well-being. In the face of mounting criticism of purebred dog breeding practices and falling registration numbers, the organization now supports independent, voluntary national certification for breeders called "Canine Care Certified."

Developed by the esteemed Purdue University Center for Animal Welfare Science, the program sets rigorous standards for the physical and behavioral health of breeding animals that, for dogs, include basic preventative care and treatment, health screening, and genetic testing. Puppies also must be properly socialized and mentally stimulated so as to promote healthy neural and physical development and a head start on training.

Facilities must provide breeding animals and puppies access to outdoor exercise and indoor protection from the weather, along with safe flooring, quality nutrition, and a host of other conditions. And there are requirements for the caretakers, too, which include continuing education in dog care, genetics, health and welfare, low-stress handling, and best practices in client relations, such as allowing people to return dogs due to financial hardship or because of temperament or health problems. All of the requirements are subject to third-party audits of the kennels.

Despite getting a bad rap from the public and the press, the American Kennel Club is moving in positive directions. It is the largest single funding source for dog health research in the United States. And it has added activity programs for herding, flyball, agility, obedience, tracking, and more, so that people can do more with their dogs besides parade them around the show ring. They have opened many of these events to mixed-breeds. In sum, they are conscious that they have a responsibility to more than just the show fancy.

Individual breed clubs, too, play a key role. They can choose to address problems in their breeds, or stick their heads in the sand. Dalmatian breeders provide a good example of responsible action. Virtually all Dalmatians suffer from a propensity to form bladder stones. The gene responsible for the dogs' characteristic spotted coat also results in high levels of uric acid crystals, which can coalesce to form stones that block the urinary tract, a potentially fatal condition.

In 1973, geneticist Robert Schaible at the Indiana University School of Medicine began breeding Dalmatians with English pointers. He then bred generations of the offspring with other Dalmatians. After 15 generations, the AKC allowed Dalmatians from this healthier pedigree, spots intact, to be registered.

New genetic knowledge offers the prospect of restoring health to dozens of dog breeds. But there has to be a willingness on the part of breed clubs and national kennel clubs to problem solve, and sometimes, the necessity of reaching outside closed gene pools to improve overall genetic health.

My own breed, the Aussie, represents an example of how people can take positive steps to improve the lot of their dogs. During the epilepsy epidemic of the 1990s, concerned individuals formed the independent Australian Shepherd Health and Genetics Institute, which provides information to breeders and pet buyers, and also provides funding for research into the causes of diseases, including epilepsy.

C. A. Sharp, one of ASHGI's founders, said that the problems in dog breeding start with human nature.

"People often fail to think in the long term. They think only about the next litter, the next blue ribbon. Most people aren't analytical about what they do. The most successful breeders pay a lot of attention to all the things they do. That's the reason they enjoy success," she said.

Carol Hartnagle put it another way when she said, "There are commercial breeders who only want to make money. There are show breeders who only want to win ribbons. And there are people, like my family, who want to be stewards of our breed."

SIX

PITY THE PIT BULL

The only thing dangerous about pit bulls is an uneducated opinion.

—Pro pit bull T-shirt

L angley, Washington, is a village made up mostly of antiques stores, chic boutiques, fine-dining restaurants and tourist shops that sell taffy and T-shirts. It's a popular getaway for Seattleites to visit in the summer, including the Nordstrom family and Microsoft billionaire Steve Balmer, who have vacation homes on Whidbey Island. The chamber of commerce proudly boasts that Langley is the place where "history and hipness meet."

Incongruously nestled amid the quaint gingerbread buildings that line First Street is a hulking, abandoned, barn-red tavern.

Opened in 1908 as the "Olympic Game Club," the place catered to the rougher characters of Whidbey Island's past—loggers and fishermen, mill workers and longshoreman. They came to the Olympic to drink, play cards, and sometimes wager on prizefights. Beginning in 1921, the club featured a new entertainment: dog fighting. These events were so popular that people began calling the place "The Dog House."

During Prohibition, the management called off the fights because they drew attention to the building's parallel function as a speakeasy. The Dog House is believed to be the last dog fighting parlor in Washington to close. But dog fighting's sordid past on the island—and indeed, across America—lives on in the form of the pit bull terrier.

A century after the Olympic was built, problems with fighting-bred dogs came to light in the *Whidbey News-Times*. It was reported that two roving pit bulls had attacked and killed four Shetland sheep belonging to a Langley couple. Earlier that year, three pit bulls fatally attacked a Labrador retriever farther north, in Oak Harbor. This attack had followed another in which two pit bulls broke through a wood fence and fatally attacked a Shetland sheepdog in another family's backyard.

But even before the stories broke, local animal control officials had a foreboding that trouble with the fighting breed was brewing. Island County Animal Control Officer Carol Barnes responded to a 911 call about a pack of stray dogs. She corralled four pit bulls and brought them to the Whidbey Animals Improvement Foundation (WAIF) shelter.

"I began looking at them and noticed they were all scarred," recalls shelter manager Shari Bibich. "And it dawned on me that they were being used for fighting."

A woman who worked for Microsoft on the mainland called to claim the dogs. When she came to pick them up, two of the dogs attacked a third pit bull bitch right in front of Bibich. Bibich refused to release the animals to the woman, whose sedan provided no means to keep the dogs from staging another brawl inside the car. The woman left in a fit of anger.

Bibich soon learned from a shelter volunteer that this woman and her partner were keeping thirty or more pit bulls chained to trees in a remote area of South Whidbey Island. When animal control officers and law enforcement went to check on the allegation, the dogs had all mysteriously vanished, leaving only chain-scarred trees and worn-down patches resembling small crop circles.

Fighting dogs had returned to Whidbey Island with a vengeance. And the problems were just beginning.

In 2007, NFL quarterback Michael Vick's conviction on felony charges of operating an interstate dog fighting operation opened the lid on the roiling pot of illegal dog fighting in the United States. Numerous sources, including the Humane Society of the United States (HSUS) and the American Society for the Prevention of Cruelty to Animals (ASPCA), describe the activity as "ubiquitous." Even unapologetic defenders of the pit bull admit that dog fighting—which relies almost exclusively on pit bulls—is still prevalent.

"Dog fighting is pervasive. No town, city, county or state is immune," wrote Karen Delise in her book, *The Pit Bull Placebo*, a defense of the dog fighting breeds.

According to the most recent HSUS estimates, 40,000 people are involved in organized dog fighting in the United States. Another 100,000 take part in illegal street fights. Each year, more than 250,000 dogs (mainly pit bulls) are bred and used for illicit fights, contributing significantly to the overpopulation of the breed as a whole.

Dog fighting has existed since ancient times. The Romans often used Molosser dogs, ancestors of pit bulls, in the Coliseum, pitting them against bears, bulls, lions, and the occasional gladiator. The sport was revived in twelfth century England, when the practice of "baiting"—releasing dogs into the ring to fight chained bears and bulls—became a common and highly popular entertainment.

King Henry VIII was a fight fan and had a dog pit at his palace in Whitehall. Queen Elizabeth I had an official master of bears and dogs and bred her own line of mastiffs for bear-baiting contests. But by the 1800s, England's stomach for blood sport began to turn, at least officially. In 1835, the English Parliament outlawed the sports of bull baiting, bear baiting, and dog fighting.

But outlawing the contests only had the effect of making dog-on-dog fighting, the most portable and easily concealed of the battles, more popular. In 1913, pit bull breed historian Theodore Marples noted, "the appetite of the populace, and also the gentry—not forgetting the undergraduates of Oxford and Cambridge—for a more vicious form of entertainment was not extinguished with the abolition of bull baiting, which sport was largely substituted by dog fighting . . . which was, of course, carried on clandestinely."

In the mines around Staffordshire, the sport literally went underground. Dog fighting flourished in the mining district, where the bloody spectacles could be conducted in the mine pits, away from public view.

Whereas bull or bear baiting favored big, heavy dogs such as the English mastiff, pit fighting put a premium on agility and quickness. Fighting dog breeders turned to the British "butcher's dog," a working breed. With their heavy heads and compact but powerful bodies, the muscular and brave "bull dog" would tenaciously hold on to a bovine's snout. With the bull or cow's attention diverted, the butcher could rush in with a hammer or knife and dispatch the animal.

Beginning from that foundation, the breeders meticulously altered the dog for efficiency in the fighting pit. In a 1913 publication of *The Dog Fancier*, Theodore Marples wrote that "for this sport, a different type of dog was required to the Bulldog—viz, a dog with a longer and more punishing jaw, and more agility, yet game and powerful."

Breeders found that they could cross the butcher's dogs with terriers, which were at the time bred as vicious, fearless hunters of small game. The bull & terrier, as the hybrid breed became known, proved to be a fierce, tenacious fighter. Years of selective breeding refined by the merciless, bloody fighting pit solidified its traits.

Bull & terriers provided the template for today's pit bull. Now, as then, the typical pit bull head is large and broad to accommodate powerful jaw muscles that mass like thick cables atop the blunt, wedge-shaped skull. The body is deep in the chest, with prominent muscles that bulge and ripple under a short, slick coat. When breed standards were created, provisions were made to allow ear cropping, performed to prevent the ears from being grabbed, torn, and shredded by opponents.

A pit bull is less a breed of dog than a type of dog, just as scent hounds, shepherd dogs, and retrievers are types of dogs. All dogs referred to as pit bulls—including the American pit bull terrier, the Staffordshire terrier (England), the American Staffordshire terrier and the American bulldog—trace their ancestry back to the bull & terrier dogs developed in England for pit fighting. Staffordshire, of course, refers to the mining area where interest in fighting dogs was especially keen.

Dog fighting came to America during the Civil War, when miners from Great Britain immigrated to the Appalachians to mine coal. Though it would achieve its greatest popularity in the South, dog fighting was a popular entertainment on both sides of the Mason-Dixon Line. After the war, it travelled with immigrant trains to the West.

As a group, nineteenth century dog fighters were secretive, especially in regard to their dogs' breeding and bloodlines. The finest dogs were passed only to family and the most trusted friends. The secrecy of their lineages was closely guarded, and any pedigree papers that existed were often falsified. Nobody wanted to give an "edge" to the competition, especially with hard-earned money on the line. But that philosophy changed with a "dog man" named John Pritchard Colby, who would become the most successful popularizer of dog fighting and pit bulls in America in the early twentieth century.

Colby was born in Newburyport, Massachusetts, in 1875, his ancestors having come to America from England. The port town where he was raised gave the young man ample exposure to the immigrants from his ancestral homeland, whose sparse possessions included the game fighting dogs, the so-called bull & terriers. Colby came to own his first pit bulldog in 1888, at the age of thirteen. That same year, the book *The Dog Pit*, by Richard E. Fox was published, detailing the *National Police Gazette* rules governing dog fighting and further popularizing the activity throughout America.

Police of the era frequently participated in dog fighting, which at the beginning of the twentieth century was still legal in most states. Today, pit bull advocates sometimes point to historical photos of police with their pit bulls, implying or outright stating that the animals were used for police work. Doubtless, some were used to intimidate vagrants and street criminals, but the proud policemen mainly used the dogs as fighters. The *Police Gazette*, a tabloid with lurid tales of bank robberies, murders, Wild West outlaws, and depictions of scantily-clad burlesque performers and prostitutes, helped keep the cops and the public informed on upcoming dog fighting matches.

One famous match in 1897 established young Colby's legitimacy and fame as a breeder and "dog man." The match held in Boxford, Massachusetts, pitted one of his dogs, Spring, against a champion named Crib. The marathon bout lasted three hours and fifteen minutes, with Spring the bloody victor. The dog would go on to be a foundation sire for the Colby line of fighting dogs. Colby proudly displayed Spring on his business envelopes for years.

Colby's reputation spread rapidly, but what made the young dog breeder the fountainhead for fighting dogs across America, and indeed, throughout the world, was his willingness to not only breed them and fight dogs, but to sell them.

"John P. Colby broke . . . tradition when he began to offer stud service and quality bred pups for sale to the 'common man,'" wrote E. L. Mullins in *The Registrar for International Sportsmen*, a magazine dedicated to the American pit bull terrier. "That was to be his crime."

As a breeder of fighting dogs, Colby would take out half-page ads in *The Dog Fancier*, the leading breeders' magazine of its day. Amid the country gentlemen's soft-mouthed retrievers and the city dweller's effete poodles, one could find line drawings of Colby's heavily muscled and lean fighting dogs. At that time, dog fighting was considered as legitimate a pursuit among breeders and dog fanciers as any other. Typically the ads boasted, "John P. Colby has bred and sold more fighting dogs than any one man in America" and touted his dogs' greatest attribute: their gameness.

In the pit fighter's estimation, gameness is the most prized quality of a dog. A dog may be a vicious fighter, or as a "dog man" might say, a "punisher," but if he quits fighting, he's likely to be tossed on the refuse heap as a disreputable "cur." It's the willingness to fight through pain, injury, and exhaustion that makes a dog game. As Colby himself said, "It's easy enough to get good lookers and good fighters, but it takes a game dog to win."

In regard to gameness, Colby's dogs were the Rocky Balboas of the canine world. He'd boast of their game nature in his ads, writing such things as, "John P. Colby bred and sold Bruce Connell's 36-pound dog Sandy that licked Reddington's Boxer at Pittston, Pa., in 3 hours, thirty minutes, over $3,000 changing hands."

Standards for Colby's breeding dogs were strict and brutal. It's said he admitted only one outside dog into his breeding program, and then only after it was made to fight three of his top dogs on the same day. The dog lived, but it took many weeks for him to recover from the "test."

Colby bred such dogs from 1889 to 1941—more than fifty years. His son, Joseph, claimed that his dad had raised more than 5,000 dogs. Colby bloodlines can be traced as far back as records of fighting breeds exist in America, back to their origins in Ireland and England.

Today, pit bull breeders boast of having Colby dogs in their pedigrees—including the Colby family itself. Although their dogs are not explicitly sold for the fighting pit (it's now a felony in all fifty states to participate in dog fighting, and sellers always deny that they are involved in pit fighting), the Colby family's pit bull website offers for sale direct descendants of John P. Colby's famous fighters, noting that "the strain is still known worldwide for tops in conformation, temperament, and gameness."

Throughout his sordid dog fighting career, Colby sought legitimacy for his breed, helping to form the Staffordshire Club of America, which, to paraphrase the words of author E. L. Mullins, was instrumental in "forcing" the American Kennel Club to accept the breed in 1936. This was an astute move; with more and more states outlawing dog fighting, a breeder like Colby could not only avoid scrutiny by participating in the legitimate activity of conformation showing, but also sell unsuitable fighting dogs to show ring fanciers.

In a shrewd bit of obfuscation, when the American Kennel Club finally bowed to pressure and accepted the breed in 1936, they changed the breed's name from "American pit bull terrier" to "Staffordshire terrier," thus distancing the dogs from the purpose for which they were bred: explosive, deadly combat in the fight pit. Colby's Primo, an American pit bull terrier, was one of the foundation dogs chosen to exemplify the Staffordshire terrier breed standard in the AKC.

"It was exactly the same dog as our American pit bull terrier," said Andy Johnson of the rival United Kennel Club in a 1987 *Sports Illustrated* article. "They even opened their registry to our dogs. The AKC didn't want anything in their name that would remind people of the fighting history of the pit bull. It was like a family denying that it had horse thieves in its past." Or that it had pathological killers.

On February 2, 1909, John Colby's two-year-old nephew, Bert Colby Leadbetter, wandered into his uncle's yard, where the dogs were kept. One of the dogs attacked the boy, grabbed him by the neck and "ferociously shook him like a rag," according to an account that appeared in the *Boston Daily Globe*. The dog let loose of the boy then snapped at other parts of his body, inflicting numerous and severe wounds.

Colby ran out, drove the dog away and carried the child into the house, where the boy died. A medical examiner found that little Bert Colby Leadbetter's "backbone and spine had been broken at the base of the brain."

Colby's sister Elizabeth, the article explained, was "prostrated." But John Colby was secretive about the death, choosing not to call the police. However, word spread about the attack and a sheriff's marshal investigated. In the end, no action was taken against the dog or its owner.

Colby had every reason to be circumspect about the murder. In his day as well as now, the myth spread by fighting dog breeders was that the dogs may be merciless in the pit, but are gentle, loving pets. If word had gotten out that the Colby dogs were child killers, the carefully constructed lie would be destroyed. Other incidents give support to the notion that at least some of Colby's famous dogs were "man biters." In 1906, the *Boston Globe* reported that a Colby dog on the loose had been shot dead by police after attacking and biting a boy and girl.

Curious whether today's dog fighters adhere to a "code of ethics" that calls for culling dogs that bite humans, I went in search of a modern day John Colby. Given the secretiveness of the underground pit-fighting society, I thought this would prove difficult. But as it turned out, I had only to look as far as my own kitchen.

Glenn is a handyman who does work on my rented house. One day while he was repairing some plumbing, I started talking about pit bulls and the problems that surround them. Immediately, Glenn began a long and passionate defense of the breed and their use for fighting.

As he saw things, fighting was necessary to prove a dog's instincts and breeding.

"It's just like your herding dogs," he said. "If a dog is bred to herd, you don't really know if it is any good unless you put him in a pen with some sheep. Same with a pit bull. If you don't fight them, how do you know if they're any good?"

Turns out the ex-Marine, Vietnam veteran, and avid biker had owned dozens of fighting dogs. Coy about whether he actually fought them, he nonetheless began telling me detailed stories of fights he'd seen and explaining how the whole underground dog fighting world functioned.

I was curious to know whether the dogs ever bit their owners.

"Sure," he said, rolling up the sleeves over his heavily muscled forearms and showing me the scars of past bites.

"But the worst one I got is here," he said, pointing at his cheek. There were two distinctive divots near his mouth, one just below his bottom lip, the other higher up on the round part of his cheek. "One day I was over at a friend's house and he asked me to look at his new dog," he said. "I bent down to give him a look over, and when I turned away, the son-of-a-bitch bit me right here in the face."

Once the pair got the dog under control, Glenn and his buddy went into the house and cracked open a couple of beers. "I didn't think the bite was bad, but then I realized that the beer was flowing out of the hole at the bottom of my mouth."

Glenn said that he was reluctant to go to a doctor, fearing the bite might draw authorities. "I didn't want to get my friend in trouble or have his dog taken away," he said.

However, when the cut became infected and his face swelled up to the size of a grapefruit, he finally had to go to an emergency room. He advised his friend that the dog needed to be put down. He offered to shoot it if his friend didn't want to.

"But the son-of-a-bitch was in denial," Glenn said. "He kept telling me it was a nice dog and that it wouldn't hurt anyone. I couldn't fricking believe it. Here I was with two holes in my face, he'd seen the dog attack me, but he kept on insisting that the dog was fine.

"I mean, that's just not right. If a dog is a man biter, you just have to put it down," he said, echoing the "dog man's" unwritten code of ethics. To this day, he says, he doesn't know what became of the dog that bit him, but he has seen many instances of dog fighters who have kept man-biting dogs in their breeding programs.

"The old timers had a code. But not anymore. If a guy has a dog that bites, he's likely to just keep on breeding it. Or maybe he'll sell it to somebody who don't know better," he said. "But yeah, I've been bitten plenty of times, and so have guys I know."

Spectating at a dogfight is a tricky thing, from a legal standpoint, like being present during a drug deal or joining a group of ecoterrorists on the high seas to stop a Japanese whaler. In Colorado, where I live, it's a felony crime to simply be present at a dogfight. While the journalist in me toyed with the idea, the animal lover, dog trainer and chicken-shit when it comes to law breaking rebelled. I really didn't want to see dogs locked in mortal combat, tearing muscles from bone and yelping in pain. So, I decided to experience it vicariously, through Glenn.

So one day, over beers and burgers, he described the scene of a typical, professional dogfight. This particular bout took place in the unincorporated rural area of Pueblo County, Colorado, where law enforcement is as sparse as icebergs in the desert. Pulling off the main highway, a driver follows a hand-drawn map to a dirt road leading to a long driveway. At the property entrance, a gateman checks the names of the occupants against a list; if you bring an uninvited or unknown guest, you are turned away. A gate fee of $20 is charged to each person.

At the end of the driveway sits a barn surrounded by cars and pickups, some containing portable dog crates. Men, mostly white and Hispanic, stand around in the glow of a yard light, drinking beer, smoking cigarettes, and spitting tobacco juice.

"You'll get all kinds around here," says Glenn. "Lots of white trailer trash, military, but also business types, some professionals. And Mexicans. There are a lot of Mexicans who like the dog and especially cockfights," he says.

Inside, men mill about, talking to the dog owners and making bets. A makeshift ring made of plywood sheets is set up in the far end of the barn, with lights hung from the rafters for illumination. The ring is sixteen feet square, with three-foot high walls bloodied from earlier bouts. A carpet is laid on the packed dirt floor so that the dogs can gain traction for their paws, even when slick with blood. Each dog is weighed, and the handlers exchange dogs and bathe them with buckets of soapy water.

"That's so they can be sure neither dog has poison on its coat," says Glenn. "It's an old tradition, but necessary. Both the fighters usually lay down anywhere from $1000 to $10,000 on a fight; I've heard it can go to $50,000 or more when drug money is involved."

Each man takes his dog to a corner behind two "scratch lines" painted on the rug. The men hold their lunging animals by the collars until a ring man signals the start of the fight. The dogs are released, rushing at each other, colliding with a thud. Usually, one of the dogs will grab hold of the other on the face, neck, shoulder, sometimes leg, grinding at the other animal's flesh.

A dog owner may command a dog to release the other so that it can improve its position. Glenn says the fights are more like wrestling matches than the frantic fights that occur in a chance encounter between two dogs on the street.

Depending on the stamina and fight in the two dogs, a bout can last from a few minutes to, on rare occasions, hours. According to Glenn, the dogs are almost eerily silent, never barking or growling, though sometimes they will howl in pain.

If the dogs break apart or one quits fighting, a situation called a "turn," the handlers separate them. The dogs are then taken to their corners and the ringman commands the handlers to "scratch." If the dog that turned rushes to the other corner to attack his opponent, the fight continues. But if the dog refuses, it is branded a cur—an almost certain death sentence among committed dog fighters.

Electrical extension cords with clips on the ends attached to batteries serve as an impromptu execution device, to be used on losing dogs. Sometimes a dog is simply taken out behind the barn and shot. Michael Vick and his buddies were said to have hanged some of their losing dogs.

Some matches end in death, but such outcomes are rare. Typically, Glenn says, the ringman or the dog fighters themselves call an end to a match. "Sometimes a good dog will simply be outclassed. You can stop a fight if your dog is obviously beat. And the dog lives to fight another day."

"I've seen dogs that had broken legs drag themselves to get at the other dog," says Glenn. "That's what a fighter calls a 'dead game dog.' Some of 'em just won't quit."

Win or lose, both combatants typically sustain injuries. Most of the "dog men" carry veterinary kits—suturing thread, needles, tapes, splints, antiseptic drugs, and painkillers. Intravenous solutions are often used to restore fluids to the depleted battlers. At home, steroids are commonly used to build muscle and some fighters administer drugs—amphetamines and cocaine are common—before fights. A fighting dog cannot be taken to a veterinary hospital because the nature of its wounds would lead to questions and possible arrests.

"A guy has to get pretty good at veterinary care," says Glenn. "I'd say there isn't much I can't do when it comes to treating an injured dog. All the dog fighters are pretty good that way."

And dog fighters sometimes see injuries that veterinarians rarely, if ever, deal with: pit bulls hold on so tenaciously, they can tear the skin off the face or body of another dog. And, Glenn says, they will hold a muscle for so long and with such tearing force that "it turns to red jelly."

Characteristic of pit bulls as a product of fight breeding is an exceptionally high tolerance for pain. Any veterinarian can attest that pit bulls have a much higher pain tolerance than other breeds. Lark Gustafson, DVM, in Coupeville, Washington, told me in an informal interview that he often saw pet pit bulls with broken bones, severe infections, and other typically painful conditions that went untreated for days or weeks because the owners never saw the animals display any pain symptoms.

"Pit bulls are, by far, the most pain-tolerant dogs I see in my practice. It's not even close," said Lark. "I've had pit bulls that were hit by cars and presented with broken bones and lacerations but showed no signs of pain."

Despite the gore, the pain, and the suffering that they cause their animals, Glenn says "dog men" like himself love their dogs.

"Yeah, I'd say I loved my dogs. Most of 'em, anyway. They made me proud. They had heart, like warriors. And it's what they're bred to do. They love to fight," he says.

Men like Glenn love the dogs . . . up until the moment a dog loses and is taken behind the barn to get a bullet between the eyes.

At 6:00 A.M. on July 9, 2009, agents from the FBI, USDA, Missouri State Highway Patrol, US Marshals Service, and an assortment of local police departments staged raids on suspected dog fighting operations in an eight-state area. They arrested twenty-six people, charging them with more than one hundred felonies, and collected over four hundred dogs from properties across the Southeast. The rescued dogs were taken to a temporary shelter in an undisclosed St. Louis warehouse; of those dogs, twenty-one were pregnant, eventually giving birth to one hundred fifty-three puppies.

Overwhelmed by the sheer numbers of dogs and puppies, the Missouri Humane Society contacted the American Humane Association's Red Star Service team, requesting that they send highly skilled dog handlers to lend assistance to an army of local humane society workers, police, and volunteers charged with overseeing the pit bulls. A sort of Red Cross for domestic animals, Red Star Services responds immediately in emergencies and disasters to help feed, shelter, and provide veterinary care for lost, stray, and abandoned animals.

When the call came to the American Humane Association, Tracy Reis of the Denver office of Red Star Services packed her bags for St. Louis. A husky woman with a cheerful, relaxed demeanor, Reis had begun her career as an animal control officer in Fort Collins, Colorado. She was no stranger to dog fighting. Twice she had helped break up pit bull fighting rings in Colorado. She told me that she'd never feared for her life around dogs and had been bitten only once in her career.

But the pit bull situation in St. Louis was different from anything she'd ever encountered, either as an animal control officer or while directing the Red Star program. Row upon row of the animals were housed in cages. Most of the adult dogs having been in fights, many were missing ears, teeth, eyes. The bitches were typically so reactive that they had been bred using "rape stands," restraints that prevented them from attacking the males when they were mounted. Temperament testing had been conducted by specialists for the Humane Society of Missouri and served as a criterion to decide which dogs would be given the needle and which would be placed in new homes.

"What we were told was that the 'severely human-aggressive' dogs were to be euthanized, while the others would be placed selectively in approved shelters and rescues around the country," Reis told me. "There wasn't any criteria set for those that were dog-aggressive. They almost all had that."

Reis particularly remembers a bitch named Fay. Part of Fay's face and most of her lips had been torn off, so she appeared to be perpetually baring her teeth.

"She was as sweet as could be with people, but when she was around another dog . . . a light switch just seemed to go on. She was the most dog-aggressive dog I have ever seen. She'd be walking with a volunteer by one of the cages and with no warning, she'd just turn on a dime and attack that cage.

"With pits, there is one speed and one pedal, zero to sixty and all teeth," she said.

Even the puppies, who were handled regularly by the volunteers and had been born in the shelter, were often inherently vicious.

"One group was just four weeks old and had to be separated to feed on their own. You could watch them 'lock down' on another puppy in their play and not let go. And they went right for the other puppies' throats," she said.

"Unfortunately, what a lot of people don't understand is, aggression is an inherited behavioral trait. People are seldom killed by Labradors or golden retrievers, although it has happened," said Reis. "But you won't see a Lab breeder selecting for aggression. They won't perpetuate that aggressive trait. But pit owners tend to be the exact opposite. The *most* aggressive dogs are the ones they pick to breed, both dogfight professionals and backyard breeders."

I asked Reis hypothetically if she would take a risk and adopt a pit bull from a shelter—any shelter.

"Even with all my work, even with all my training and experience, I would be hesitant to adopt a dog or puppy from such a situation," she said. "Fear of these dogs is not necessarily unwarranted. With all the bad bloodlines and breeding for aggression, you just never know. You can't tell if a dog comes from a fighting bloodline or fighting dog breeder."

Because of both the perceived and real danger that pit bulls represent, it is not unusual for them to languish in shelters for months, even a year or longer. Dogs that are normal and behaved on intake often become neurotic, fearful, or aggressive as a result of their prolonged stays, said many of the shelter workers I spoke with. Whereas thirty years ago, a dog would typically be euthanized within ten days if unclaimed, today's shelter ethic of "no kill" or "slow kill" can mean that a dog remains in a shelter for months on end. Long stays for pits are the rule, not the exception.

Confinement takes its toll mentally on the dogs, and takes a toll on the scarce financial resources of the shelters, themselves.

Jan McHugh-Smith, president and CEO of the Humane Society of the Pikes Peak Region in Colorado Springs and former director of the Humane Society of Boulder County, Colorado, told me that the average annual cost to keep an animal in a publicly-operated shelter or non-profit runs about $3,500, or slightly less than one-tenth of what it costs to imprison a human in a federal penitentiary. At McHugh's facility, HSPPR, adoption fees vary from nothing on "adopt a cat free" days to about $300 for a desirable purebred Dalmatian or golden retriever.

Increasingly, pit bulls are soaking up a disproportionate amount of public funds and private donations at all-breed animal shelters and rescues across the country, says Merritt Clifton, a journalist and editor of the animal shelter industry weblog *Animals 24–7*. Clifton, a reporter and activist in the animal welfare movement and a statistician by inclination, has followed the progress of the international shelter community since the 1970s.

"Each year, about one-third of the total US pit bull population enters an animal shelter, a phenomenon never before seen with any other dog breed," Clifton said. While other breeds and even mixed-breed mutts (excluding those with a pit bull for a parent) have a 60 percent or better chance of being re-homed when placed in a shelter, pit bulls and their mixes at the same shelters are killed nearly 60 percent of the time.

Because of this, no-kill, slow-kill, and "traditional" shelters go to extraordinary lengths to place pit bulls. No dogs are shown more often in animal shelter adoption advertising. Ads typically try to counteract the dog's negative reputation, often showing young children cuddling and kissing pit bulls—a message which contradicts every tenet of education involving dog bites.

Advocates for the breed (some of them active in the dog fighting community) are skillfully employing the Internet to remake the dog's image and sell the dogs as wholesome, loving, protective family pets that wouldn't harm a kitten. In fact, one of the most common photo clichés on pit bull advocacy websites such as www.realpitbull.com and www.happypitbull.com (besides the already-mentioned small children cuddling adult pit bulls) is a photo of a pit bull nuzzled up with a small kitten. Or, in one example I ran across, bunny rabbits.

Despite claims that the dog is a cream puff, a nanny, a kitten-cuddler, and a loving family pet, the breed's reputation as unpredictable attacker is supported by news reports of vicious mayhem-making. These are not fiction, as the breed's supporters would like the public to believe. Statistics gathered from the media stories bear out the assertion that the pit bill terrier is by far the most dangerous and deadly of all popular dog breeds in North America today.

In 1979, when Merritt Clifton was a reporter for the Sherbrooke Record in Quebec, he began investigating a local exotic cat breeding and trafficking business. As part of the assignment, he began tracking news reports of fatal and disfiguring attacks by exotic pets. In 1982, he added dog breeds to the attack statistics. Thirty years later, Clifton had amassed an impressive data set of 3,498 reports of fatal and disfiguring dog attacks. During the thirty-year period, pit bull terriers and pit bull crosses accounted for 60 percent of all fatal attacks and "felonious" disfigurements.

Using search criteria to aggregate more than three million want-ad listings, Clifton ranked the relative popularity of various breeds. He then went on to correlate dog breed popularity with fatal and disfiguring dog bite attacks.

"Pit bulls make up about 5 percent of all dogs in North America, but account for 60 percent of all fatal and disfiguring dog attacks," he told me. "From an actuarial [insurance] risk standpoint, pit bulls are by far the most dangerous of all dog breeds. Compared to other breeds, they're off the charts."

Pit bull advocates frequently criticize Clifton's thirty-year study, whether in personal letters to the journalist, letters-to-the-editor columns, or on the Internet. One point often made is that pit bulls are frequently misidentified in attacks. But Clifton points out that news stories are derived from animal control reports, police reports, hospital reports, and other official sources, often allowing for cross-verification from multiple sources. And he strongly defends the validity of his research.

"There is a persistent allegation by pit bull terrier advocates that pit bulls are over-represented among reported dog attack deaths and maimings because of misidentification or because 'pit bull' is, according to them, a generic term covering several similar types of dog," Clifton writes. "However, the frequency of pit bull attacks . . . is so disproportionate that even if half of the attacks in the pit bull category were misattributed, or even if the pit bull category was split three ways by breed, attacks by pit bulls and their closest relatives would still outnumber attacks by any other breed."

Clifton also pointed out to me the illogic of the argument that the media was somehow "out to get" pit bulls and their owners.

"If a Pomeranian killed somebody, *that* would be national news. The more unusual a story, the more likely the press is to pursue it. Pit bull attacks, on the other hand, happen almost every day in North America. If anything, I think, they are underreporting these incidents," he told me.

It so happens that Merritt Clifton lives on Whidbey Island, less than five miles from the WAIF shelter. It was not long after the first news stories of pit bull attacks on the island broke that a "perfect storm," of events, as Shari Bibich called them, conspired to fill the facility with unwanted pit bulls.

A group of young people were breeding litter after litter of pit bulls and selling puppies in a grocery store parking lot; at about the same time, the Naval facility in Oak Harbor banned pit bulls among its personnel, and the naval town passed an ordinance requiring pit bull owners to get special licenses and insurance policies. Consequently, apartment managers adopted breed-specific rules that prevented people from owning the dogs.

Soon, WAIF was brimming with abandoned pit bulls. There were only forty-four kennels among the shelter's two facilities, all of them filled, and WAIF was taking in five or six new pit bulls a week. Some days, the staff took in several pit bulls in a single day.

"We had nowhere to put them. We talked to every no-kill shelter in the area and they wouldn't accept the dogs. The dogs weren't being adopted, and when people found out we had nothing but pit bulls, they stopped coming in to look. And that meant cats were going unadopted, too!"

Some of the strong, agile, and determined dogs in the satellite facility in Oak Harbor escaped over the cyclone fences. Fights were a common, almost everyday occurrence. One night, two puppies from the same litter who were placed together fought viciously, and when shelter workers arrived, the dogs were lying in pools of blood. Finally, Bibich went to the shelter's board of directors, made up mainly of volunteer animal lovers from throughout the community.

"I said, 'Look, I need help! We are just keeping these dogs caged until they become kennel crazy. We cannot keep putting these dogs through this. We place a handful of dogs while the rest linger here and suffer. What we are doing is inhumane . . .'"

WAIF's board decided to add an addendum to the existing "minimum kill" policy, which specified euthanasia only for dogs that are sick, dangerous, or have behavioral problems making them unsuitable for adoption. To this they added a new category: dogs that are unadoptable. In effect, euthanasia became a "last resort" for the dogs (and under this new policy, all were in fact pit bulls) that had spent months and months caged, waiting for an owner who simply never came.

In the end, nearly all of the pit bulls ended up being euthanized.

"During that period, I saw in every person that worked here a plea in their eyes every time someone walked in the door with another pit bull. That plea was, 'please, don't come here,'" said Bibich.

"If there is one thing I can put out there, speaking for myself and everyone who works at WAIF, it is that we love animals. And the heartbreak we feel when having to put an animal down is real. There is not one person here that doesn't die a little each time; you want to make a commitment to every animal."

Bibich remembers one puppy in particular, Dan, who was returned after a successful adoption. The puppy was behaving oddly, spinning in circles, his head tilted to one side.

"An x-ray showed that his brain was filled with buckshot. It broke my heart. I held Dan when we euthanized him. And I held him before when he was just a happy little puppy and loved everyone. And I made a commitment to never put these animals in situations like that."

Whidbey Island represents a microcosm of a problem found across America. It is a problem entirely man-made, a problem directly related to breeding decisions. Since Roman times, people have bred special dogs to fight—people like John Colby, who as his family proudly boasts, raised more than 5,000 pit bulls during his lifetime, probably resulting in the births of tens of thousands if not hundreds of thousands of fighting dogs. These were dogs for whom the injuring, killing, and maiming of other dogs and animals was the primary reason for existing.

Just like people attacked by pit bulls, the dogs murdered at the WAIF facility—and at facilities just like it throughout the country—are victims. They're victims of a warped set of values by people who have placed an emphasis on murderous violence as a criterion for owning, breeding, and ultimately fighting their dogs. Shelter workers like Shari Bibich, her employees, and the community volunteers of WAIF are victims of this bloodlust, too.

Before I leave the WAIF shelter, I take a look at descriptions of shelter dogs placed in the last week: Abby, a rat terrier. Allie, a black lab mix. Disco, an Australian shepherd/border collie cross. Happy, a Labrador retriever. All had been at WAIF for less than two months; a few, less than a week. Then, I look at the sheet for

Tessa, a pit bull I met earlier that day while touring the facility. The sweet-faced girl had been there for eleven months.

Before leaving, I double back to take another stroll amid the kennels. Some of the dogs bark and lunge at the chain link kennel doors, vying for my attention. I come to the cage of Tessa. She enthusiastically wiggles to the kennel door and, with kind brown eyes, looks up to me. Her tail wags. My heart melts. Unguardedly, I reach out to her cage and offer a hand. She licks it through the metal fence wiring. In a moment of impulse, I think, "I could take her home."

Then I think about my dog, Onda. I think about all I know about the pit bull breed and the risks associated with it. I think about a recent incident in Oak Harbor in which a rescued pit bull attacked a small Corgi then bit the hand of an elderly man when he tried to break up the fight. And I think about Darla Napora, a 32-year-old woman who lived in Pacifica, California.

Napora was a supporter of Bad Rap, a pit bull rescue and advocacy group that helped to evaluate quarterback Michael Vick's dogs, rehabilitating and finding homes for them. Napora, who was pregnant, was attacked by her adopted pet pit bull, Gunner. She and her unborn child died from shock and loss of blood. Her husband, perversely, vowed to bury the dog's ashes beside his wife and unborn child.

The moment passes, and I bid Tessa goodbye.

"I hope you find a good home," I say. "Be safe."

SEVEN

LET SLEEPING DOGS LIE

Where will the puppies come from?
—Doctor Emily Weiss, ASPCA

I t's a sunny Sunday in February and our spirits are running high. We're back in Colorado, headed to the Denver Coliseum for the Twentieth Annual Rocky Mountain Dog Show and a long-awaited reunion with Onda's breeder, Carol Ann Hartnagle. I've got a coffee in the cup holder and I'm singing along with Tom Petty on radio. Bright and alert, Onda is riding shotgun, peering out of the RV's enormous windshield at a city still fast asleep.

On Brighton Boulevard, we pass by historic brick warehouses that contain abstract art galleries, hipster brew pubs, and skunky marijuana-growing operations. Onda sniffs the air, cocks his head quizzically, then returns to his gazing. The timeworn concrete coliseum is now in view.

To my left, I catch the first rays of dawn striking a billboard. It shows a sullen, nondescript hound dog locked inside a stainless steel cage. It reads: "AKC breeders kill shelter dogs' chances. Always adopt, never buy."

My mood slips a notch and there's a bitter taste in my mouth . . . and it's not the coffee. It's bile. Because I know that sign is a lie. And the savvier people in the animal adoption world do, too.

The sign implies that there's a dog overpopulation problem, and that the problem is the fault of irresponsible and profligate AKC dog breeders. The lie was more explicitly stated in a press release sent to Denver media in advance of the show by the sign's sponsor, People for the Ethical Treatment of Animals (PETA).

"Dog shows promote breeding and prompt interest in 'purebred' animals while animal shelters overflow with millions of lovable, healthy dogs—both mutts and purebreds—whose lives depend on getting a second chance," it read.

But shelters today aren't overflowing. Truth be told, shelters in many parts of the country—Denver included—are having to go outside their state borders and even beyond the borders of the United State to find enough adoptable dogs. In fact, the year prior to PETA targeting this show, the state of Colorado imported more than 17,000 shelter dogs to meet demand; in the year ahead, they'd need another 24,000.

Today's reality is that no dog overpopulation crisis exists in America. And while there is a shelter problem—one that caused 670,000 dogs to be killed in 2016—it's not due to overpopulation. And it's not caused by AKC show breeders—who are, for all their faults, the *most* responsible group of dog breeders in America today.

I know, you think I'm crazy. For decades, every humane group, every animal rights organization, every shelter blog, every self-anointed pet expert, and every media story focusing on pet adoption has said exactly the opposite.

"Every year millions of companion animals are euthanized in shelters around the country because there just aren't enough homes."—Sylvia Ottaka, Senior Director of Shelter Operations at North Shore Animal League America.

"Some dog lovers feel that buying a purebred dog is ethically questionable because of health problems associated with overbreeding and inbreeding. At the same time, two million to three million shelter dogs in the US are put to death every year."—*The New York Times*.

"Dog overpopulation is not a fairy tale."—celebrity dog trainer Cesar Millan.

But it has *become* a fairy tale. Shelter populations and euthanasia counts have dropped drastically in the past several years, and the rhetoric has failed to catch up to the reality. Finally, the change is something people are starting to acknowledge.

Journalist Kim Kavin spent more than two years researching and writing *The Dog Merchants*, an exhaustive investigation of the global dog industry. In it, she debunked the myth of dog overpopulation contributing to shelter deaths.

"Dog lovers could give a home to every single dog who has been abandoned in every single shelter, and millions more pups would be needed to annually satisfy consumer demand," she wrote. "The notion that America's homeless dogs face an 'overpopulation problem' does not match up against the available statistics. Supply is not exceeding demand."

Indeed. The most recent figures supplied by shelters, the pet products industry, veterinarians' associations, and animal welfare organizations bear this out. Each year, people in the United States bring home between seven and eight million new dogs, including roughly six million puppies; many are replacement pets for the millions of pet dogs that have simply died from old age.

In the 1970s, a time when fewer than 10 percent of Americans spayed or neutered their pet animals, public shelters became stretched beyond capacity and were euthanizing as many as eleven million dogs a year—about one in every ten dogs in America. Shelter managers began using the phrase "pet overpopulation" to describe the rivers of puppies, kittens, dogs, and cats flowing through their doors in cardboard boxes and on leashes, only to exit through the backdoors in trash bags.

When I was still a kid, I recall the heroism of a cowboy I knew who walked into a shelter in Texas. After he'd looked at all the dogs, the clerk asked him which one he'd like to adopt. "I'll take the next one in line to die," he said. It was a spunky Jack Russell terrier named Danger, and it rode with him in his pickup for a decade. Sadly for the dogs, cats, kittens, and puppies of that generation, there simply weren't enough cowboys to go around.

That was when we had a serious, serious dog overpopulation crisis. But today, thanks to largely successful efforts to educate people about the importance of spaying and neutering family pets, about 91 percent of American dogs are sterilized. This has significantly cut down on the numbers of unplanned, unwanted litters.

Today, Dr. Emily Weiss, DVM, who writes an ASPCA blog for shelter professionals, says she loses sleep not over how many puppies are getting euthanized in shelters, but over where we're going to get enough puppies to meet anticipated consumer demand.

"In many communities around the country, we're reaching a crisis point—that is, if you believe that people should have an opportunity to have a dog in their life, and that they should have the opportunity to choose what type of dog to be a part of their family," she said. The big challenge, she believes, will be to find more sources for *humanely* raised puppies. One solution likely will come from the building I am about to enter, where the dog show is taking place.

Since the release of *Pedigree Dogs Exposed*, the BBC exposé about genetic diseases in purebred dogs, interest in pedigreed purebred dog breeding has plummeted. Annual registrations with the American Kennel Club have fallen from a record of 1.7 million in 1992 to just over 530,000 in 2011—the last year figures were publicly released. In 2008, when the film was shown in the United States, AKC registrations stood at about three-quarters of a million puppies; since then, registrations have fallen by two hundred thousand dogs a year, or about two million dogs over a decade.

And rightfully so, some would say. As the documentary strongly showed, many of the practices that had become commonplace in the dog show world were harming the dogs and in need of change. But as I wind my way through the maze of rings, looking for Carol Ann's little compound of dogs, dog crates, and grooming table amid the hundreds of competitors at the show, I see encouraging signs of improvement and hope in the dog show business.

First, dog shows are becoming more open and multi-dimensional. At Denver, for instance, participation in the agility competition is enormous, requiring three rings be run simultaneously on a sunup to sundown schedule. That's a good outcome—it's bringing more dogs and dog owners through the door and giving them a chance to compete.

When the Westminster Kennel Club added agility to its roster in 2014, the event became an instant hit, gaining millions of viewers online and on television. In 2017, Mia the beagle, a masters-level agility contestant at Westminster, caused a sensation when she improvised her own course rather than follow her master's guidance. More than three and a half million Facebook viewers watched the routine, over twice as many people as viewed the televised Best in Show contest. Unlike the meticulously groomed show dogs standing like Greek statues for inspection, the less-than-perfect

Mia was a dog people at home could relate to; after all, dogs are only human.

Denver's three agility rings are, of course, filled with pure-breds. Herding breeds—whip-smart border collies, cattle dogs, shelties and Australian shepherds—rule in this canine version of steeplechase, which demands athleticism and the willingness to take commands. But there's hardly a variety of dog you won't see in the contest, including lumbering hounds and plenty of "Heinz 57s"—all-American mutts. Yes, in a break from tradition, the AKC allows all comers, whether registered or not, to compete.

As I hasten by the ring, I see that they are running the small dogs. With a jump height set at eight inches, the class is dominated by speedy Jack Russell terriers and shelties. But I am heartened to notice a middle aged Asian-American woman coaxing a Chihuahua through the obstacle course. As I pause to watch, the Chihuahua tiptoes to the edge of the teeter-totter board and peers over the brink as he begins the long descent to earth—or what I imagine seems like a very long distance for such a small dog. When he finally touches ground, I hear a shimmer of applause from the crowd enjoying the teacup-sized competitor's performance.

Dog shows are increasingly adding events like agility that put more to the test than mere appearances. The number of agility events sanctioned by the American Kennel Club has doubled in five years, growing to more than 3,700 competitions across the United States. And a raft of other events are becoming popular, too.

Performance-based dog show competitions, including flyball (a team relay race for dogs), barn hunting (a search for caged white lab rats amid hay bales), and "nose work," a game of olfactory hide and seek, are taking their places beside Victorian-era conformation showing. Other activities include "earthdog" trials designed to test burrow hunters like small terriers and dachshunds, "fast cat" sprint races for greyhounds and whippets, and traditional herding and hunting dog trials.

Giving dog lovers more activities focused on performance rather than conformation is important, not only because people today want to do more with their dogs, but because it can help focus breeders on the original purposes of breeds. Australian shepherd breeder Ernest Hartnagle often told me, "performance is the yard-stick." What he meant was, appearance and written standards only go so far in judging a dog's merit as a breeding animal. We need to consider the whole picture, including the animal's ability to actually do the thing for which he or she was bred. More and more people in the dog show world seem to be getting that.

Finally, I find Carol Ann's grooming area. She's cloaked in a blue smock meant to shield her show outfit from the loose fur she's brushing and clipping from Lena, a two-year-old black female Aussie with white and gold trim.

"Welcome back to Colorado, stranger!" she says, giving me a hug, her scissors still in hand. She reaches down to pet Onda, who is dancing sideways and whining for her attention.

"And how is the little man?" she says to him. He leaps up and licks her on the face in reply. Carol laughs heartily. Then, as expected, I am swept up into Carol Ann's tornado of show activity. She hands me a variety of grooming supplies and says, "Can you take Lena's leash and meet me at ring eight? I need to check myself in the ladies' room . . ."

Popping Onda into one of the empty travel crates, I lead Lena, whose formal name is "Reverie Primavera of Las Rocosa," to the ring. Carol takes a brush from her pocket, makes a few last minute swipes to Lena's coat, spritzes it with show-shine mist, then hands me her blue smock. She's got on flat shoes and one of her conserva-tive show suits, but it's an eye-popping shade of canary that flatters her blond hair and Lena's shiny black coat—and is bound to catch the judge's eye.

As usual, the Aussie class is one of the biggest at the show. But notably, a lot of the top dogs and professional handlers aren't there. The Denver schedule happens to overlap with the Westminster

Kennel Club Dog Show, and the "big dogs" are all in New York. With less competition, Carol has a strong chance to claim a Best-of-Breed win, as Lena is a very "typey" dog (meaning her features adhere closely to the breed standard) with charisma that's bound to impress the ring judge.

As if to prove the point, Lena wins her class, females bred by exhibitor. This means that later, she'll return to the ring to compete for Best of Bitches. (Even after two years around the shows, I still find myself uncomfortable saying that word, though no one else gives it a thought.) If she wins there, she'll be considered for Best of Breed.

During the break, Carol and I discuss breeding Onda. As he was en route to earning his show championship, two judges in the Australian shepherd club expressed interest in using him as a stud. That's a big honor, because they're people who look at thousands of dogs a year and have decided he's an especially good choice for their own programs. Ultimately, the decision is up to Carol. Per our mutual agreement, I defer all breeding decisions to her superior expertise.

Before we consider the next step, however, Carol suggests I get Onda's eyes, elbows, and hips tested to rule out any reasons why Onda might not be a good breeding candidate. Fortunately, eye testing is available on-site, so in the interval before Carol Ann's next class, I take Onda down to the clinic under the coliseum bleachers to see if I can squeeze an exam in. There's a line of dogs and owners already there, waiting for a chance to see the ophthalmologist. While I wait in line to make an appointment, I check out pamphlets from VetGen, a genetic testing service with a booth adjacent to the eye clinic.

Eight health tests are available for diseases common to the Aussie; knowing the results could help in determining if a bitch is a good potential match. Inevitably, at least one or two of the disorders will appear in any pairing, so that should be factored into any decision. I take a pamphlet so I can discuss with Carol Ann which tests might be worthwhile.

One of the tests I find amusing is for the bobtail trait. Onda was born a "natural" bobtail. What that means is, he carries alleles for the dominant gene. One of the things Carol Ann has taught me is that crossing a natural bob tail with a natural bob tail will likely result in a few pups with spinal disorders. It's that kind of knowledge, which is often absent among casual breeders and puppy mill operators, that a skilled show breeder brings to bear when planning a litter.

Largely due to the success of *Pedigreed Dogs Exposed*, many people today hold a negative opinion of show breeders and "hobby" breeders, people involved in dog activities like agility, herding trials, and canine disc competition, who breed for love of animals. Because of negative publicity, it's widely believed that their blindness or indifference to the consequences of linebreeding and inbreeding jeopardizes purebred dogs' health. Kona, my epileptic Aussie, is certainly a case that proves the point. But after spending two years at dog shows getting to know the people, I have come to recognize that breeders are far more aware of genetic problems in their breeds than the public gives them credit for, and they are also the most likely breeders to take precautions such as genetic testing and outcrossing with different bloodlines to control for negative outcomes.

A great deal of ink has been spilled arguing over which are healthier, purebred dogs or mixed bred mutts. Naturally, dog show breeders are sensitive to the subject because they invest a lot of passion, care, and money in their litters and want people to know that they are raising healthy dogs. Shelter adoption advocates, on the other hand, want to bolster their argument for adoption by claiming that mixed breed mutts are a healthier choice.

In 2013, a study at UC Davis vet school involving 27,000 dogs compared the incidence of twenty-four genetic disorders in mixed versus purebred dogs. It found that the incidence of ten genetic disorders (42 percent) was higher in purebreds. But in the case of the other fourteen diseases, there was no difference.

"A new study by researchers at the University of California, Davis, indicates that mixed breeds don't necessarily have an advantage when it comes to inherited canine disorders," concluded a press release announcing the study's conclusions.

Still, a higher incidence of ten disorders suggests that the shelter advocates and others who criticize purebreds are partially right: purebreds as a whole do have a higher likelihood for some genetic diseases. But reading through the study's fine print, I noticed this caveat:

> This study suggests that subpopulations of the purebred dog population are more likely to exhibit certain inherited conditions while other subpopulations do not differ statistically from mixed-breed dogs in terms of how common these diseases are.

In short, some breeds are healthier than others, and in the healthiest breeds, there is no substantive difference between purebreds and mutts.

Furthermore, genetic testing has begun to make it possible for breeders to make informed decisions that can lower incidences of genetic disorders in their breeds. And breed clubs also are sharing information and cooperating with members to clean up some of the past mistakes that resulted from an incomplete understanding of genetics as it relates to purebred breeding. These days show breeders are capable of being part of the solution, rather than a cause of the problem.

Elaine Ostrander, a geneticist with the National Human Genome Research Institute, heads the institute's Dog Genome Project, making her one of the world's foremost researchers in canine genetic diseases. She received post-doctoral education in molecular biology at Harvard and was instrumental in having the dog genome sequenced.

An opportunity to speak with her candidly about canine health helped me gain a greater appreciation for purebred dog breeders.

Ostrander told me that her family raised purebred dogs, and that with all she knows, she has no qualms about obtaining dogs from *quality* purebred dog breeders.

"Show breeders are not hobby breeders. The dogs they produce are typically long-lived and meticulously cared for. They're the people most likely to get tests done, understand what they mean, and apply that knowledge to their breeding programs," she said. "They're open about their dogs, and the problems in pedigrees and bloodlines are well known."

The belief that "breed-blending" (the purposeful crossing of two purebred parents from different breeds) creates healthier dogs is part of the reason "designer dogs" like goldendoodles, morkies, and puggles have become so popular. It's also why breeders are able to ask inflated prices for dogs that aren't purebred. While the UC Davis study seems to support the view that mixed breed dogs have a better chance at healthy outcomes, Ostrander takes a typically scientific position. She wants to see more data.

"It's a good question. We're currently in the process of collecting labradoodle data. We know, though, that certain diseases exist across breed lines. For example, hip dysplasia is common in labs and goldens, a common cross. Is there a reasonable chance the offspring will get hip dysplasia? Well, yeah."

"In the end, you can have a [designer dog] with hip problems and this and that. And you can have a purebred that lives to be 19. A lot depends on the breeder. So, I don't think crossbreeding is a panacea," she concluded.

Because Ostrander believes that the care breeders put into their litters is paramount, she cautions against buying dogs without first learning everything possible about the breeder.

"Personally, I'd never buy a dog from a pet store. You don't know anything about the puppy, and there's no way to access that information. Anyone buying a puppy should ask lots of questions of the breeder. Expect to be scrutinized—a caring breeder wants to know that the puppy is going to a good home," she said.

It seems that many people are taking her words to heart. What surprised me, as I dug into the data, was the fact that pet store sales aren't as big a part of today's multi-billion-dollar dog business as I had supposed. In 2016, pet shop sales made up less than 4 percent of all dog acquisitions, down from 5 percent in 2013.

Still, close to one million puppies are being bred each year in USDA-licensed dog facilities, many of which are so-called "puppy mills." And it's likely millions more are being bred without USDA knowledge or oversight, being sold direct to consumers via online ads and pet adoption websites like petfinder.com. And according to author Kim Kavin, even rescues now serve as fronts for unscrupulous and unregulated puppy-raisers to sell their wares.

If your goal is to bring home a healthy puppy, Ostrander has one piece of advice that should serve as a golden rule: Before you pick one and take it home, go see its parents.

Unfortunately, that's getting harder to do. A decade of wearying criticism has thinned the ranks of American Kennel Club breeders, making it tougher than ever before to find pups from small-scale breed enthusiasts as opposed to large-scale puppy mills and unscrupulous Internet sellers out to make an easy buck.

As mentioned before, AKC registry numbers have plummeted drastically in the face of anti-purebred dog campaigns mounted by all of the nation's leading animal rights groups, plus the release of the film *Pedigreed Dogs Exposed*. Things have gotten so bad for the AKC that they no longer publish their overall registration figures for new puppies. As mentioned, the last numbers I was able to obtain showed that, in 2011, the AKC registered just 536,611 new dogs. The AKC hasn't made more recent statistics available to the public, but if the trend of the last ten years has continued, it's surely lower.

Meanwhile, puppy mill breeders continue to churn out dogs in high numbers, pedigree or no pedigree. If the market demands mixed-breed designer dogs like puggles, labradoodles, and morkies, such breeders are more than happy to oblige. It's they who are least likely to do any of the planning or testing that characterizes the best practices of today's AKC show breeders.

While it's impossible to know how many AKC dogs come from show breeders and breed enthusiasts versus large commercial puppy mills (the AKC accepts registrations from both), it's nevertheless a discouraging trend to see fewer and fewer registrations of purebred dogs. Because, as the ASPCA veterinarian who is losing sleep over a looming puppy shortage points out, we're gonna need as many ethical, quality breeders as we can get.

Even though the largest percentage of dogs being taken home by Americans will always be puppies (a statistical necessity, since at least half of all "new" dogs must at least have a birth home), there's encouraging news for older dogs in need of homes. Americans are taking home more rescued pets, and abandoning their dogs at lower rates, too.

According to the ASPCA, fewer dogs than before are coming into shelters and needing homes. In fact, the number of dogs has fallen from about 3.9 million in 2011 to about 3.2 million in 2016. Well over half found homes with new families.

Even the rates of euthanasia for dogs show reason to be optimistic. For the first time in more than half a century, the number of dogs killed in shelters in the United States has dropped below the million mark.

Shelters euthanize dogs for any number of reasons. A percentage of these dogs have unsolvable health issues, including diseases caused by old age, that make them unsuitable for rehoming. In many cases, people give older pets up because they cannot afford to pay their veterinary bills or simply don't wish to pay the costs associated with private euthanasia. Many other dogs enter the shelter system because of dangerous behavioral problems, which include biting people or attacking other animals, that prevent shelters from placing them in new homes.

However, figures from the Humane Society of the United States show that about 80 percent of dogs brought into shelters and euthanized could have been placed in new homes, but were not. When people talk about overpopulation, it's this group that they're discussing. And it is in this one segment of the shelter world that we have an ongoing crisis.

I dedicated an entire chapter of this book to one breed of dog, the pit bull, for good reason. According to Merritt Clifton, a journalist who has covered the animal shelter and humane community for more than three decades, about one-third of the estimated 3.2 million stray or abandoned dogs in shelters are either pit bulls or pit bull mixes. But I didn't just take his word for it.

To corroborate this information, I surveyed a number of shelter websites, beginning with Petfinder, the Internet's largest pet adoption site. The searchable website lists dogs and cats available from more than 11,500 animal shelters and rescue groups, providing a more than ample data set.

On the day I conducted a breed search of the more than 100,000 dogs available for adoption, I found that pit bulls and pit bull mixes made up one-quarter of all dogs seeking new homes. In other words, from the glass half-empty perspective, they made up the largest number of dogs being abandoned. By comparison, all dogs of the retriever type, the AKC's most popular breed category over the past twenty-six years, comprised just 18 percent. Chihuahuas, another dog with major abandonment issues, came in third, at about 10 percent.

The same sad story came through at Best Friends Animal Society, in Kenab, Utah. Based on the shelter's own descriptions of their adoptable dogs, 34 percent were pit bulls and pit bull crosses.

Back home in Colorado, I spoke with Jan McHugh Smith of the Humane Society of the Pikes Peak Region in Colorado Springs. Consistent with Petfinder and Best Friends, HSPPR's internal shelter statistics showed that pit bulls and Chihuahuas made up the largest percentages of the abandoned dogs.

Jan told me that the shelter has little problem finding homes for the Chihuahuas, non-pit bull mixes, and non-pit bull purebred dogs that pass through its doors. And it's high "live release" rate, the ratio of animals re-homed to those euthanized for reasons other than health or owner request, was running close to 85 percent—an indication that there was no shortage of people taking home the purebred and mixed breed dogs available for adoption. But the same wasn't true for the pit bulls. The shelter, she told me, euthanizes as many as one-quarter of them for "behavioral problems," most involving aggression, and struggles to find homes for the rest.

"I think a pit bull overpopulation problem exists all across America, and it's worse in some communities than in others," she told me.

Sadly, of all dogs euthanized in America, about two of every three is a pit bull or pit bull mix. There is no other dog as promiscuously bred, frequently abused, or wantonly abandoned. No other breed as likely to be killed . . . or to kill.

On the morning I wrote this, an adopted pit bull named Blue killed a ninety-year-old Virginia woman, Margaret Colvin. The unprovoked attack occurred just hours after her daughter had adopted the fifty-pound dog from the Forever Home Rehabilitation Center in Virginia Beach. From all appearances, the shelter had done everything right prior to the placement.

"Blue went through our three-month board and train program and was a favorite amongst all of the staff members and volunteers. Blue loved other dogs and didn't know a stranger. He never showed any aggression while at our facility and passed his final evaluation with flying colors," said the shelter in a media statement.

Margaret Colvin joined the list of more than three hundred Americans killed by this breed since 1998, including nine victims between January and June of 2017, when her death occurred. She was killed less than five weeks after Lisa Green, thirty-two, of Upper Macungie Township, Pennsylvania, was likewise fatally mauled by a pit bull, this one adopted from Peaceable Kingdom fostering network in nearby Allentown.

Is it any wonder that people are reluctant to adopt these dogs? Especially when the alternative is a shiny new puppy, or a graying retriever-mix, or a Chihuahua in need of a home?

Before I began this book, I held no opinion about pit bulls and had had few actual encounters with them. Denver, my home, had banned the breed in the 1980s following two highly publicized fatal attacks, one involving a nine-year-old boy and the other a middle-aged pastor. The ban has been effective not only in preventing attacks—there hasn't been a single fatal dog attack in the city since the passage of the legislation—but also serves to keep down the number of unwanted dogs in shelters. As I mentioned, Colorado had to import 24,000 dogs to meet demand for shelter pets in 2016.

It seems to me that for too long, the humane and shelter organizations have been eager to blame purebred dog breeders for the problems that beset shelters all over America, while failing to acknowledge the number one overpopulation problem: the profligate overbreeding of pit bulls by pit bull owners. By and large, the pit bull advocacy and animal rights communities both oppose common-sense measures like mandatory sterilization laws and pit bull bans that could not only lower the risk of fatal and disfiguring attacks (close to one thousand pit bull attacks involving disfiguring mauling occurred in 2016 alone), but would also reduce the numbers of unwanted, unadoptable pit bulls being euthanized in America every single year.

Typically, community attempts to ban pit bulls or sterilize them have resulted in the organized opposition of hundreds of the breed advocates, many associated with pit bull rescue groups. Thankfully, some communities are standing up to this response with a counter-movement. In 2006, following the fatal mauling of twelve-year-old Nicholas Faibish by two pit bulls, San Francisco passed an ordinance that required pit bull owners to sterilize their dogs. Within eighteen months, the pit bull population in the city's shelter dropped from three-quarters of the dogs to less than one-quarter, and the number of pit bulls euthanized fell by 24 percent.

In 2006, the city of Springfield, Missouri, passed a pit bull sterilization ordinance. The breed was not banned. Owners simply had to get them registered, spayed or neutered, and microchipped, in addition to posting a sign about their dog(s). Before the ban, the city had been picking up and euthanizing hundreds of pit bulls a year; in 2016, just twenty-six were put down.

After Beaufort County, South Carolina, passed a mandatory pit bull sterilization ordinance in 2014, more than 691 pit bulls—including four hundred females—were sterilized.

"We had basically become a pit bull sanctuary—and to a degree we still are," said Beaufort County Animal Services' Tallulah Trice. But mandatory sterilization of pit bulls had stopped the births of at least several thousand pit bull puppies that likely would have ended up in shelters, she said.

If more communities would adopt similar ordinances, it would result in thousands of shelters in America emptying out. Absent the half-million or more pit bulls being bred and surrendered to shelters each year, hundreds of shelters across American would go out of business. And wouldn't that be great?

Many, though, will say that the pit bull deserves to be "saved." But what is so special about this particular package of artificially-selected traits? Throughout history, dog breeds have come and gone. Take the turnspit or "kitchen" dog. It was a long-backed, short-legged British dog bred to run on a wheel attached to a meat spit. The dog was essentially a rotisserie motor, so the breed went extinct as soon as someone had the sense to design a mechanical roasting device.

Like the turnspit, the pit bull was bred to do a job that is no longer considered humanely acceptable—fighting others of its kind to the death. Nobody mourns the passing of the turnspit dog. We should all be happy that both the job it was bred for and the work that it did no longer exist. So why should anybody mourn the extinction of the pit bull? Especially when homes are needed for hundreds of breeds and millions of dogs that weren't artificially selected over many generations for the purpose of killing their own kind?

Even if the shelters don't want to shutter their doors, the resources presently spent on caring for, promoting, and euthanizing the millions of pit bulls flooding shelters today could be dedicated to other deserving dogs—like the street dogs in Third World countries that are in great need of homes. Or the money could be put toward programs to help low-income people faced with veterinary costs, or eviction, or loss of income, to keep their dogs in their own homes rather than abandon them to shelters.

Writing for the *New York Times*, Francis Battista, co-founder of Best Friends Animal Society, said that "the only guilt-free purebred dog is one acquired from a shelter or rescue group."

But I don't agree. Not when the majority of dogs in shelters these days are of just one purebred type: pit bulls. Clearly, adopting pit bulls can't be the only ethical option Americans have when choosing canine companions. Every dog has to come from somewhere. Shaming the dog breeding community and holding them to a higher standard than we do backyard pit bull breeders and dog fighters simply isn't fair, and it isn't going to result in less suffering for animals.

If anything, we need not fewer dog show breeders and purebred enthusiasts—the people most likely to raise dogs that never end up in shelters in the first place—but far, far more of them.

It's late in the afternoon at the Rocky Mountain Dog Show. They say every dog has its day, and today wasn't Lena's. Finishing as the runner-up among the female dogs, she failed to advance to the Best of Breed competition. Carol gets a second-place ribbon, but not the points needed for Lena to finish her AKC championship. She takes the loss with her usual grace, smiling at ringside, congratulating the winner. "Well, there's always another dog show," she says to me.

Fortunately, Onda saves the day. Competing in the afternoon agility contest, Onda makes a flawless run that earns him a qualified score and the second fastest time of the day. Looking on are Carol Ann, her friend Susan Davis, and the owner of Onda's dam, Lynn Hamon. After our run, which draws a loud clatter of applause from the audience, we walk up into the stands.

The women coo and congratulate Onda, who drops onto his back to offer his belly for a tummy rub. His tongue lolls, his eyes closed in contentment as the women lavish affection on him.

As we pack up to go, I can't help but marvel at all the dogs I see. Fleet greyhounds, their speed passed down from ancient desert landraces of the ancient Middle East. Border collies, heelers and my beloved Aussies, whose intelligence and athleticism arose from shepherds' need to control livestock, along with Anatolian sheep dogs, English sheep dogs, and others whose job was to stand guard over the animals and protect them from predators. Pekingese, once the lapdogs of Chinese emperors and British Queens. Saint Bernards and huskies, who pulled carts and sleds. Retrievers and pointers and Spaniels and hounds, who all assisted in hunting.

And of course, there are the beloved mutts who are finally getting their accolades among the rest in this pageant of canine diversity. Together, they represent ten thousand years of shared history and the ingenious evolutionary ways that *canis familiaris*—the familiar wolf—has adapted itself to serve us in return for our care, understanding, and love.

CATS

*Cats were put into the world to disprove the
dogma that all things were created to serve man.*
—Musician Paul Gray

EIGHT

OF MICE AND MEN (AND CATS)

It is better to feed one cat than many mice.
—Norwegian proverb

Fifteen thousand years ago, *Mus musculus*, the common house mouse, trekked west from northern India, eventually scurrying into the campsites of Stone Age hunter-gatherers in the Middle East's Fertile Crescent, the biblical Garden of Eden.

Less resourceful in the wild than native mice but better at stealing from people (*mus*, in ancient Sanskrit meant "thief"), the house mouse's fortunes ebbed and flowed with the humans' willingness to stay put. Whenever food was abundant and people hunkered down in habitations, the house mouse flourished. But when food grew scarce and people returned to their wandering ways, the long-tailed mice lost ground to native rodents.

Then, about twelve thousand years ago, Neolithic farmers began to put down roots. Literally. The switch to agriculture (and perhaps the subsequent discovery of fermented beverages) demanded a more stationary way of life based on permanent villages, cultivated fields, and grain storages. In these unnatural environs, where food was abundant and predators scarce, house mice thrived. So much so that they jeopardized the cultures people were striving to create.

Since time immemorial, rodents have beset human efforts to save and store. In the Old Testament, God sent the Philistines a plague of mice for stealing the Ark of the Covenant. In ancient Greece, Aristotle wrote about mice outbreaks that often destroyed farmers' harvests.

"They go to work with such speed that owners of small farms notice one day that it is time to start reaping . . . only to discover the entire crop has been devoured," he lamented.

Not only could mice eat a farmer out of farm and field, they would invade granaries and spoil what remained of the harvest with their urine and excrement. Given the devastating impact mice could have on farmers' livelihoods, the earliest crop growers must have welcomed cats' arrival on the scene like an emancipating army.

Until recently, it was widely held that the ancient Egyptians were the first to domesticate wildcats, selectively breeding them to produce a distinctive new species, the house cat. Egyptians buried alongside their pet cats date back as many as six thousand years, and tomb paintings show them curled up under their mistresses's chairs more than four thousand years ago. But an increasing body of evidence suggests that even before the inception of Egyptian civilization, cats were human hangers-on as rodent hunters *par excellence*.

In the early 1980s, scientists unearthed an eight-thousand-year-old cat jawbone on the Mediterranean island of Cyprus. Wildcats are not native to the island, and it seems unlikely that the late stone-age pioneers would have taken non-domesticated wildcats there. As the writer Desmond Morris, author of *Catworld: A Feline Encyclopedia* remarked, a "spitting, scratching, panic-stricken wild feline would have been the last kind of boat companion they would have wanted."

In 2008, French scientists discovered more ancient Cyprian cat remains. Around 9,500 years ago, islanders buried a man with a variety of his treasured artifacts—including a cuddly eight-month-old kitten. To the archaeologists, this implied a more than passing relationship between the man and his trusty mouser, and a desire that it accompany him in the afterlife.

"The first discovery of cat bones on Cyprus showed that human beings brought cats with them to the islands, but we couldn't decide if these cats were wild or tame," said Jean-Denis Vigne, of the National Museum of Natural History in Paris. "With this discovery, we can now decide that these cats were linked to humans."

The domestication of nearly all economically important animals occurred in the Fertile Crescent, a scimitar-shaped area of land in the Middle East that encompassed the Tigris-Euphrates River Valley, the eastern edge of the Mediterranean Sea, and Egypt's Nile River. According to Carlos Driscoll and a team of co-researchers at the National Cancer Institute in the United States, it's almost certain the cat got her start there, too.

Curious to determine the domestic cat's ancient origins, Driscoll's team looked at cat DNA as part of a side project of their main research goal, which is to study the genetic basis of human diseases by comparing similar diseases found in cats.

Driscoll's team spent six years collecting wildcat DNA from locations as distant as Scotland, Israel, Namibia, and Mongolia. The DNA they collected identified five subspecies of closely related wildcats, *Felis sylvestris*, each corresponding to a different geographic region: Europe, South Africa, the Middle East, Mongolia, and Eastern China. The genetic blueprints for each of the subspecies were compared to those of hundreds of domesticated cats, including feral cats, household pets, and pedigreed, purebred show cats.

The comparison revealed that the world's domestic cats share gene patterns exclusively with wildcats from the Middle East. The nearest matches were from wildcats captured in Israel, Saudi Arabia, Bahrain, and the United Arab Emirates—countries clustered within or proximate to the ancient boundaries of the Fertile Crescent. It's proof that this area of the Middle East, often referred to as "the Cradle of Civilization," was also the cradle of the household cat.

Driscoll believes that a population of wildcats gained a claw hold among the earliest farming settlements, beginning an extended domestication episode. Once a tame cat population was established and began to spread, a handful of other wildcats likely took advantage of the easy village life and became part of the gene pool. According to Driscoll's DNA research, all of today's six hundred million cats owe their ancestry to just five wildcat matriarchs.

Driscoll contends that humans had little to do with the process; nobody likely said to himself, "I'll try and domesticate a wildcat." Instead, the cats chose domestication.

"The cats were adapting themselves to a new environment, so the push for domestication came from the cat side, not the human side," he told *The New York Times*.

Driscoll's views are gaining support among evolutionary biologists. Performing similar research involving eleven hundred cats from across multiple continents, a group from the School of Veterinary Medicine at the University of California, Davis, was able to confirm Driscoll's Middle Eastern wildcat hypothesis and even narrow down the area of origin.

"Our data support the Fertile Crescent, especially Turkey, as one of the origin sites for cats," said Dr. Leslie Lyons, who led the UC Davis group. "Turkey was part of the Fertile Crescent and hence was one of the earliest areas for agricultural development." Lending even more support to this view is the current belief that Turkish farmers were the first to colonize Cyprus.

The mechanism for domestication—mouse catching—has been verified, too. In China, scientists looking into a well-developed agricultural village that flourished 5,500 years ago discovered cat bones. Analyzing the bones, they determined that the cats there fed on rodents that, in turn, had been raiding the villagers' stored millet crops—clear evidence the felines had a job in the local economy.

"It's very hard to find, archaeologically, exactly what relationship caused domestication," said Fiona Marshall, who worked on the study. "It's been speculated that . . . cats were attracted to early farmers, but it wasn't known for sure. But what this shows us is, yes, there was food for cats in ancient farming villages, and that they helped the farmers out . . . by eating rodents."

From an evolutionary standpoint, taking up residence in villages was a win-win for humans and cats. Farming cultures gained from the sly little felines' help protecting their crops, ensuring they had more to eat. And cats gained protection from larger predators, plus easy access to mice, sparrows, certain insects, reptiles, and other small prey that had found a comfortable niche to exploit in the artificial world of human settlements.

But this new arrangement forced the cats to adapt, in an evolutionary sense, to novel and challenging circumstances. Cats in the wild live solitary lives and are territorially defensive by nature. They profoundly dislike and distrust people. Some species, like the Scottish wildcat, are so antisocial that they're all but impossible to tame. But in the village, cats had to live closely among other cats and learn to get along with people.

Simply moving into the village created natural selective pressure for tameness, which altered the behavioral gene pool so that people-friendly cats found it easier to survive and bear offspring than their nastier-natured sisters. With their preference for tameness in animals, people likely accelerated the natural domestication process by choosing especially friendly cats as pets to be fed, cared for, and even traded with people in distant lands.

The social transformation of cats during domestication is important. Unlike dogs, which underwent profound changes in form following domestication, cats of today remain little altered in appearance from the wildcats from which they sprang. If you were to compare wildcat and domestic cat skeletons, as I did one day at the Denver Museum of Natural Science, you'd find it virtually impossible to tell one from the other. And if someone were to let a Middle Eastern wildcat loose in the wilds of a Boston suburb, people there would doubtless mistake her for someone's pet. But woe be to the person who tries to catch her and take her home.

"There's a big difference between house cats and wildcats. A house cat will sit on your lap, but a wildcat will hand you your behind," says geneticist and feline researcher Stephen O'Brien.

But once it got right with its attitude, the cat was perfect in every regard for its role as a rodent assassin in service to mankind. The cat is what's known as an obligate carnivore, which is to say, it's obligated to eat meat. Cats' digestive systems can't process plant nutrients and carbs efficiently, and they've even lost the ability to taste sugars. (Because of this, cats should not be fed a vegan diet. For a pet that aligns with a vegan's ethical stance against meat, there's the bunny rabbit).

For early farmers, cats' carnivorous proclivities were a boon. With no interest in fruits, vegetables, or grains, cats required few food sacrifices from humans besides the occasional offering of surplus animal products, such as souring milk or the discarded bits of raised or hunted animals or fish, that served to bridge times when prey was scarce and encouraged cats not to seek prey elsewhere.

But the cat's appeal to humankind, of course, extended beyond mere utility. It couldn't have escaped early farmers' notice that cats also made for appealing companions. With their childlike faces, inquisitive eyes, soft fur, and (in time) their ability to develop affection toward people, the cat ingratiated itself into human life. Yet, unlike the dog, which would be profoundly changed through its association with human masters, the cat managed to keep three paws firmly planted in the wild.

NINE

CAT CULT CULTURE

When a man smells of myrrh, his wife is a cat.
When he is in distress, she is a lioness.
—Ancient Egyptian philosopher Onchsheshonqy

O ne morning in the fall of 1934, a British Army officer with an interest in Egyptian antiquities invited a shifty and suspicious trader to his Cairo flat. The man had a sack of mostly valueless ancient artifacts wrapped in paper and rags. Nevertheless, he revealed each item slowly and with ceremony, using an age-old technique for building dramatic tension. A long pause followed the last item. Major Robert Gayer-Anderson broke the silence.

"Is that all?"

Taking his cue, the trader fumbled among the wrappings and brought out an object of considerable size and weight. He unwrapped it carefully and then, with a graceful flourish, offered his patron a life-sized statue of a cat.

The collector caught his breath. Although he'd never held an ancient Egyptian bronze cat sculpture in his own hands, he instantly recognized the exquisite piece as a temple offering to Bastet, the cat-headed goddess beloved by ancient Egyptians.

"To my practiced eye it was obviously a work of the greatest refinement and beauty of form, a bronze of great rarity and value," he recalled.

While the trader shared the story of how he'd discovered the object at a massive burial site in the ancient city of Memphis, Gayer-Anderson studied the piece with feigned coolness. He knew there was no equal to the cat. Not in Cairo, London, or New York.

As a lengthy bargaining session commenced, each man privately thrilled at the possibility of striking a fantastic deal. In the end, Gayer-Anderson paid one hundred Egyptian pounds for the merchant's entire lot—a ludicrously small sum for such a treasure. But the trader likely felt he'd gotten the better of his patron—he could go home without constantly glancing over his shoulder for the police.

For nearly a year, Gayer-Anderson painstakingly restored the statue, delicately chipping away at the crusty patina of verdigris to reveal the subtleties of the bronze beneath. Fine ornamentation, most of it religiously symbolic, began to reveal itself: an incised silver "collar of Isis" circled the neck four times; attached to it was a pendant with the Eye of Horus set inside a rectangle. Below this was a beautifully etched drawing of a winged scarab beetle holding the disc of Ra, the Sun God. Another scarab beetle adorned the cat's forehead—it was thought Ra favored scarabs because they rolled dung across the ground just as he rolled the sun across the sky. Within each of the cat's ears the artist had incised a Feather of Truth, symbol of the goddess Maat, mistress of heaven and earth and bestower of justice.

To complete his restoration, Gayer-Anderson repaired a crack that threatened to break the statue in two. He used jewelry of correct age and origin to replace the gold rings that had once pierced the cat's nose and ears, but left out the stone eyes that, he felt, would only steal from the statue's aloof dignity.

Getting the object out of Egypt would prove tricky, but Gayer-Anderson used his connections and know-how to repatriate the statue. He never revealed whether his methods were legitimate or illicit, though one suspects some laws were bent and bribes were paid.

"Suffice to say that in the summer of 1936, I carried this treasure ashore at Tilbury with a feeling of triumph and accomplishment, unspoiled by any twinges of conscience," he wrote in his journal.

Back in England, Gayer-Anderson entertained offers as high as three thousand British pounds (about $500,000 in current US dollars) for the find. But in the end, he refused to sell. He'd acquired enough antiquities to literally fill his own museum in Cairo, but he came to regard the bronze statue as his greatest and most adored acquisition.

After having three exacting copies made, he committed to donating the original figure to the British Museum in 1939. However, the collector took his time parting with it. Afraid the Nazis might succeed in invading England or perhaps in bombing the British Museum in London out of existence, he kept the cat well hidden (in a well, in fact) on a Suffolk farm until the war ended in 1945 and the cat's safety was assured.

Today, the "Gayer-Anderson cat" ranks among the British Museum's best-known and most beloved art objects. As iconic Egyptian sculptures go, in the public's mind it ranks in awareness just below the Great Sphinx of Giza and King Tutankhamen's gold sarcophagus. Simply looking at something as familiar as a cat with such obvious ties to an ancient culture seems to forge an immediate, visceral connection between the present and the past.

What did the cat goddess statue mean to ancient Egyptians? What was its purpose? To understand, we need to go back in time

2,500 years, to a raucous and ribald party taking place on the eastern bank of the Nile Delta.

The festival site was called Per-Bast, "the domain of Bastet." For thousands of years, a city of that name was the cult center of Egypt for the feline-loving goddess revered by all as a protector of Lower Egypt and its people.

In Per-Bast's early centuries, Egyptians believed the goddess Bastet to be a fearsome lioness, or a lioness-headed protector. Her name meant *a female devourer*. As such, the people believed she would protect them from invading attackers. A similar goddess, Sekhmet, who also took the form of a lioness, protected Upper Egypt, which was established as a separate and often antagonistic kingdom.

Eventually, the unification of Upper and Lower Egypt would lead to Egyptians regarding the two feline goddesses as sisters and as the daughters of Ra, the mighty Sun God. Each daughter served as Ra's eyes, projecting the rays of sunlight. Sekmet projected the cruel, searing heat of destruction while Bastet provided the warm, life-giving powers of the sun.

Though the worship of Bastet as a lioness began early in Egyptian times, one would labor in vain to find a *cat-headed* goddess on the walls of the earliest pyramids and burial tombs. Domestic cats appear not to have arrived on the scene until Egypt's Middle Kingdom, when its important deities were already well established. And it was not until the last thousand years of ancient Egypt's greatness that the cat would rise to renown.

The cat first appears in Egyptian art in the tomb of Baket III, around 1950 B.C. Amidst drawings of everyday life—women weaving on looms, butchers slaughtering cattle—is a drawing of a cat about to battle a field mouse. The cat stands next to a man, indicating it belongs to him.

The rodent is an important detail. Egypt was about to enter its period of greatest power, with which the rise of the cat coincides. Egypt's fortunes depended on grain, the single most important commodity in its economy.

Before the cat arrived, rodents were an insolvable and vexing problem for Egyptians. When the highly-regarded Egyptologist Flinders Petrie described a nineteenth century excavation of Kahun, a village that existed two thousand years before Christ, he observed that "nearly every room had its corners tunneled with rats, and the holes are stuffed up with stones and rubbish to keep them back."

Not long after, the domestic cat arrived on the scene . . . doubtless with the same welcoming it earned in the homes of other neolithic farmers. Its ability to slay mice and rats, to protect grain bins, and to save lives by hunting poisonous scorpions and snakes must have made it seem magical. And the fact that it hunted its own food, kept itself clean, and buried its feces in the desert sands surely made it even more welcome.

However, as a relatively late arrival in Egypt, the humble cat had to literally claw her way into the hierarchy of Egypt's divine and sacred animal community. But when she did, in the guise of the goddess Bastet, she surpassed all the other animals in worship and esteem.

A twist of fate likely helped elevate the cat goddess to a position of unmatched idolatry in Egypt during its final millennia of greatness. Around three thousand years before the present day, Egypt was struggling through a period of foreign invasion, disunity, and unrest. In 943 B.C., a military leader, Shoshenq I, seized control of Lower Egypt and became pharaoh. His home was Per-Bast, and his ascension to power made the city central to Egyptian government, culture, and trade for nearly two hundred years.

It's likely that Shoshenq was the first to link the goddess Bastet with the cat, changing her face from that of a fierce lioness to one of a domesticated feline. In any case, Shoshenq encouraged this change in appearance because he understood the powerful hold that the domestic cat had over the Egyptian populace at large.

A story widely circulated among Egyptians helped to explain why Bastet chose Per-Bast as the place of her shrine. The goddess had fled to the Nubian Desert, where she hid in the form of a lioness. When her father, Ra, needed her to return, he sent some of his messengers to persuade her. Angry to leave, she cooled her temper in the waters of the Nile, emerging as a mild-mannered domestic cat.

She then sailed down the Nile to the acclaim of the many Egyptians lining the banks until she came to Per-Bast. There, a celebration was held, establishing Per-Bast as a sacred place where periodic feasts were held to honor her. And in this way, the cult of the cat got underway.

The cat's appeal lay in her humble origins and affectionate behavior, which brought the animal adoration and prominence in the day-to-day worship of ordinary people. While the wealthy and powerful had private temples that allowed them to pay homage to long-established and mightier animal gods, it was possible for average Egyptians to have a goddess figure in their own homes simply by owning a cat.

When the cat came to take the lioness' place as goddess, Bastet's role as a warrior became less significant (the job now taken by her sister, Sekhmet), and she assumed the part of protectress of the home—a natural, given the cat's importance in ridding grain storages and households of mice, along with venomous snakes and insects. Significantly, people believed Bastet also protected them from diseases—a protection that likely stemmed from cats' ability to control disease-carrying mice.

Bastet's worshippers also ascribed to her other cat-like attributes. Cats, or course, are known for having many kittens, so Bastet also symbolized fertility and family. Women who wanted children would wear amulets showing Bastet with kittens at her feet, each signifying the number of children the woman hoped to birth. Children might also be tattooed with Bastet's likeness or given simple amulets to gain her protection.

Naturally, fertility went hand-in-hand with sexuality. Cats are well known for noisy, boundless nocturnal coupling. Likewise, Egyptians regarded Bastet as a sexual being: she took three husbands and also slept around with other gods and goddesses. So, Bastet also became associated with sexual pleasure, seduction (she was the lady of perfumes), music, and celebration.

Which brings us back to the party at Per-Bast. Shoshenq and his successors invested lavishly to renovate the Temple of Bastet to one of unsurpassed beauty. Most of what we know about the temple comes from an account written by the Greek historian Herodotus, who visited the site centuries after the Per-Bast rulers had fallen from power. Even long past the height of its glory, it remained a fantastic place.

Per-Bast was set in a hollow, so that the center of the city could be seen from any vantage point. Two channels from the Nile flowed into the city, forming a peninsula that comprised the temple grounds. Each waterway was a hundred feet wide and shadowed by trees; people coming in by boat from the Nile would pass through either of these two broad, placid canals.

Worshippers coming from town would approach the temple from the city's vast public market, walking on a stone-paved road that was four hundred feet wide "with trees on either side, reaching to Heaven," according to Herodotus. The temple grounds were surrounded by a marble wall adorned with figures of gods and goddesses carved in relief. Inside was a garden of tall trees that shaded the temple.

Bastet's temple was square and ran 220 feet on every side—about the same length but twice the width of the famed Parthenon in Athens. Inside was a massive shrine to the goddess, attended year-round by female and male priests. The priests were acclaimed for their dancing, which often involved disrobing . . . making them, perhaps, the first professional strippers.

During quiet times, temple attendants distributed food, provided medical help and advice, counseled people in legal, business, and personal affairs, and assisted worshippers in their daily devotions. They also cared for a cattery, which housed sacred cats that people believed could, at any time, carry the spirit of Bastet.

But every April, the Temple of Bastet witnessed a massive five-day festival in the goddesses' honor. It was, in a word, epic. Whether your touchstone is Carnivale, Mardi Gras, Coachella, Burning Man, or the original Woodstock, the party at Per Bastet would stand tall as a contender for sheer extravagance, spectacle, and excess.

In the days leading up to the festival, people would come from throughout all of Egypt, floating or sailing in boats filled to capacity with revelers. Women carried in their hands the sistrum, a musical noisemaker like a rattle or castanet. Some played flutes. Everyone danced to the music, clapping and singing and shouting.

When a boat passed a town, the women would jeer those who had not yet joined the procession, and would lift their skirts and display their, em, kitties. It was an invitation to the licentiousness and abandon that was soon to come.

At the festival, anything went. Historian Geraldine Pinch, citing Herodotus, said that "women were freed from all constraints during the annual festival." It was a time to cast aside inhibitions, and this included not only feasting and drinking (Herodotus remarked that Egyptians consumed more wine during the festival than during the entire remainder of the year), but also dancing, flirting, singing, and having sex with whomever one could seduce. More than 700,000 people took part in the orgiastic party each year, making it among the most popular celebrations, if not the most, on the robust annual Egyptian religious festival circuit. (Children, it should be noted, remained at home).

Amid all the revelry and sexual abandon, the festival had its moments of solemnity and great beauty. On the final evening, all would gather in silence at the temple. A single candle would be lit. From this light, other candles were given flame so that the light spread from the center outward, illuminating the entire crowd in a growing circle that must have been spectacular to behold from the heights.

During the festival, one of the important duties of the worshippers was to present gifts to the goddess Bastet. If a family cat had died during the year, it was embalmed and mummified, to be buried in a massive temple graveyard. When the temple at Per-Bast was excavated in 1887, more than 300,000 mummified cats were found there.

If one didn't have a cat to bring, mummified cats could be bought as votive offerings. In addition, people shopped for jewelry made of precious metals and stones to be left as temple offerings, worn as amulets, or taken home and placed in family shrines. Gifts to the goddess were often accompanied by requests, or prayers, that the women might have children, or that the home might be protected from disease.

An especially wealthy patron might present a statue like the Gayer-Anderson cat as a votive offering. This sculpture would likely have been displayed in a prominent location until such time as it was replaced with one of greater beauty and value. Statues like these were often inscribed with messages or requests to the goddess.

Bastet was popular among men as well as women, as every man had a mother, wife, sister or daughter who benefitted from the care the cat goddess provided. Furthermore, Egyptian society recognized women as equal in status and rights with men. This helps explain why a cat goddess who protected women, helped them conceive children, protected the household, and guarded women's secrets could attain such high standing.

Because the Egyptians believed that their gods and goddesses could choose to inhabit the bodies of the animals they favored, cats enjoyed the protection of society as well. Foreigners who visited Egypt during the waning years of its power commented on the extraordinary protection that cats received from everyday Egyptians.

It's often said that a person in Egypt who killed a cat, even by accident, put himself in a position of grave mortal danger. Greek historian Diodorus Siculus wrote about his visit to Egypt just a few decades before the birth of Christ. He remarked that if a person were to kill one of the sacred animals, whether a cat or an ibis, "he is certainly put to death, for the common people gather in crowds and deal with the perpetrator most cruelly, sometimes without waiting for a trial."

He then related an account of a hapless Roman soldier stationed in Egypt during the late Ptolemaic Dynasty. The Egyptians were courting the Romans' favor to avoid war with the great foreign nation when the soldier killed a cat. A mass of Egyptian citizens stormed his house to exact revenge on behalf of Bastet.

"Neither the officials sent by the king to beg the man off nor the fear of Rome which all the people felt was enough to save the man from punishment, even though his act had been an accident," wrote the historian. To quell any question of his truthfulness, Siculus noted that he'd witnessed the soldier's death with his own eyes.

The Macedonian writer Polyaenus and Greek historian Herodotus both described a battle between the Egyptian army and that of the Persian king, Cambyses II. Craftily but cruelly, the Persian invader turned the Egyptians' reverence for cats against them.

To defend the fortified city of Pelusium, an eastern gateway to Lower Egypt, the Egyptian army deployed catapults to hurl rocks, missiles, and fire upon their foes. In response, Cambyses gathered cats, dogs, ibises and other sacred animals before his troops, whose shields had been painted with the image of Bastet.

This cat-centric counter-offensive compelled the Egyptians to cease their shelling, as they feared offending their sacred goddess. The Persians then took the city without a fight. (In Herodotus' account, only cats had been used to shield the Persian forces). Cambyses then rode through town in a chariot, tossing cats at the people to show his scorn for them. He then ordered the temple walls at Per-Bast destroyed.

The loss of Egyptian independence under Rome following Cleopatra's death in 30 B.C. dealt a blow to traditional Egyptian religion from which it would not recover. Rulers abandoned the ancient, animistic gods and goddesses, replacing them with humanistic Greco-Roman gods. But to the common people, worship of ancient, animal-loving deities, especially the popular ones like Bastet, would continue for hundreds of years more.

Theirs was a losing faith. In the fourth and fifth centuries, the Christian orthodox leader Shenute waged war against pagan worshippers to rid Egypt once and for all of its polytheistic past. His zealotry swept aside the last remaining cult worshippers of Egyptian animal deities.

After a glorious period of protection and worship (which some say felines have never forgotten), the cat returned to its humble role of domestic animal and pet. In Egypt, at least, it did not fare poorly. The cat remained much beloved and later would receive the blessing and protection of Egypt's new religious leader, the Prophet Mohammed. Well into the medieval period, people made donations to feed the homeless cats of Cairo. Most notably, in the twelfth century, Sultan Baibars willed a part of his fortune so that a sanctuary could be built near his mosque solely for the upkeep of Cairo's destitute cats.

Elsewhere, it was a different story.

TEN

PUTTING THE EVIL IN MEDIEVAL

*The devyl playeth ofte with the synnar, lyke as
the catte doth with the mous.*
—Fifteenth century publisher William Caxton

A s with all things concerning the domestication and spread of
pets and barnyard animals, scientists debate the cat's timing
and manner of arrival in Europe. A plausible explanation as for
feline proliferation across the European landscape during ancient
times is that Phoenician traders carried cats aboard their ships as
mouse-catchers and trade goods.

In the millennia preceding Christ's birth, Phoenician ships
sailed across the entirety of the Mediterranean Sea to the Straits

of Gibraltar and beyond, stopping off in the Iberian Peninsula and the islands of Sardinia and Sicily. At any of these ports, cats might have jumped ship or traders could have sold them as exotic pets, just as is done today with wild animals like macaws, meerkats, pythons, etc.

Although they never colonized Britain, Phoenicians traded British tin for grain from the Middle East, especially Egypt. Doubtless, mice hitched a ride with the grain. Therefore, it's plausible that Phoenicians brought cats to the British isles to clean up a problem of their own making.

But significantly, the Bible contains not a single mention of cats in the Old Testament—making it likely they were still little known outside Egypt. Therefore, it's conjectured that the cat didn't make its way north into Europe until the outset of Greco-Roman rule in Egypt, which began with the Greek conqueror Alexander the Great in 332 B.C.

Whether brought overseas by Phoenicians or by land via Greeks or Romans, cats were scarcely remarked upon in Europe in the early centuries following Christ's death. It was not, in fact, until the fifth century that the word *cattus* first appeared in Latin. (The Egyptians had used the delightfully onomatopoeic word *miu* instead, as well as *caute*, the likely source of the Latin version).

As opposed to the animistic gods of Egypt, the Greeks and Romans worshipped humanistic deities. Bastet's nearest equivalents were the Grecian virgin huntress, Artemis, known for her untamed nature, and her Roman counterpart, Diana. Like Bastet, both were revered by women as goddesses of fertility, childbirth, and the home, as well as being curers of disease. However, neither was intimately associated with cats. As hunters, both favored dogs for companionship.

Likely this shift reflects the fact that neither the Greeks nor the Romans were as enamored with cats as were the Egyptians. For the most part, they employed tame ferrets to control mice, rabbits, and black rats, the latter of which arrived in Rome during the height of the empire and likely brought with them the plague-infested fleas that proved to be Rome's coup de grace.

Cats did make a mark on Greek art, however, where they can be seen chasing ducks on wall frescoes and playing with string on silver coins. These were but fleeting impressions. It's not in art but rather in the thoughts and words of Greeks that cats begin to take on personalities. Egyptians may have shaped the cat and given it reverence, but Greek literature gave it soul.

Greek fables of the kind written down by Aesop include numerous stories about cats, many depicting them as tricksters or deceivers. In "The Cat's Birthday Party," for instance, the animal invites birds to the celebration—then closes the door and devours them. And in "The Eagle, the Cat, and the Wild Sow," the cat convinces the bird and the pig that if they leave their homes, the other will take their young. Tied to their places, the animals starve—and the cat eats their babies.

The cat also enters into a particular ancient Greek myth, an earlier version of which likely accompanied it out of Egypt. The myth went something like this: The powerful god of war, Zeus, seduced the beautiful Princess Alcmene, who became pregnant with their illegitimate child, Heracles (Hercules, to Romans). In a jealous rage, Zeus' wife, Hera, persuaded another goddess, who was responsible for childbirth, to sit outside Alcmene's door and cross her legs tightly, which cast a spell on Alcmene that blocked Heracles' birth.

As the labor endured over several days, causing Alcmene great distress, her clever maid-servant, Galinthius, hatched a plan. She told the goddess guarding Alcmene's door that she'd failed, and that the baby had already come forth. When the goddess stood up, the spell over Alcmene was broken and Heracles was born.

Hera was furious not only that her foe, Alcmene, had delivered Zeus' illegitimate child, but that she'd been outsmarted by Galinthius, a mere mortal. To exact revenge on the faithful servant, she turned Galinthius into a cat, then banished her to the underworld.

There, the goddess of magic and darkness, Hecate, took pity on Galinthius and made the creature her personal, sacred pet. This often-told myth, which associated cats with darkness, transformation, the underworld, and dark magic, would prove tragically unfortunate for European cats in the centuries to come.

Following the decline of the Greco-Roman empire, the cat enjoyed a period of high status within the evolving European kingdoms. In Scotland and Ireland, for instance, the people considered cats to be magical, only in a positive sense. And in Norse mythology, the goddess Freya rode the sky in a chariot drawn by two giant cats—a fantastic proposition, given cats' poor reputation for teamwork, but nevertheless . . .

Along with pagans, the earliest Christians seemed inclined to regard cats with affection, judging, at least, by a bit of ancient folklore. The tale goes that the newborn baby Jesus was shivering in his manger when a mother cat lay down next to him and provided him with warmth. Mary awoke and stroked the cat's forehead in thanks, marking it with an "M" that tabbies carry to this day.

A similar story is shared in the Muslim faith, in which a tabby cat warned Mohammed of danger. In thanks, the Prophet affectionately petted the cat, leaving *his* first initial on the forehead, as well as stripes on the back where he stroked the fur. Both the Christian and Muslim stories, in turn, likely originated from an ancient Egyptian tale in which the "M" signified the legs of the scarab beetle, the sacred mark of Ra the Sun God, father of Bastet.

Any affection early Christians in Europe may have felt for cats, however, was about to take a dark turn. At the end of the twelfth century, the cat appeared for the first time in Christian literature in diabolical form. This tale involved Saint Bartholomew of Farne, a Benedictine priest who wandered Europe performing miracles before settling down to a miserable life as a hermit in Britain.

During his wanderings, Bartholomew battled the Devil, who appeared to him in a number of animal forms, particularly as a cat. Animals were commonly used as religious symbols in medieval art, and in this case, the shorthand for St. Bart's battles with Satan became a cat toying with a mouse. Coincidentally, the Latin words *cattus* and *capturer* made for a nice play on words in Latin, so ecclesiastical writers seized on it too.

As a result, the cat torturing a mouse became an often-used medieval allegory, or what we might today call a "meme." Manuscript artists used it often when illustrating Holy Bibles and Books of Psalms. An example is the Psalter at St. Augustine's Abbey circa 1220, in which a letter "C" encloses a rather diabolical cat clutching a mouse. More than a century later, an almost identical illustration appears in The Luttrell Psalter, also from England.

Another popular use was in bestiaries, basically field guides to medieval animals and fantastical beasts that were used to teach moral lessons. Priests in their sermons and theologians in their tracts likewise employed the parable of the cat toying with the mouse to reinforce the fear of the Devil—and cats—in parishioners' hearts.

Portrayals of cats as devils in disguise coincided with increasing persecution of non-believers—atheists, pagan worshippers, and heretics—which intensified and became institutionalized beginning in the twelfth century.

Religious persecution under Christianity had first gotten underway in 391, when the Emperor Theodosius I banned all pagan worship, including cults devoted to the Roman goddess Diana and her Egyptian counterpart, Bastet. But for hundreds of years, people living beyond the Vatican's reach maintained ancient pagan religions passed down and adapted from pre-Christian cultures.

Over time, elements of the native religious practices fused with Christian doctrine, resulting in hybrid religions regarded as heretical by the Church. By the eleventh century, these religions were gaining ground as people resisted the oppressive, greedy and capricious authority of the popes and their bishops. Threatened by the independence of the sects and coveting the lands of their worshippers, the Church and secular authorities under various Catholic kings began to systematically annihilate their adherents.

Among the first to feel the Church's wrath were the Cathars, who by 1150 had gained a wide following in Southern France, as well as Flanders (in Northern Belgium), and parts of Germany, Northern France, and Northern Italy. Something like hippies in their '60s heyday, high-ranking Cathars practiced veganism, worshipped nature and animals, and opposed violence, property ownership, and oath taking. Quite unlike hippies, high-ranking Cathars professed to abstain from sex.

Although the name *cathar* had its roots in the Latin word for chaste, *casta*, the medieval author Alain de Lille equated it with the Latin *cattus*. According to the French cleric, Satan appeared to Cathars in the form of a cat, or a man with fur-covered cat legs. During sacred rituals, initiates were said to literally kiss the ass of Satan, who appeared in the form of a huge black cat with his tail held high. Festivities were said to conclude with orgiastic banquets.

Fantastical claims like these served to justify a merciless campaign to wipe out heretical sects. The Cathars first came under attack in 1209 under the ironically named Pope Innocent III, who called for a crusade against them. In the first day of battle, twenty thousand men, women and children were killed. The persecution campaign against the Cathars continued for two decades. Raphael Lemkin, a Jewish lawyer who coined the word *genocide*, referred to the battle to destroy the Cathars as "one of the most conclusive cases of genocide in religious history."

Others, like de Lille's contemporary Walter Map, a Welshman, linked heretics with cats by using almost identical descriptions of cat-kissing initiation rituals. Inflamed by the heretics' alleged association with felines, in 1233, Innocent's successor, Pope Gregory, issued the *Vox In Rama*—in effect a declaration of holy war against heretical sects. It contained the same cat-kissing imagery, this time related by a sadistic German inquisitor who doubtless cribbed *his* notes from the others.

Vox In Rama served to kick off the Inquisition, a sort of papal police force and kangaroo court whose job became to root out heretics and torture confessions from them using unspeakably painful and often lethal methods—all for the sake of saving their souls.

Since all but a handful of Cathars had already been killed, scattered, or "converted" by Pope Innocent when *Vox In Rama* was written, the same cat-kissing rituals they'd allegedly practiced became the boilerplate used against other heretical groups— Waldensians, Luciferians (a German sect who really were quite wicked), and, a century later, the venerable Knights Templar, who had been allied with the Church during the Crusades but then fell out of favor.

Rumors about the Templars' secret initiation ceremony provided reason not to trust them, and King Philip IV of France— deeply in debt to the order—took advantage of the situation to destroy the Templars. In 1307, he had many of the order's members in France arrested, tortured into giving false confessions, and burned at the stake. Like other heretics, many were damned by false confessions of Devil worship involving cats.

Bishops in the German kingdoms, meanwhile, were so keen to associate cats with heretical sects that their nickname for heretics became *ketzer*, from the German word for cat, *katzke*. Even more to the point, some even called heretics *katzenküssers* (cat kissers).

Given the superstitious nature of the Dark Ages, it's understandable that the Church would choose to associate cats so closely with heretics. In the King James version of the Old Testament, it was written "Let us make man in our image, after our likeness, and let them have dominion over the fish of the sea, and over the fowl of the air, and over the cattle, and over all the earth, and over every creeping thing that creepeth upon the earth."

Cats are, by nature, very independent creatures, not inclined to bend to man's will. They sleep all day, and so were deemed indolent. They didn't depend upon people to care for them, nor did they perform useful tasks (beyond their self-supporting hunting), and didn't yield to human authority, as did dogs. Cats are highly sexual and indiscriminate love-makers, and their yowling and screaming during love making must have offended pious sensibilities more than did dogs' silent humping. It's easy to imagine that, in the dead of night, being awoken by their discordant caterwauling might have seemed like a foreshadowing of life in hell.

In short, cats weren't good Christian role models. Add to this the cat's ancient symbolic associations with the underworld, magic, and the mysticism of ancient Egyptian cults, and it was easy to see why church authorities seemed eager to regard cats as Satan incarnate.

Heaping yet more scorn on felines, ecclesiastical writers of the day attributed to them all sorts of diabolical powers. Their teeth were said to be venomous, their flesh poisonous, their hair lethal and capable of causing suffocation, and their breath infectious to the point of destroying human lungs.

Of course, people didn't recognize those "evils" for what they really were: allergic reactions caused by cat saliva, dander, and urine. About one in ten Europeans and Americans today suffers from cat allergies, whose symptoms affect the eyes, skin, and respiratory system. In severe cases, reactions may include deadly asthma attacks and anaphylaxis—whose sudden onset among cat allergy sufferers must have frightened people in the Middle Ages.

Superstition, fear, and religious persecution led to widespread cat killing and cat massacres throughout Europe during the Middle Ages. At this time, communities began holding annual cat celebrations whose main purpose was to round up and kill feral cats. Millions of cats are thought to have died as a result.

But then, after a century of ill-treatment at the hands of Catholics, some say cats exacted divine revenge in the form of the Black Death—humankind's greatest catastrophe.

In 1346, a virulent form of bubonic plague known as the Black Death arrived in Europe. Carried by rats' fleas aboard Italian trading ships, the disease made its way from the Black Sea to Mediterranean port cities, then inland across the entirety of Western Europe and North Africa.

According to Ole Benedictow, emeritus professor of History at the University of Oslo, Norway, the Black Death swept away something like 60 percent of Europe's population, reducing it from around eighty million to just thirty million. A popular theory to explain this phenomenon (especially among cat lovers) is that the Catholic Church's persecution of cats enabled mouse and rat populations in Europe to burgeon. A population explosion of rodents created ideal conditions for spreading the disease. When the Plague arrived in a new place, it would kill off the area's now abundant rats and mice; as the rodent population crashed, the disease-carrying fleas would naturally jump to humans.

Little doubt exists among medical historians that a sharp decrease in cat population would upset the predator/prey balance, resulting in an increase in rodents. And it has been established that such a decrease occurred in the years preceding the arrival of the Black Death. Rodent fleas, the natural breeding ground for the bubonic plague bacteria *Yersenia pestis,* landed in Europe just as a rodent irruption, caused by an absence of cats, made conditions for their attack ideal.

While there's a definite logic to this, there's also a line of thought suggesting that cats weren't able to gain justice against their tormentors in such straightforward fashion. Those reasons were laid out by Abigail Tucker in her acclaimed cat book, *The Lion in the Living Room.*

First, nobody knows for certain how many cats were killed during the purges. While certainly some towns suffered near-total cat population collapses, others were less vigilant and more kitty-tolerant.

Further, as everyone knows, cats are both highly adaptable and unusually fecund creatures, and would have been nearly as quick to replenish their population as were rats and mice. Tucker says it's doubtful that that an eradication effort based upon rounding up and tossing cats from tower belfries or burning them in bonfires (the preferred eradication methods of the time) would have made much of a dent in Europe's overall cat population.

Still, many will argue that cat persecution played a part in Europe's distress. For them, there is the disturbing but also powerful story of the European Jewish community during the years of 1346–1351, when Black Death was most aggressively reaping souls.

According to historical accounts, Jewish communities resisted the worst excesses of the Pandemic. Sadly and tragically, this fueled a fire among Christians to blame Jews for the Black Death. Christians' hysteria led to acts of Jewish persecution in towns and cities throughout Europe. These culminated in Christians rioting against Jews in Mainz, Germany, where they set fire to the entire Jewish enclave, resulting in the murder of six thousand Jewish residents.

Jewish scholar Yonassan Gershom believes the reason so many Jews escaped the ravages of the plague was simple: they refused to participate in killing cats.

"In contrast to medieval Christians who were killing all the cats as demons, Jews kept *shul katze* (synagogue cats) around to hunt rodents and protect the holy books from mice," he explained. *Chatul*, the Hebrew word for house cats, also kept away flea-carrying rats and mice in Jewish homes.

Unlike Christians, Jews had never viewed cats as evil or demonic. Judaism forbids a belief in omens, so the faithful weren't inclined to be superstitious, as Christians were. Further, Jewish cultural experiences with cats extended back in time to ancient Egypt, when cats were looked upon with reverence. Since cats were neither strange nor threatening to the Jews, they felt less conflicted about keeping them as pets.

"Unfortunately, since nobody back then knew how plague was spread, this difference just reinforced the idea that Jews were witches with demon cats who had brought the Plague as a curse on the Christians," Yonassan Gershom concluded.

Ironically, the Black Death served to undermine the power of both the Catholic Church and the feudal kingdoms. The dramatic loss of lives during the first wave of Plague, along with that of subsequent waves, created a labor shortage across Europe. Since the disease affected lords and paupers alike, when landowners perished, peasants fortunate enough to survive often gained their freedom. Many abandoned the countryside in favor of towns and cities, where there was opportunity for a better life.

As Europe's population plummeted and people left the peasant manors, land formerly used for crops was converted to grazing land held in common, allowing those who remained to raise livestock and to prosper. This led to the greater production of wool cloth, one of the earliest foundations of a fledgling industrial economy. Their economic power would eventually undermine medieval governance centered upon ecclesiastical and royal authority.

Concurrently, the Black Death caused many people in Europe to lose faith in the Christian God and the Catholic Church. (Many astute people observed that Rome had been better off under the management of its myriad of gods and goddesses than under the Christian God). So, ironically, paganism made a comeback in some regions. In others, disillusionment with the powers in Rome helped set the stage for the Protestant reformation. Liberated from Christian thought, people also turned to the study of ancient Greek and Roman culture, which helped kick-start the Renaissance.

In spite of all this, superstitious beliefs about cats that had been seared into the minds of Europeans during the Middle Ages continued well into modern times. In 1486, Pope Innocent VIII began another round of religious persecution, this one aimed at eradicating Europe of witches. He specifically pointed to cats as witches' "familiars," animals that aided people using magic.

From Pope Innocent's time forward, the iconography of cats and witches became inseparable. An example of this appears in Shakespeare's play *Macbeth*. In the opening scene, one of the three witches planning to meet with Macbeth suddenly announces, "I come, Graymalkin." The witch is responding to the summons of her familiar, or guardian spirit, which is embodied in the form of her gray cat.

Although superstitious Europeans believed that many animals could serve as familiar spirits inhabited by magic (toads, for instance), cats were especially singled out as witches' pets because of their prior associations with heretical sects and ancient pagan worship, including the cult of Bastet in Egypt. Now, though, in addition to the Catholic Church targeting and torturing cats, the recently formed Protestant churches, along with secular authorities all across Europe, also got in on the action. They did this by holding witch hunts and trials.

According to Kathleen Walker-Meikle, author of *Medieval Cats*, the first cat mentioned in the record of an English witch trial was a white-spotted feline named (appropriately) Satan. The cat was reputedly a gift to its owner, Elizabeth Francis, given by her grandmother upon the young woman's vow to renounce God. Satan, it appears, spoke with Elizabeth "in a straunge holowe voice" and possessed great powers. For every evil deed it did, Elizabeth paid the cat with a droplet of her own blood.

One of the more common claims made in late Middle Age literature was that witches could transform themselves into cats and vice-versa—a belief that can be traced back to the Greek story of the maid servant, Galinthius. Echoes of the ancient Greek myth led many to believe that beating a witch in cat form would reveal her identity the following day, when she would appear as a woman (rarely a man) with the same injury.

This shape-shifting interpretation appeared in a popular tract about witches and witchcraft called the *Maleus Maleficarum* written by a particularly sadistic German bishop during the time of Pope Innocent VIII. The widely read document helped usher in the infamous witch hunts, which came in waves from the fifteenth to the late eighteenth century, making an appearance in the American colonies during the infamous Salem witch trials of 1692.

The quasi-legal religious trials throughout Europe were said to result in forty thousand to one hundred thousand executions, plus another hundred thousand vigilante deaths between the years 1480 and 1750. Most of those executed were women. In some cases, the courts would even try animals accused of crimes.

For instance, on September 5, 1379, two herds of pigs at a French monastery grew agitated and killed a man named Perrinot Muet. All were sentenced to die, but after the trial verdict was reached, the Friar appealed the convictions of the animals that had merely observed the act, instead of taking part. His appeal managed to save their bacon.

Cats, toads, and other animals implicated as witches' familiars were seldom tried in court, but instead tended to be swept up in the witch trials and burned alongside their owners without recourse to legal counsel or court process.

Hanging was the preferred method of dispensing justice on criminals, but burning at the stake was mainly reserved for witches. It was established doctrine that witches were not witches by their own choice, but by Satan's, and so burning them at the stake would purify them by pain so they could enter Heaven. As familiars, cats were subject to the same legal logic.

Religious leaders purportedly believed, and led the populace to believe, that it was doing witches a favor by torturing them and burning them to death. It mattered not whether the witches were in human or feline form. At annual festivals, it became a widespread practice to place cats into baskets and burn them *en masse* with the idea that their hideous screams would warn other witches and demons to stay away lest they suffer the same fate.

Black cats, which had been stigmatized in the early Papal bulls regarding heretics, paid the steepest price for witchcraft. It is only in the last century that black cats have regained a representative proportion among Europe's cat population.

Though witch hunts ran out of steam by the mid 1700s, the persecution and torture of cats in Europe would continue into the nineteenth century. One of the last places to officially do away with sanctioned cat massacres was Ypres, a market town in Belgium. Before coming to its senses, the entire city would gather for an annual celebration of ritual cat torture dating back to the Middle Ages.

In medieval times, Ypres prospered as a center of cloth making. The city's warehouses stored acres of imported wool, which were woven into finished cloth sold at the annual Lenten fair. The warehouses attracted rats and mice, so cats were kept to prevent such rodents from chewing on the goods. But the cats also multiplied, eventually overwhelming the city with feral felines that were themselves a problem.

Ypres' solution was to designate a day during Lent as "Cats' Wednesday," which included a city-wide feast, celebration and parade—and ended with cats being thrown off a tower. The practice became more popular as superstitions linked the cats to witchcraft and devil worship. The celebration wasn't unique to Ypres—history shows many European towns dealt with their cat populations similarly. Paris, for instance, held a similar event, attended and paid for by the King. But Ypres held on to its tradition well into modern times, earning itself a cruel reputation.

Thankfully, things there took a turn for the better in 1817, when a lucky tabby is said to have survived the fall. Seeing this as an omen, the people of Ypres decided to cease tossing cats from the heights. But they continued to ring the bells on Cats' Day and in the 1930s revived a kinder, gentler version of the traditional celebration.

Every three years, Ypres hosts Kattenstoet, the "Cats' Parade." Perhaps to make up for so many years of ill treatment, the modern festival is a celebration of the furry pet. It includes cat-themed lectures, music, dance and theater, along with a grand procession to the bell tower, where plush stuffed toy cats plummet harmlessly to earth.

The parade, of course, features cat-themed floats. In an ironic twist of fate, the idea of the parade float dates from ancient Egyptian times, to the boats carrying revelers in the annual procession to the Temple of Bastet.

ELEVEN

CATCHING A BREAK

One day, we shall see the merit of cats generally recognized.
—Eighteenth century poet
Francois-Augustin Paradis de Moncrif

While the fates of cats during the Dark Ages seemed particularly, well, dark, even during the depths of persecution and hysteria, the animal was never without its defenders. Medieval book illustrators, for instance, often amused themselves by filling the margins of sacred texts with drawings of cats frolicking or at leisure, and sometimes even playing musical instruments!

Laws show that, at various times and places, people in the Middle Ages valued cats highly for their service. In early medieval Ireland, for instance, a cat was assigned a value equal to that of three cows, provided it purred and hunted mice (its value was half that if it wasn't a mouser—an indication that people likely enjoyed them simply as pets). Similar laws existed in Wales and in Saxony—in the latter, the penalty for mortally injuring someone's cat was reckoned in sacks of grain, which emphasized the cat's role in protecting crops from mice.

According to Kathleen Walker-Meikle, author of *Medieval Cats*, nuns favored the animals as pets, though the practice may have been frowned upon—according to the writer, the nunnery of Langendorf, Saxony, specifically forbade dogs and cats "as they distract from seriousness." But in an early thirteenth century instruction book written for the nuns of the Ancrene order, the women were advised to keep no pets *other* than cats—though it cautioned that the nuns not become affectionate with them, lest their hearts be distracted from piety.

In monasteries where monks were employed copying manuscripts, cats may have been "necessary evils" kept as pets under the guise of protecting the documents from vermin—just as they did in Jewish synagogues and as cats still do today at Russia's famous Hermitage Museum in St. Petersburg.

Since the mid nineteenth century, the Hermitage has maintained a colony of seventy-four cats who live in its basements and protect its more than three million items from the ravages of mice. One of the world's great museums, the Hermitage is part of a complex of historical buildings that includes the Winter Palace, a former residence of Russian Emperors. During the reign of Empress Elizabeth in the early eighteenth century, the palace became infested with mice, which raided the royal kitchen and gnawed on the building's fine woodwork. The Empress ordered that cats be brought in to eradicate the rodents, and the solution proved so effective, they've been maintained there ever since.

In modern times, royalty would play a role in restoring dignity and humane treatment to the cat, not only as protectors of the home (or palace, in the case of Russia's Empress Elizabeth), but also in the minds of modern people. To understand how the cat went from being a reviled henchman of the Devil to a favored household pet of all classes, one must begin with the Renaissance.

The upper class's dramatic change in attitudes towards cats can be seen in Renaissance artwork. Though religious symbolism remained important, artists felt more freedom to depict cats at play and at leisure. This license probably came from the fact that, in many cases, the wealthy people who commissioned the works also kept dogs and cats as pets, and wanted their likenesses included in the paintings for which they paid.

"Cats were fully acceptable pets for the aristocracy," notes art historian Lindsey Nicole Blair. "Instead of being seen as objects, animals earned empathy and formed tangible bonds with their owners."

The concept of the household pet emerged among upper class Europeans between the fourteenth and sixteenth centuries. The Oxford English Dictionary recorded the first use of the word "pet" in 1539. Though the origin is not known, its meaning was understood to be "an animal kept as a favorite."

Even though the upper class in the late Middle Ages and the Renaissance began to come around and accept cats in a familiar and affectionate way, efforts at gaining greater respectability for cats did not prove altogether successful, even as we approached the modern age in Europe.

In 1727, French poet and author Francois-Augustin Paradis de Moncrif wrote the first comprehensive book on the subject of cats. *Le Chats* consisted of eleven letters to a wealthy patron (her name was not revealed in full, only expressed as Madame la M. de B), along with ten poems.

"One has heard since the cradle that Cats are treacherous by nature, that they suffocate infants, that perhaps they are sorcerers. Succeeding reason may cry out in vain against these calumnies," he wrote, before ending the volume on a hopeful note: "One day we shall see the merit of Cats generally recognized. It is impossible that in a nation as enlightened as our own the prejudice in this regard should prevail much longer."

It appears, however, that Moncrif's optimism failed to sway the minds of many of his literary contemporaries. According to Desmond Morris, author of *Cat World: A Feline Encyclopedia*, the debonair court figure was lampooned and ridiculed for his effort by peers, becoming the subject of savage skits and biting satires. Admitted to the French Academy, that esteemed arbiter of French language and culture, he was in the process of giving his maiden speech there when one of the lauded academicians released a stray cat in the room.

The cat was said to have meowed pitifully, and the room full of learned men burst out in laughter. Whether Moncrif wrote *Le Chats* to mock the seriousness of those same academicians or whether he did so as a sincere effort at scholarship and literature is debated. But it's said that he withdrew the book from circulation in the face of the withering ridicule; ironically, it remains his best-known work.

If some members of the upper class were slow to accord the cat respect, common people were even slower, just as they had been slower to accept the cat's supposed evil in the first place. Age-old superstitions about cats have persevered in the populace well into the modern era.

Given the affection many of us feel for cats today, it may be difficult to grasp that entire classes of people still see cats as evil and demonic. But I was reminded of this when one day I called a friend, Carolina Tarraga, whose family lives in Barcelona, Spain. I was researching cats and the Catholic Inquisition, which became part of our conversation.

"Oh, I have a cat story to share," she said. "My grandmother was religious, but not too strongly. Hell, she married a left-wing atheist. But she was raised a Catholic. And she would tell us that cats were the Devil's incarnation and would not have them around her.

"When my mom was pregnant with me, my dad brought her a beautiful Siamese cat as a gift. My mom was not warm about the cat, but she didn't want to seem ungrateful and decided to make it work. A few weeks after I was born, though, I was nursing when the cat attacked my face, piercing my lip. My mom took the cat's paw and removed it from my lip. I think she would have wrung its neck right then, but instead she took the time to comfort me. I wasn't too happy!"

When Carolina's father came home, her mother showed him the injury. That night, the cat "disappeared" from the house and was not seen by the Tarragas again. Presumably, the cat took a dirt nap.

"I think the lack of compassion my mom showed for the cat may have come from my grandma's views about them. Apparently, it was a very beautiful cat, but it made one mistake. Maybe it *was* the Devil's cat," she concluded, with a voice that betrayed her own dismissal of her family's lingering superstitions.

Still, it was striking to hear of such superstitions just one generation removed from Carolina, a twenty-first century businesswoman with advanced degrees in software engineering. To me, the story validates the notion that superstitious beliefs originating a thousand years ago with a cat-hating Catholic pope still echo across the centuries, shaping the way people think about cats to this day.

Fortunately, something changed to make people view cats in more benevolent terms. To mark that turn, one can point to an event that occurred in 1871, when the common cat got its own public relations ambassador. That person was the Baroness Angela Burdett-Coutts.

An alluring English woman who, in modern times, would likely have gained acclaim as a model, Coutts had an hourglass figure and an oval-shaped face framed by raven-black hair. Her beauty was accentuated by the elegant clothing one would expect of a woman known as "England's wealthiest heiress." Born in 1814 into a banking family, she inherited her grandfather's fortune and set about becoming a philanthropist of renown.

In 1871, Queen Victoria conferred on her the title of Baroness in recognition of her philanthropic efforts on behalf of children, the poor, and domestic animals; among her many accomplishments, she helped co-found the London Society for the Prevention of Cruelty to Animals. That same year, she collaborated with a well-known artist, Harrison Weir, to improve on what is believed to be the world's first pedigreed cat show, held at the renowned Crystal Palace in London.

The cat show had begun three years earlier under the direction of Fred Wilson of the Crystal Palace's Natural History Department. Weir had been brought in as a judge, helping to create a points system and judging criteria for the various breeds known at that time in England. In fact, there were so few that Weir padded the field by including cats of different colors.

Still, when it was observed that there were few entrants, and that most of those were owned by people of high birth and privilege, Burdett-Coutts—who knew Weir through their mutual friend, Charles Dickens—suggested they create a special class for "workingmen's cats." She even contributed prize money for the competition.

The announcement of a cash prize sent Crystal Palace janitors scurrying to capture cats on the show grounds that they could exhibit. The sight of workingmen proudly displaying their "pet" cats proved to be a huge success, establishing a precedent at the National Cat Show for many years to come. Hundreds of thousands of people would attend these shows and others like them held across England and abroad, helping elevate common cats to a place of esteem as pets among average people.

In 1899, winners of the National Cat Show's "workingmen's class" continued to claim their awards beside the "blue bloods"—both cats and aristocrats. Though this celebration fell short of the worship it had achieved in ancient Egypt, the cat had finally returned to a position of dignity and esteem by royalty and commoners alike.

TWELVE

LIFE IN THE GREAT INDOORS

*It's easy to understand why the cat has eclipsed
the dog as modern America's favorite pet. People
like pets to possess the same qualities they do . . .
Cats are mean for the fun of it.*
                                    —Author P. J. O'Rourke

When World War II ended in 1946, Navy veteran Ed Lowe
returned to Michigan and went to work for his father's bulk
delivery business. One of the products his family sold was Fuller's
Earth, a kiln-dried clay that mechanics used to soak up spilled
motor oil. Able to absorb many times its weight in liquids, it made
cleanup of garage floors a snap. Lowe realized that the product

worked equally well for absorbing chicken manure. So, he bagged up some of the clay and set out in his '43 Chevy coupe, intent on selling poultrymen on his "Chicken Litter."

The twenty-seven-year-old wannabe entrepreneur didn't find any buyers. Chicken farmers simply couldn't see the advantage of spending money for clay in place of the free straw bedding they could gather from their fields. Discouraged, Ed returned to his home in Cassopolis, where the unsold bags languished in his vehicle's trunk.

But one day a neighbor named Kaye Draper stopped by. Her cat's outdoor sand box had frozen, she explained, and she wondered whether she could get some sawdust to use instead. In a moment of inspiration, Ed suggested that she try some of the clay pellets he had in the trunk of his car.

A few days later, Mrs. Draper came by for more. She commented on how well the material absorbed her cat's urine and praised its ability to knock down the strong ammonia odor. Ed Lowe realized he might be on to something. So he scrawled the name "Kitty Litter" on ten paper sacks filled with Fuller's Earth and took them to a local pet store. The owner doubted that people would pay Lowe's price of sixty-five cents a bag. After all, cat owners could buy sand for just one penny a pound. So Lowe suggested he give them their first bag for free. When the customers returned and asked for "Kitty Litter" by name, a business and a brand were born.

In early 1947, Ed began filling the trunk of his Chevy with bags of Kitty Litter and traveling the Midwest, convincing owners of pet shops, feed stores, and grocery markets to find shelf space for his product. He cleaned cat boxes at pet shows in exchange for booth space and a chance to convince still more new customers.

In a matter of years, Kitty Litter would make Lowe a very wealthy man. When he sold the family business in 1990, Lowe's company dominated the industry he'd created, selling an estimated two hundred million dollars worth of Tidy Cat kitty litter and subsidiary brands per year. His story is still told in business schools as an example of a man creating an entire industry . . . from scratch.

Ed's timing had been perfect. When he began selling Kitty Litter, the United States was in the midst of an economic transformation. In the 1930s, more than half of all Americans still lived on farms where animals were expected to earn their keep, including cats in barns. But as America ramped up its industrial might during the Second World War, people left the countryside by the millions to join the war effort. When the conflict ended, the flight from rural America accelerated as soldiers returned from overseas, started families, and found well-paying jobs in the cities and inexpensive homes in the suburbs. This lifestyle demanded new and more intimate logistics when it came to keeping pets. And it fostered a new way of thinking about them, too.

Ask any farmer during the 1940s if he thought of his barn cats or hunting dogs as family members, and he'd have looked at you as if you were crazy. Speaking from personal experience, I can attest that barn cats seldom get much attention, much less love.

On the 6,500-acre Colorado horse farm where I worked in the 1980s, cats came and went like the seasons. In the springtime, deer mice would move in from the fields, scurrying across barn rafters, tunneling through stall bedding, and invading our corrals in search of grain spilled from feedbags, feed sacks, and even from horses' mouths.

About that time, new litters of kittens would be born. We'd go into the barn to find that the calico cat was nursing a new litter in a clump of hay she'd hastily piled in a corner. Soon, she'd be carrying live mice to the kitty enclave, instructing her kittens in the art of mouse hunting.

As summer progressed, the cat population that had swelled in the spring would begin its inevitable decline. The tamest and cutest kittens would go home with ranch guests. Less fortunate littermates would fall prey to coyotes, rattlesnakes, barn owls, or hawks, never to be seen again. One or two inevitably died of disease or got hit by vehicles on the farm road. By autumn, it was likely that only one breeding pair remained to carry on.

In this environment, you learned not to become too emotionally attached to cats. We never named them, for instance. But I must admit to a certain admiration that fell just shy of affection for the survivors, who I felt lived rich and natural (if not always long) lives. They had all the freedom a large farm could offer and filled their days happily chasing mice and sparrows, lapping up the occasional saucer of fresh milk, and relaxing in the sun that filtered into the barn through windows and holes in the roof.

This is the best explanation I can come up with for why I never became a "cat person." Like most rural people, I just never thought to bond with felines any more than I'd have thought to bond with the barn swallows or prairie dogs. Cats were simply part of the landscape.

Lowe's product transformed the relationship most Americans had with cats. Prior to Kitty Litter, only people with an abiding affection for felines and high tolerance for the stench of their cat boxes kept their kitties indoors. Kitty Litter gave felines carte blanche to live in people's homes, initiating a hostile takeover of the American household—at least in the eyes of the cat's nemesis—the dog.

Though it took more than half a century, the cat has replaced the dog as America's No. 1 pet. Counting only "owned" cats, not free-living feral cats, the American Pet Products Association estimated in 2016 that there are now more than 85 million cats in American homes, versus about 77.8 million dogs.

Cat-box litter not only enabled millions of urbanites and sub-urbanites to keep cats indoors, the invention helped create today's billion dollar annual business in kitty laser pointers, stuffed mice, scratching posts, cat carriers, cat furniture, high-tech cat water fountains and automated cat feeders, etc., all designed to keep bored indoor cats nourished, exercised, and entertained.

Given my own somewhat indifferent relationships with cats, I was amused when I moved to the city to work as a journalist and began befriending cat lovers whose relationships with their animals were quite beyond my experience. Take New Yorker Paul Rosa, for instance. Rosa is a former standup comic who lives in Manhattan. When we met, there was no question that his cat, Jesse, a stray that had been gifted to him by his sister, was the center of his universe.

Jesse had a special bed perch in the window where she could watch the world. She had tiny stuffed mice to bat around, and Paul kept a laser pointer by the TV remote to entertain her in games of chase. Paul conversed with his cat. He shared photos and videos on Facebook of Jesse asleep on his head or his stomach. I'm pretty certain that if she fell asleep on his coat before he headed out the door to promote comedy clubs in Times Square, he'd cut off a sleeve rather than wake her. In her waning days, Paul administered intravenous fluids to flush Jesse's failing kidneys, spending thousands of dollars in veterinary costs to prolong her life a few extra years. Thanks to Paul's fastidious nursing, Jesse lived to the remarkable age of twenty-three. Paul is now equally doting when it comes to his new cat, an adopted black-and-white spotted stray named Ché.

Though both Paul and I are baby boomers, we symbolize opposing generational attitudes towards cats that bookend both of us. I doubtless reflect the prejudices of my grandparents' pre-World War II farming generation, who viewed animals less as pets than as unpaid laborers. Paul, on the other hand, presaged the relationship that today's millennials have with their pets, especially cats. For nobody loves and dotes on their felines quite like this young generation who came of age after the turn of the twenty-first century.

In 2015, pet food maker Nestlé-Purina conducted an extensive survey about people and their pets. What they found was that millennials, the massive cohort of Americans born between 1982 and 2004, own more cats, and at a higher percentage for their respective age group, than any previous generation. Nearly 50 percent of millennials own at least one cat, compared with just over one-third of my generation, the baby boomers. (Oddly, the generation bridging baby boomers and millennials, so-called "Generation X," has much lower pet ownership rates than either group.)

What's more, millennials have a particularly familial relationship with their cats (and dogs) that may be unique in history.

"Pets are becoming a replacement for children," said Jean Twenge, a psychology professor at San Diego State University and author of *Generation Me*, a book about millennials. "They're less expensive. You can get one even if you're not ready to live with someone or get married, and they can still provide companionship."

The millennial generation's feline affinity likely stems from the economic times that shaped their perspectives, especially the economic downturn that occurred during the Bush administration and profoundly impacted the generation's outlook on life. As many reached adulthood, they found themselves in an unwelcoming and unstable job market. A decade later, the job market had rebounded, but a sense of insecurity remains. This makes it harder to plan a future, and a family.

Less than one-quarter of millennials marry before their thirties, compared with more than one-third of baby boomers and a whopping two-thirds of the so-called "Greatest Generation," people who came of age before and during the Second World War. Millennials are also delaying parenthood and demanding flexible work arrangements, such as working more from home—all of which, researchers say, has translated to higher rates of pet ownership.

Many millennials find themselves changing jobs, homes, and even cities frequently, forcing them to interact with an ever-revolving door of colleagues and friends. In a rapidly changing social environment, pets provide companionship and a sense of stability.

Cats seem tailored to the millennial lifestyle. They're independent by nature; you don't have to shape your day's schedule around their needs as you do with dogs that need to be walked and fed at regular intervals. Their small size and cleanliness makes them well suited to small homes (nearly half of all millennials rent and live in apartments). When compared with dogs, cats' grooming needs are fewer, they require only minimal training, and their veterinary needs tend to be less frequent and less costly.

All this goes to explain why millennials have formed such deep bonds with cats; it's a relationship that people of my parents' generation, or even my own, might find, well, a bit strange. To a millennial, for instance, being called a "cat lady" or even a "cat man" isn't a pejorative, but rather a badge of distinction. (Sixty percent have no objection to these labels.)

Half of millennial cat owners share secrets with their cats. They view themselves and their felines as kindred spirits, identifying with their cats' independent yet social natures; 57 percent said that their cat is as important in their lives as their friends; two in five consider their cats their "new best friend." Nearly 90 percent feel that their cats are "in synch" with their active lifestyles—though two-thirds of the cats never leave millennials' homes.

Regardless of what generation they hail from, most Americans consider their pets to be part of the family. But millennials take it steps farther, agreeing, for instance, that it's essential to dine with their pets, take them places for entertainment and exercise, and keep tabs on them during the workday via technology that includes baby cams placed in the home.

Even millennials who don't own cats lay claim to the feline zeitgeist as the world's foremost consumers of social media. About 60 percent of Internet users watch cat videos, but the numbers are even higher among millennials. Enthusiasm for cat videos has elevated felines to web superstardom on par with that of the Kardashian sisters.

The trend began around 2006 with a grainy video of "Keyboard Cat," a piano-playing ginger tabby named Fatso. The original short film was created in the 1980s by Charlie Schmidt, a visual artist whose intention was simply to amuse himself and friends.

In the early twenty-first century, YouTube was just gaining widespread attention when a friend suggested that Schmidt post a digitized copy of Keyboard Cat there. He saw it as a way to share the neglected videos with his daughter. In a few months' time, Keyboard Cat had gone viral. Schmidt's video has been viewed more than forty-seven million times.

"I didn't really know what YouTube was. It was like the Internet was ready; the cat was already way ahead of the times," he reflected.

Keyboard Cat's popularity took Schmidt by surprise. Since the original cat was long gone, he found a younger stand-in that went on to appear in a Super Bowl ad and overseas ads for the Cartoon Network, Snickers candy, and a passenger safety film for Delta Airlines. But the potential of cats in the Internet age wasn't fully realized until 2012, with the appearance of Tarder Sauce, a runt of a feline owned by former waitress Tabatha Bundesen.

The cat is better known by its meme name, Grumpy Cat. An endearingly cute dwarf tabby with an underbite that gives her a realistic resemblance to the cartoon cat Garfield, Grumpy Cat debuted as a photo posted by Bundesen's brother on Reddit in 2012. People questioned whether Grumpy Cat's expression had been digitally altered for effect, so the Bundesens filmed a series of videos to satisfy critics. Grumpy Cat blew up with a following that eventually grew to seven million Facebook likes. Her fame reverberated in ways incomprehensible in any previous age, setting off a seemingly insatiable demand for merchandise, a film, books in fifty-seven foreign languages, and more. Grumpy Cat has earned her owner in excess of one hundred million dollars.

Hot on her tail have been dozens of other charismatic Internet cats such as Lil' Bub, a dwarf mutant with extra toes and a lolling tongue, and a two-faced "chimera" cat named Venus. As of 2015, there were more than two million cat videos on YouTube with an average of twelve thousand views each—a figure higher than that of any other YouTube category. If you want to try cashing in on the fame, there's a book out now called *How to Make Your Cat An Internet Celebrity: A Guide to Financial Freedom*. Here's an excerpt:

"The time to grab your slice of the furry pot is now. Actually, it is way past now because while you've been not getting rich off your cat, the web has been populated with the likes of Ceiling Cat, Maru, Li'l Bub, and Grumpy Cat. Their owners already understand the guiding principle of the twenty-first century, which can be summed up in a single sentence: No financial investment will give you a better return on investment than your cat."

While there are not, as yet, any studies that measure the impact of social media on cat ownership, recent surveys hint that millennials adopt pets not merely for companionship, but for the online social status they might confer. Owners post photos of their cats at twice the rate of selfies on popular social media apps like Facebook, Snapchat, and Instagram.

According to Nathan Richter, a partner at the marketing firm Wakefield Research, millennials were twice as likely as baby boomers to buy clothing for their pets, a phenomenon he attributes to their insatiable use of social media and a need for status affirmation from peers.

"The clothing is, for them, an opportunity for performance— they put it on their dog or cat, take them for a walk, post a picture on Facebook," Richter said. "It's increasingly about getting a digital stamp of approval."

Growing up in a world in which their lives are under constant electronic scrutiny, it's little wonder that millennials are interested in pets that are stylish, rare, or at least quirky (the most famous Internet cats tend to be mutants with unique features or coloration) and that make a statement about themselves and their lifestyles.

It's a trend that has some in the pet adoption world concerned. According to the Best Friends Animal Society, millennials are more likely than older Americans to seek pets through pet shops or breeders (especially those advertising online) rather than though more traditional brick-and-mortar shelters and local rescues.

But overall, it's hard to find fault with the young generation of cat owners, at least from the perspective of cats. According to the ASPCA, millennials' sheer numbers and their high degree of interest in pet ownership have fueled the current nationwide rise in overall animal adoptions. Even if some prefer to buy rather than adopt, the net result of so much interest in pets has been millions of shelter cats and dogs being saved from euthanasia.

And that same trend is occurring in England and India, both of which are witnessing large upticks in pet adoptions in recent years. In a survey of eight thousand English pet owners conducted by the Pet Manufacturers Association of Great Britain, it was discovered that British men, in particular, are providing homes for more cats. By the survey's estimation, UK men took in nearly one million cats over a two-year period. Today, British men are twice as likely as women to own cats.

The reason? Writing a tongue-in-cheek piece for the British webzine Metro News, blogger Ellen Scott ventured that it's all about getting dates.

"Men who love cats are hot," she wrote. "And not just because we're using them for snuggle time with their moggy. (Fine, we're using them a bit. But all's fair in love and the pursuit of purring)."

But the idea doesn't appear far-fetched. Peter Gray, an anthropologist at the University of Nevada in Las Vegas, decided to test a basic tenet of evolutionary psychology: women tend to allocate more resources to child rearing, while men devote more time to pursuing mating opportunities. Based on this, he and his team hypothesized that men who were better caregivers—to pets—would be more enticing to women. And, on the flip, that men would be more likely than women to use pets to attract partners.

Gray's team surveyed more than twelve hundred single pet owners. Lo and behold, nearly one-quarter of men admitted that they used pets as "date bait." And millennial men in their thirties were the most likely to flaunt their pet ownership, with more than one-third saying they used pets to attract women. It does seem to be a winning strategy: one in three women in the survey said they were more attracted to a pet-owning fella. (Hint to guys: women find it sexiest if you adopt your pet from a shelter).

We don't often think about the big-picture cultural issues when we decide to bring home a pet. But from the earliest days of domestication, styles of animal keeping have been shaped by human culture and typically operate on a subconscious level.

Throughout the entirety of history, cats were considered an outdoor species. Their main function was to control rodents. It was this very function that led to the conditions of their domestication. But, thanks to innovations like Kitty Litter, packaged cat food, and the Internet, our social relationships with cats have changed, almost entirely for the better. They've moved indoors to become part of the family. Which has led to a question unthinkable just a half century ago: Should cats be allowed outdoors at all?

THIRTEEN

ALLEY CAT BLUES

Get a shoe thrown at me from a mean ol' man,
get my dinner from a garbage can.
> —*Stray Cat Strut*, by the Stray Cats.

When Disneyland opened in 1955, Walt Disney wanted to create a special experience for guests passing through its iconic Sleeping Beauty Castle. He and a group of Disneyland "imagineers" were walking through the building when they came upon scores of flea-ridden, abandoned cats who'd taken up residence in the yet-to-be built interior. Something needed to be done so that the work could progress, but Walt knew that simply "eliminating" the cats would cause a public uproar. So instead, he had workers trap the cats and find adoption homes for them among Disneyland employees.

Meanwhile, the outdoor theme park's 160 acres of former orange groves, now landscaped to simulate rustic environments, was also nurturing rodents—and not just the expected ambassadors, Mickey and Minnie. After studying the problem, the folks at Disneyland came to realize that the cats already on the property provided a cost-effective and natural means of keeping non-celebrity mice in the park to a minimum. Better, in fact, than any human exterminators were likely to do. So rather than evict the cats, as they'd done in the castle, it became Disneyland policy to provide and care for them.

Though occasionally a guest would spy a cat sunning himself on Grizzly Peak or strolling across Main Street, Disneyland's cats went little noticed and unremarked upon for decades. But in 2011, actor Ryan Gosling brought nationwide attention to them during a televised appearance on *Late Night With Conan O'Brien*. Asked about his frequent Disneyland visits, Gosling raised the cat situation as an example of his love/hate relationship with the famous theme park.

Disneyland, he alleged, was breeding an army of cats. And not just ordinary cats, but ones with a special set of skills. "They're like commando cats," he mused. At night, the actor claimed, these cats left their "cat barracks" and descended on the park to wage war on mice. "Which is what I love about Disney, because they are so weird and they think about everything . . ."

"The thing that is so messed up about it . . . and why I hate them . . . is that the whole empire of Disney is built on the back of one mouse," Gosling quipped with deadpan irony. "If you're a mouse and you go into Disneyland, you are not leaving alive."

Gosling got some of the particulars wrong. Well, most of them. There is no special covert cat-breeding program. And getting hundreds of cats to return daily to a "cat barracks" would be like, well, herding cats. But it's true that a stable population of about two hundred cats resides in Disneyland, roaming the park and ridding it of rodents after the gates close. The cats don't receive commando training and are, in fact, handled as little as possible to prevent them from becoming too friendly with park guests. Overly social cats usually get re-homed with crew members.

Given many people's cultish devotion to Disneyland, and to Gosling, the cats inevitably earned a social media presence, with a web site, a Facebook page, a Twitter account, and an Instagram page with fifty-three thousand followers. People write fictitious bios about the cats that list favorite foods and rides, plus actual information about the cats' preferred haunts in the park. One popular cat, a long-haired tortoiseshell with arresting green eyes named Francisco, even has a "Francisco Friday" feature, where fans post photos and accounts of sightings; a Francisco sighting is considered a coup, like finding a hidden Mickey Mouse icon in the park.

When it opened, Disneyland featured a place called "Tomorrowland" which was meant to give people a glimpse into the future. Its creators accurately foretold the coming of moon walks, microwave ovens, an Interstate highway system, and video phones. But Disney was an equally bold predictor of the future when it came to feral cats. Disneyland's practice of trapping, sterilizing, and releasing its feral cats so that they could remain at large proved decades ahead of its time.

Cat advocates in England began experimenting with the practice of trapping, neutering, and returning feral cats to communities in the 1950s. TNR, as the practice became known, gained widespread attention in the 1960s when a popular British model for *Vogue* named Celia Hammond began a crusade to popularize radical new ideas about animal rights and animal welfare.

A vegetarian since her teens, Hammond ironically became one of Europe's leading fur models. But after witnessing a seal hunt first-hand, she vowed she'd never again model fur and persuaded other top models of the day to stop, too. She advocated for animals in a publicity-grabbing fashion, at one point chaining herself inside a cage on London's Regent Street to call attention to the plight of factory-farmed chickens.

After discovering an abandoned cat and her three dead kittens in a British flat, Hammond began to use her celebrity to bring attention to abandoned pet cats. She developed her own equipment to trap feral cats, housing some on an estate she shared with guitarist Jeff Beck. At first she tried taming and rehoming the animals, but ditched that approach when it proved, in her words, "hopelessly inefficient."

Reluctantly, she embraced the practices of trapping, vaccinating, neutering/spaying, and returning the animals to their outdoor homes. In this way, she reasoned, she could help control future populations of cats while providing a better life for those already living precariously outdoors.

Hammond's efforts came at a time when most people in England and elsewhere held free-living, unowned "nuisance" cats in low regard. These cats' noisy breeding, fighting and noxious territory-marking habits often provoked calls to animal control offices, and their diseases raised public health concerns. "Humane" solutions mainly involved death by needle, poison, shooting, lethal trapping, and ghastly decompression chambers.

Hammond frequently battled local animal control authorities and environmental health departments to carry on her TNR program. But gradually, she turned the tide on public opinion almost single handedly, elevating feral cats in England from near vermin status to animals worthy of humane treatment and public compassion.

Meanwhile, America remained mired in the past. As the twenty-first century approached, the prevailing ethos of feral cat control in American could be summarized simply as "capture and kill." It was a century-old approach used by virtually every municipal and county animal control authority. Furthermore, the practice was endorsed by all the large national animal rights organizations, including the American Humane Association, the Humane Society of the United States, American Society for the Prevention of Cruelty to Animals, and PETA.

In a scathing indictment of the animal control system circa 1989, animal activist and author Edward Duvin penned an influential article, *In the Name of Mercy*, for the publication *Animalines*. It is now regarded as a seminal manifesto of the "No Kill" shelter movement. In it, Duvin described community animal control as "a convoluted system that places a higher operational priority on 'painless execution' than preventative education."

"Shelters cannot continue to be slaughterhouses and friends of animals cannot continue killing healthy beings in the name of mercy," he concluded.

That was the environment in which Becky Robinson found herself in 1990 when she and a friend, Louise Holton, took a shortcut down an alleyway in the Adams Morgan neighborhood of Washington D.C. and discovered a feral cat colony. Rather than call animal control, which would have meant almost certain death for the cats, they decided to do something themselves. Holton already had experience with feral cats as an animal advocate who'd worked with TNR feral cat programs in her native South Africa in the 1970s.

With help from other volunteer caregivers, the women began capturing the cats and kittens. They spayed and neutered the cats to ensure no more litters would occur. The kittens and the more people-friendly cats they placed in homes, returning the remainder to the alley to be watched over by kitty caregivers.

In addition to stabilizing the cat population, the volunteers observed that spaying and neutering helped curb obnoxious behaviors associated with mating, fighting, and roaming, making the cats less objectionable in the neighborhood. The addition of cat litter-box stations, regular feeding schedules, and food deliveries based on the population size (important so that the food would not attract "outside" cats or feed wildlife) further helped to quell complaints from non-feline loving neighbors.

Through natural attrition and the removal of adoptable cats and kittens, the cat population dwindled from more than fifty-four cats to just six after seven years. The last cat from the colony died in 2007, at the age of seventeen.

Meanwhile, media attention and word of mouth brought a deluge of would-be cat rescuers and information seekers to the women's doorstep. Within months of taking responsibility for a feral cat colony, the women formed the non-profit Alley Cat Allies to provide support and know-how to others. Little did the women realize they were starting a revolution that would drastically change the lives and fortunes of cats—and inflame the passions of people who'd rather see the cats dead.

Cat myths and superstitions from Europe's Middle Ages persist today: Just think about black cats and Halloween or the storyteller's common trope of the villain's evil cat. (Consider Austin Power's archrival Dr. Evil and his naked cat, Mr. Bigglesworth: "When Dr. Evil gets angry, Mr. Bigglesworth gets upset. And when Mr. Bigglesworth gets upset, people die!")

To these, cat opponents have added legitimate concerns about the threats to health, safety, and the environment that free-roaming outdoor cats present. The concerns focus on outdoor cats, especially unowned feral cats, as nuisance animals—noisy, noxious, and disease-ridden—as well as non-native super predators that kill millions (some claim billions) of small animals each year, especially birds.

Ornithologists, in laymen's terms professional "bird watchers," began documenting the widespread depletion of bird populations around the turn of the twentieth century. Among the most influential was a devoted chronicler, Edward Howe Forbush, who served as Massachusetts state ornithologist from 1908 to 1929. In 1916, he penned the book *The Domestic Cat: Bird Killer, Mouser, and Destroyer of Wild Life*. The screed still serves as a template for many feral cat opponents' writings and research reports.

Forbush used anecdotes from fellow bird watchers along with quasi-scientific studies to implicate cats as a primary cause of bird losses throughout America. Despite the scientific tone of the work, the science itself was dubious. For instance, Forbush greatly exaggerated the fecundity of cats, doubling the typical number of litters they produce while omitting to mention that half of all feral cats die before weaning.

At one point, Forbush contradicted his own observation that free roaming cats kill about ten birds per year by dwelling on claims from twenty-five other observers, all birding enthusiasts, who claimed cats under their watch killed between twenty and fifty birds per year. Forbush also failed to account for habitat depletion as a primary cause of bird losses, and insecticide intoxication as a secondary one.

Despite errors like these, Forbush's book became the basis for generations of birders' arguments regarding feral cats; as recently as 2011, the University of Nebraska extension service published a feral cat control document that one reviewer described as "a dumbed-down paraphrasing of the Forbush tract, with updated references."

Nevertheless, it would be wrong to make light of the threats to birds' survival, including predation by cats. In an annual report prepared by the US Fish and Wildlife Service, along with a variety of conservation groups, it was determined that one-third of all North American bird species need urgent conservation action in order to avoid extinction. Of the 1,154 bird species, a whopping 432 are at risk.

There is no debating that feral and outdoor cats add to birds' burdens. Cats, which are considered a non-native invasive species throughout most of the world, have been linked to the extinction of sixty-three animal species, including forty birds, twenty-one mammals and two reptiles. (Ironically, when it comes to extinctions caused by non-native invasive species, cats are topped only by their enemies, mice and rats).

According to the Humane Society of the United States, which has taken on the herculean task of compiling accurate statistics on companion animals available in America, there are an estimated thirty to forty million stray and feral cats in the United States and tens of millions more owned cats that venture outdoors to hunt small birds, reptiles, and mammals. Likewise, scientists have tried to estimate the number of mortalities these cats have caused—with wildly varied results.

Prior to 2013, the most frequently cited number for cat-caused bird mortalities in all of North America put the figure at five hundred million, or roughly half the number attributed to window strikes. But in 2013, the Smithsonian Institution and the US Fish and Wildlife Service funded a study by researchers Peter Marra, Scott Loss, and Tom Will that greatly challenged this figure. The study, published in *Nature Communications*, claimed that outdoor cats kill as many as *3.7 billion* birds in the United States alone each year—a seven-fold increase from previous estimates.

According to the researchers, more than 70 percent of these mortalities are caused by unowned feral cats. In 2016, Marra, head of the Smithsonian Migratory Bird Center, would publish the controversial book *Cat Wars: The Devastating Consequences of a Cuddly Killer*, which advocated trapping, poisoning, or shooting feral cats as public policy—the same prescription offered a century earlier by Forbush.

If you buy Dr. Marra's figures, outdoor cats, mainly ferals, murder as many as one-fifth of all birds in the contiguous United States in a given year. That assertion alone caused cat defenders and some journalists to cry "foul!"

"Cats are hunters and other creatures do fall prey to them in significant numbers," wrote Barbara King for National Public Radio. "And yet there are serious reasons to suspect the reliability of the new, extreme cat killer statistics."

One of the biggest assumptions the authors make concerns the size of the feral and outdoor cat population itself. Marra used an estimate of 30 to 80 million. The Humane Society of the United States estimates a more conservative 30 to 40 million. But nobody has done a comprehensive study of feral cat populations in decades, so nobody really has a clear picture of their numbers. That number is critical to any estimate of bird deaths caused by free-roaming cats.

Furthermore, the authors' headline-grabbing claim that "free-ranging domestic cats kill 1.4–3.7 billion birds and 6.9–20.7 billion mammals annually" in the United States raised serious questions of credibility. Their figures for bird mortalities, for example, represent an astonishing 28.5 to 75.5 percent of the estimated 4.7 billion land birds in all of North America. (Land birds, as opposed to water birds, are not adapted to live continuously where aquatic conditions predominate, and are therefore more susceptible to water-phobic cats).

"Were these figures even remotely accurate, the continent would have been devoid of birds long ago," said Peter Wolf, the cat initiatives analyst for the Best Friends Animal Society and author of the pro-cat blog *Vox Felina*.

Concurrent with the Smithsonian study was one conducted by Canadian government researchers which showed that cats killed anywhere from 100 to 350 million birds each year in Canada, and that an estimated 60 percent of those were taken by feral cats. But the researcher in charge of that study, Peter Blancher, proved less willing to commit to the data's accuracy than Marra and his co-researchers.

First, Blancher admitted, the figures on prey taken were largely derived from studies conducted outside of Canada (mainly the United States, but also Europe), and second, the number of feral cats in the nation—a figure crucial in any country-wide extrapolation—were "very crudely estimated."

From Forbush's published study to these most recent works, predictions of enormous predation attributed to cats have relied upon small, often flawed studies. Results are based upon highly variable, local situations extrapolated to encompass huge territories, such as states, countries, and even continents.

In short, our quantifiable knowledge of outdoor cats' impact on populations of wildlife, especially birds, amounts to informed guesses. Furthermore, they're guesses that make sweeping generalizations based on the premise that because cats in some areas threaten birds and biodiversity, they constitute a threat across all habitats, everywhere.

Take the already-mentioned bird extinctions. Virtually every case linking cats to extinctions of native fauna involve islands, which are highly fragile environments with delicate predator-prey relationships. There is, as yet, no data to suggest that cats have caused extinctions outside these unique environments. And yet many people opposed to free-roaming cats would like the same strict eradication policies employed in places like Chicago as they would on an uninhabited island in the South Pacific.

Counter-arguments by TNR advocates often point out that in cities, where birds have co-evolved to cope with cats over centuries, even millenniums, it is dubious to claim that cats upset the ecological balance. In fact, eliminating cats might do more damage than good, as cats perform the economically valuable service to humans and birds of reducing rodent populations. Furthermore, argue many cat defenders, feral and outdoor cats mainly prey on the sick, the aging, and the young, leaving healthy breeding birds to continue reproducing.

Even so, with tens of millions of free-roaming cats in North America, both feral and owned, it's impossible and foolhardy to deny that cats contribute greatly to the human-related dangers birds face. Pesticide poisoning, wind turbines, high tension wires, communications towers, oil waste pits, oil spills, fishing nets and hooks, collisions with vehicles and building windows, and yes, cats, are all parts of a human-dominated world that isn't kindly caring for its avian inhabitants. But to make cats out to be the principle culprit in bird declines and extinctions is to ignore the eight-hundred-pound gorilla in the room, admit even those who fight on birds' behalf.

"To me, the top three threats to birds overall are habitat loss, habitat loss, and habitat loss," says Ken Rosenberg of the Cornell Lab of Ornithology. "We're losing the battle acre by acre."

Gary Langham of the Audubon Society agrees. "Certainly to this point, loss of habitat is the number one problem," he says. "In some cases, say in California, we have removed or converted up to 99 percent of riparian [streamside] habitat and 95 percent of wetlands. Those losses have huge impacts on birds."

"We should stop arguing about how many birds cats eat," says Julie Levy, professor of shelter medicine at the University of Florida College of Veterinary Medicine. "We should just decide they eat a lot and agree we want fewer cats roaming the community—and then look at what our options are to make that happen."

Indeed. Since at least the time of Dr. Edward Howe Forbush, the dominant policy of feral cat control advocated by ornithological societies, wildlife defenders, animal control authorities, and wildlife managers has been to kill free-living felines *en masse*. But this approach hasn't proven to be particularly effective. In fact, the best-known, most painstakingly documented large-scale success in eliminating a feral cat population has served to discredit, rather than support, the idea that mass killing is a viable solution for cat control.

Just over 1,350 miles southeast of Cape Town, South Africa, Marion Island rises out of the pounding waves of the South Indian Ocean to form an impressive volcanic cone. Millions of sea birds inhabit its 112 square miles of sparsely-vegetated terrain, along with large numbers of penguins and a smattering of fur seals. Offshore, wintering whales pass nearby. The presence of these commercially valuable sea mammals is what caused Marion Island to be swept up in the fervor of nineteenth century whaling and seal hunting.

Around 1810, a ship landing or a shipwreck brought the first house mice to the island. The mice were left alone to thrive for more than a century before scientists established a meteorological outpost on Marion Island in the late 1940s. Alarmed by the ecological damage the rodents were causing and the nuisance they presented to the researchers themselves, the station staff imported five cats as mice exterminators. Nobody thought to sterilize them.

By 1977, the Marion Island cat population had exploded to more than 3,400. The cats did indeed catch mice, but were also devastating local populations of burrowing petrels, killing as many as half a million of the birds a year. In 1977, the scientific authorities overseeing the island began a program aimed at total feline annihilation. It was to prove anything but humane.

For the first phase, they infected ninety-six cats with a highly contagious feline distemper virus, setting off an epidemic which killed half the population in just eighteen months. Over time, however, the cat population rebounded and became immune to the virus. As a result, a variety of other methods were tried, including poisoning, trapping, and hunting the cats with dogs. All to little or no success.

Eventually, eight two-man teams of hunters equipped with shotguns and spotlights were hired. Three years later, five two-man trapping teams got involved. During the final year of eradication, the trappers deployed 1,387 leg traps, which also ensnared hundreds of birds. Additionally, thirty thousand day-old chickens were stuffed with poison to lure the few remaining cats to their deaths, causing untold poisonings of native species.

All told, it took two years of study, fourteen years of on-the-ground eradication efforts, and countless millions of dollars to eliminate the Marion Island cats. In 2002, a similar effort took place on Ascension Island off the Argentinian coast of South America. That program eradicated 635 cats over twenty-seven months at a cost of $2,200 each. Nearly 40 percent, it turned out, were people's pets.

As the Smithsonian's Peter Marra rightly points out, it is impossible to quantify the value of a species. The problem isn't one that can be folded into a cost/benefit analysis. Certainly, $2,200 per cat might seem like chump change compared with the cost to rehabilitate a species that's faced with imminent extinction, like the frigate birds residing on Ascension Island that have made a comeback.

As these islands demonstrate, with enough time and resources, and in a controlled environment like a sparsely inhabited island, a complete eradication effort to eliminate an invasive species can succeed. And under certain circumstances, when cats are identified as a serious threat to native wildlife, the efforts seem justified.

But Mother Nature can be a treacherous mistress of unforeseen consequences. In recent years, Ascension Island has seen an explosion in its rat population that may prove as threatening to native bird species as the cats that were displaced. Rats there have been especially damaging to sooty terns, endangered birds already weakened by falling fish stocks in the area.

"The removal of an apex predator has allowed a mesopredator to thrive," remarked University of Birmingham ornithologist Jim Reynolds, who had warned that eliminating the cats from Ascension Island could have repercussions. "And [the rats] are moving away from the mountains toward where the seabird colonies are breeding."

Meanwhile, the mice have returned in epidemic numbers to Marion Island. The conservation group Birdlife South Africa found that, fourteen years after the last cats were removed, "mice have colonized almost every corner of the island," reported Tony Carnie of the KwaZulu-Natal Mercury news. And now, the mice are wreaking havoc on the island's sea birds, including albatross chicks.

Remote, uninhabited islands are unique cases where it is possible to tightly control the introduction of new breeding animals into a population. In many of these cases that involve critically endangered species, the expense and difficulty of eliminating non-native, invasive species seems merited. It makes sense that drastic measures be taken to eradicate cats, mice, rats, foxes and other invasive species from these fragile habitats.

Equally obvious, though, is the fact that if it is this difficult and costly to control and eradicate cat populations on small islands, the possibility of controlling or obliterating feral cats in a place as vast as the United States or Australia is a fiscal, logistical, and probably a social impossibility. Not that some don't want to try.

When it comes to invasive species, Australia has suffered more than most countries, or for that matter, continents. Especially damaging are mice, rats, rabbits, red foxes and feral cats, all of which threaten native wildlife, some already teetering on the brink of extinction.

Australia has been the most aggressive advocate for lethal culling of feral cats. In July 2015, the national government declared a "war on feral cats," with the goal of killing two million of them by 2020. But to many people's surprise, the early results of this program provide strong scientific support for a key presumption of groups, like Alley Cat Allies, that argue for TNR as a better way to control feral cat populations.

Expecting to validate the use of lethal culling as a control option, Australian researchers working with the cat eradication program in Tasmania discovered that culling actually increased the numbers of feral cats hunting in favorable wildlife habitat. A survey of cats conducted at two culling sites resulted in one location having 75 percent *more* cats after the aggressive culling period, while the other site had more than *twice as many* cats.

According to the researchers, it's likely that culling led to the deaths of the boldest, most territorially defensive cats. Their absence caused other cats to thrive and allowed new cats to enter the disturbed territories and exploit unprotected resources.

What the study showed is something TNR advocates have been saying for years: the problem with trying to eradicate cats through lethal methods is that when one cat is removed, another moves in to take its place from an eternally replenishing population. Or as Billie Lazenby, one of the Australian researchers, concluded: "You may be inadvertently doing more damage than good."

It's the same conclusion reached on the other side of the globe by Kate Hurley, director of UC Davis' Koret Shelter Medicine Program. Hurley began her career working as an animal control officer in Santa Cruz, California, where it was her duty to employ lethal control methods.

"I love cats. But I believed that controlling them was for their benefit and the protection of wildlife. I trapped cats. I killed cats," she says.

But in time, she realized that the efforts were having no recognizable impact on the feral cat problem in her community, only serving to demoralize people in the field and at the shelter where captured cats were taken and euthanized.

"In order to eliminate cats, you need a massive effort to get rid of every breeding individual. And then, it comes down to the final cat, the one you couldn't lure into the trap. Well, she's pregnant," she said.

"I think a lot of people come to [TNR] because they can't imagine ever killing a cat. Personally, I would shoot cats myself if I thought doing so would save a sea otter. But it won't. It doesn't work.

"Look at Marion Island. It was fourteen years of effort. Over fourteen thousand hours of hunting cats, day and night. Trapping. Infecting cats with a fatal disease by helicopter. And that was 3,500 cats on a seventy-seven square mile island!" she said. "There are an estimated thirty to eighty million feral cats in the United States."

According to Kate, there are zero studies, anywhere, ever, that support the idea that feral cats populations can be controlled, much less eliminated completely, using a trap and kill approach. Others agree.

"There's no department that I'm aware of that has enough money in their budget to practice the old capture-and-euthanize policy," said Mark Kumpf, former president of the National Animal Control Association. "Nature just keeps having more kittens."

But there is increasing evidence that TNR can stabilize or reduce feral cat populations, and in some cases, even eliminate colonies of feral cats. For instance, in Randolph County, North Carolina, a study of six colonies of sterilized cats saw a one-third decrease in their numbers over two years; in Rome, Italy, a survey of caretakers overseeing 103 cat colonies showed a 22 percent decrease overall in the number of cats—despite a 21 percent rate of "cat immigration" that resulted from stray and abandoned cats moving into the colonies.

The best-documented case of a successful TNR community has been Newburyport, Massachusetts. Located just thirty-five miles from Boston, the town was formerly a thriving fishing community. Today, it is a popular summer destination. People flock there to view its historic Colonial-era homes, stroll its picturesque boat harbor, and spend cash in the chic restaurants and quaint shops that line its busy waterfront and cobblestone main street.

In 1992, resident Jan DeWitt was sipping coffee at the Captain's Quarters restaurant when she saw three tiny kittens scrounging in a dumpster. DeWitt took the kittens home, but she realized that dozens more would likely die during the harsh winter. So, she wrote a letter to Chamber of Commerce president Shirley Magnanti, a cat lover, asking for help from local merchants.

DeWitt's proposal called for rallying local business owners to fund a humane solution to help the hundreds of feral cats. Magnanti threw her support behind the proposal, and a committee was formed to create a TNR program. They solicited local businesses, most along the riverfront where the majority of the cats lived, to fund a campaign.

"It was a tough struggle," Magnanti remembers. "Some merchants did not want us to feed the cats; they preferred that we poison them."

Many didn't see the point in trapping cats only to release them again. Some couldn't wrap their minds around the idea that eradicating one colony would only create space for another colony to move in and claim whatever food sources existed. But the group persisted, scraping together the finances needed to proceed. A local veterinarian, Dr. Regina Downey, donated thirty free spay-and-neuter operations and low-cost vaccinations. Volunteers began trapping cats.

The newly-formed Merrimack Riverfront Feline Rescue Society created a shelter to house the friendliest cats, most of them abandoned pets, and kittens that had not yet learned to fear and avoid people. In the first year, they removed 120 kittens from the waterfront.

"There was a focus on reducing the population," said Stacy LeBaron, who served as president of the MRFRS for seventeen years. "But the primary goal was to make sure they had food, water, medical care, and shelter—to provide them with a good quality of life."

Soon, the organization began getting calls from other communities asking for help and advice. From the onset, LeBaron tells me, there was a realization that a comprehensive, community-wide education and prevention program would be required to reduce or eliminate feral cats in communities. As MRFRS expanded into nearby towns and eventually, across the state of Massachusetts, the group created educational and veterinary outreach programs, not only to help others set up TNR programs, but also to provide services to help keep more cats in homes and prevent them from abandonment or having unwanted litters.

The group carries on the work today. Services include a hotline to refer people to spay/neuter clinics, mobile "Catmobiles" that perform low-cost spaying and neutering, and Sunday spay/neuter clinics (mainly for feral cats). Additionally, the group provides grants to help low-income cat owners pay for veterinary services, "bridge" programs to provide boarding for owners in perilous circumstances, and foster programs to help house cats transitioning between homes.

MRFRS's statistics are impressive. Altogether, they've helped more than 114,000 cats, placing more than 20,500 cats in homes, spaying or neutering over 13,000 feral cats at its TNR clinics and another 53,700 owned cats with its Catmobiles. They've also helped dozens of communities create their own TNR programs, and provided valuable insights into how TNR is best accomplished.

Today, Stacy LeBaron hosts her own podcast program to share the message of TNR with communities across the vastness of the Internet. She estimates that she has worked with more than eighty community feline welfare organizations over the years. I asked her what lessons she learned from working with feral cat rescue that would be of help to other communities struggling with feral cats.

"The first priority is to make affordable or no-cost spay and neuter available to every cat owner in the community. Many middle class people know about and practice spay/neuter, but too often, people in the poorer parts of town are missing the message or can't afford the cost," she said. "It only takes one cat pair, Adam and Eve, to start a feral colony.

"Unfortunately, Adam and Eve may stray. And if they do, you want them to be spayed and neutered before they become abandoned," she said.

She believes the rise of no-kill shelters has helped, because people are more reluctant to abandon cats on the streets if they feel the local shelter will do everything possible to find them homes. She also advocates for non-judgmental intake protocols and open admissions.

"Once we became an open-admission adoption center, we stopped seeing cats being dumped at the (feral cat) feeding stations," she says.

But that doesn't mean letting people abandon cats easily. She recalls instances where soldiers needed to serve overseas, or criminals needed to serve time, or people were hospitalized for long periods. In such instances, foster care to help bridge the gap became a viable option.

"Having a variety of programs in place enables you to work like a case manager," she said. "There's no one-size-fits-all solution to every cat and human problem."

The Merrimack River Feline Rescue Society is proof that community-wide TNR programs can work. In 2009, the last cat in the waterfront colonies, Zorro, died of old age.

Despite more than three hundred local governments incorporating TNR into their animal control policies and practices and thousands of feral cat groups and individuals providing care, only about one in thirty feral cats in the United States is spayed or neutered.

The challenge, feral cat advocates and supporters of TNR say, is not to discourage people from feeding cats (about one in ten Americans already does), but rather to get them to link up with or form TNR groups that can provide vitally important spay/neuter control and other services aimed at ensuring the animals' health and wellbeing and get more of them off the streets.

"When cat populations are present, the choice is not between having cats or not having cats. The choice is between having a managed community cat population or an unmanaged one," said Bryan Kortis, program manager of PetSmart Charities.

FOURTEEN

FANCY CATS

Time spent with cats is never wasted.
—French author Sidonie-Gabrielle Colette

D enver County Fair's motto is "fairly weird." It's an apt description. The fair is less Ringling Brothers and more Cirque du Soleil, but an unpolished Cirque du Soleil with a cheesy, hipster vibe.

Created in 2011 by entrepreneurs Tracy Weil and Dana Cain, it's an urban take on the traditional county fair. The pair recognized a need for an alternative to the annual livestock show and rodeo, something hipper and more germane to Denver County's youthful and entirely urban populace.

To that end, the fair features attractions you're not likely to find elsewhere, such as the "Geek Pavilion," a celebration of fifty years of Star Trek, and the "X-Treme Breakfast," where you have the option of topping your pancakes with grasshoppers. While there's a traditional farm-to-table area showcasing the produce of local farmers, for a year the fair also hosted a controversial "grow-to-doper" Pot Pavilion, showcasing the wares of area marijuana growers. That's since been dropped for an even more popular Craft Beer Pavilion (Coloradans like their weed, but they like their beer even better).

An up-and-comer among Denver's plethora of summer events, the fair draws close to 25,000 visitors over a three-day weekend. Its promoters hoped to up those numbers in 2016 with the appearance of a celebrity guest: Venus the two-faced cat. Venus is one of the most famous Internet cats in the world. In 2012, she became an honest-to-goodness overnight sensation when her picture went from zero to 1.2 million views within twenty-four hours of going online.

What's so unusual about Venus? Half of her face is jet black with an amber eye, while the other half is traditional tabby with a blue eye. She's a chimera cat. And had she been alive in ancient Egypt, it's a good bet she would have been revered as the living goddess Bastet herself.

I first became aware of the cat not on the Internet, but through one of the fair's delightful art posters plastered all over town. At first, I thought the two-faced cat drawing was a product of some artist's fruitful imagination. But no, I soon learned: Venus is the real deal, and she was coming to the Denver County Fair. This I had to see.

So in late July, I arrived at the Denver County Fair dressed not in my typical fair attire of boots and a cowboy hat, but instead in walking shorts, flip flops, and a surf logo t-shirt. True to the fair's motto, the first thing I encountered was a children's unicorn ride. The mythical, rainbow colored unicorns topped with tots were being led by college-aged princesses resplendent in taffeta gowns and tattoos.

Consulting my schedule, I learned that I had already missed the Miss Denver County Fair Drag Queen Pageant (darn!), but that the Rocky Mountain Rollergirls would be bashing and trash-talking later in the day (bonus!). Venus was slated to take the stage in the Kitten Pavilion at one P.M. sharp.

I texted my friends, got them aboard for the roller derby, and headed for the Kitten Pavilion, the fair's largest livestock exhibition, where a cat show was already in progress. Since I'd never been to a cat show, I didn't really know what to expect. Suffice it to say, I did not anticipate cat fanciers parading their cats around the ring on leashes. I was not disappointed.

There were several rings, which were not really rings at all but rather tables fronting banks of cages. Each official was responsible for judging a variety of breeds. When a judge finished with one breed contest, which could consist of anywhere from a single cat to a dozen or more, those cats would be taken away and a new group put in the cages.

For the actual judging, the judge would approach each cage, open the door, lift the cat onto the examining table and begin his or her appraisal. One of the coolest things about the show, to me at least, was that each judge had a cordless microphone headset so that he or she could explain to the audience the history of the breed and its main distinguishing characteristics, and maybe share a little information about their judging decisions.

I homed in on an elderly, gray-haired judge whose name was Pat Harding. As she lifted a longhaired Siberian cat from his cage, she remarked, "They feed this cat solid cement!" which made all of us laugh. She then picked up a tinsel wand and began waving it around the cat, which followed its movement and tried capturing it in his paws. After a few seconds of play, Pat set the wand down and took the cat's head in her hands gently.

"Let me see your head," she said, giving it a going over. "There's sure a lot of it!"

As she stroked the cat and encouraged it to chase her wand, Pat told us that Siberian cats did duty as farm exterminators in one of the coldest, harshest climates on earth—the reason for their long, luxurious fur coats and large bodies. Originally exhibited at the first "official" Crystal Palace Cat Show in 1871, the cats disappeared from worldview throughout most of the twentieth century, not emerging from Russia until the breakup of the Soviet Union in 1990. The International Cat Association (TICA) recognized the breed in 1992, and its main competitor, the Cat Fanciers Association, did the same in 2000.

Pat carried the cat to his cage and put him away. Later, I caught up with her at the TICA booth. She told me that she has been involved with show cats for sixty-three years and that her work as a show judge has taken her all over the world. She bought her first cat, a Siamese, at a Gimbel's Department Store in New York City in 1953. In those days, cat carriers and kitty litter did not exist. (Apparently, Ed Lowe had yet to establish a market in Manhattan). She carried the cat home in a cardboard box with air holes punched in the sides and twine tied around it.

"When I brought the box in, Mom blew her top," she said with a laugh. "But I got to keep Mox. I thought he was the most beautiful Siamese every born!"

When the family moved to New Mexico, Pat carried Mox is a box on her lap in the TWA jetliner. She became interested in cat shows there and began exhibiting, only to learn the judges thought less of her store-bought Siamese than she did.

"Turns out, he was everything a Siamese is *not* supposed to be!" she laughed. "But I still thought he was beautiful."

However, now that she'd had a taste of cat showing, she imported a pair of Siamese from England and got deeper into the scene. Around 1960, the Cat Fanciers Association, the world's largest registry of pedigreed cats, asked if she would become a judge.

"I had to study the breeds, take exams, and go to shows and apprentice. But most importantly, I handled hundreds and hundreds of cats. You can only learn to be a judge with your hands," she told me.

In addition to examining the cats, she explained, a judge has to make them feel secure and safe on stage. It's a much more delicate judging procedure than what you'll see in the dog show ring, where the dogs learn from puppyhood to stand still, to move correctly, to accept the noise and commotion of an audience, and to be handled by strangers. Faced with an unfamiliar environment and handler, a scared cat can easily bolt and get lost, so a judge must literally be hands-on and aware of the cat's emotions.

"It's much more physical, judging cats. You have to be sensitive to their needs and the needs of their owners. You handle them so that they look good to their owners," she said.

According to Pat, only a few dozen breeds were recognized when she started out. Over the years, the various cat associations have added dozens more so that today, there are about eighty different recognized breeds. What surprised me is how recently many of these breeds developed. Unlike dogs, which have been selectively bred and refined for a couple of thousand years at least, it is really only in the last two centuries that cats have been selectively bred at all.

Of the eighty or so recognized cat breeds, just thirteen were known to exist prior to the mid-1800s. Some of these were what we'd call "landrace varieties," indigenous species shaped almost entirely by local conditions and climate. An example is the Persian, an ancient cat which developed a long coat to survive the frigid winters in the Zagros Mountains of Iran, Iraq, and Turkey.

Ironically, the Persian cat probably arrived in Persia as war booty after King Cambyses sacked Per-Bast, using the Egyptian cats as shields. Once in Persia, the ancestors of Egypt's sacred temple cats mated with long-haired and stockier native wildcats in order to adapt to the cold winters—or so, at least, goes the myth. It's as likely, or even more so, that natural selection in the cold mountain climate alone favored the survival of cats with longer coats.

But the vast majority of cat breeds to date were developed by cat fanciers between the 1930s and the present day. At a cat show, you will find yourself looking at breeds that may not have existed before you were born. Take, for instance, the Ragdoll, a cat popular for its extremely friendly disposition.

Ragdolls and closely related Ragamuffins are long haired cats similar to the ancient Birman breed, but with heavier bodies and differing color variations. What is unique about the cats is that, when held, they become limp and floppy and completely relaxed, like rag dolls.

The Ragdoll cat began with a single breeder in the 1960s and soon developed its own mythology. The story goes that a California woman had a non-pedigreed, white Persian-style cat named Josephine. The cat was pregnant when she was injured in a car accident. She broke her pelvis, but the veterinarian was able to save the cat and kittens. When the kittens were born, the woman found them to be abnormally limp and docile, which she attributed to the shock of the accident.

A cat breeder named Ann Baker bought some of the unusually friendly kittens and began line-breeding them to produce Ragdolls.

The story, of course, is nonsense—an accident could not have affected the genes of Josephine's offspring. But it was shrewd nonsense. People love a good story, especially when it comes to their pets, and Baker knew that her Ragamuffin cats had a pretty good story. So, in an unusual move, Ann Baker trademarked the cat breed and for years, she controlled their marketing through her own, exclusive breed association. By the 1990s, there were more than three thousand Ragdolls in the country.

People who wanted to breed and show the cats, however, were less than thrilled with this arrangement, and began creating variant breeds—Cherubims, Honeybears, and Ragamuffins. Outcrossing allowed them to add new colors to the breeds, and also to correct some of the genetic flaws that had resulted from Ann Baker's tight control over the Ragdoll breeding pool.

Checking out all the breeds at Denver, I spot my first celebrity. It's Mr. Bigglesworth, Dr. Evil's sidekick. And boy, is he ugly!

Actually, it turns out he's only one of Mr. Bigglesworth's close relatives, a naked sphynx cat owned by Megan Dickey of Colorado Springs. It, too, is a relatively new breed that, like the Ragdoll, was developed from a very small number of mutant cats.

Dickey is a textbook example of a crazy cat lady. She wears a long t-shirt dress with a naked cat on the front, and both her fore-arms have life-sized tattoos of naked sphynx cats. She even has a uniquely cat-like face, with narrow, squinting, almond-shaped eyes, arching brows, and a nose in the shape of a diamond.

Sphynx cats have no fur and are considered by many to be one of the most ugly cats alive. Dickey says they are like bleu cheese—an acquired taste. Dickey, who is a bit iconoclastic and out of the box herself, saw the breed many years ago and found herself drawn to them.

After researching the cats for several years, she finally bought one. But, owing to health problems, he didn't live long. She com-memorated him with her first tattoo, she tells me, pointing to one of her arms. After that cat's passing, she acquired two more from a breeder in Colorado, and soon found out they were "show quality." As often happens in the show world, the breeder said it would be a shame if she didn't exhibit them, so she began taking them to cat shows.

"I felt like it would raise my stature as a crazy cat lady," she told me.

Writing in *Cat World: A Feline Encyclopedia*, Desmond Morris noted that the sphynx is "the most controversial of all modern cat breeds." It's story, and the controversy, are part of the cat's lore.

In 1966, a black and white cat in Canada gave birth to a hair-less male kitten. The owner named him "Prune." A young science student at a local university heard tell of the cat and brought him to the attention of his mother, Yania Bawa, a breeder of Siamese cats. She bought the kitten, along with his mother.

Back-mating the naked male to his mother resulted in the first litter of naked cats. The breed name "sphinx cat" was chosen, the spelling later changed to "sphynx," because the strange, mutant cats looked a lot like the cat statues used by ancient Egyptians as votive offerings to the goddess Bastet.

Sphynx cats developed a number of reproductive and other problems due to the tight inbreeding, and many people felt it was cruel to own them, owing to the fact that if left outside in the cold for even short periods, the cats could become hypothermic and die. Eventually, though, other naked, mutant cats were found that added vigor to the breed, saving it from extinction.

Of course, the breed rose to even greater popularity in 1997 when a sphynx named Mr. Bigglesworth made his appearance in the Mike Myers movie *Austin Powers: International Man of Mystery* as the sidekick to Austin's archnemesis, Dr. Evil. Today, Megan tells me, a show-quality sphynx cat sells for anywhere from twenty-five hundred to five thousand dollars.

As I walk around the cat show looking at all the various breeds, I see some of the same dangerous tendencies among purebred cat breeders that have led to problems in the dog world. For example, I stop by to see the Siamese cats, which were among my favorite breeds as a kid. One of our neighbors, a crazy cat lady, kept several. Each day, she would carefully feed them liver that she chopped by hand into small, bite-sized cubes.

I remember them having round faces and robust bodies. But the show cats here at the Denver County Fair were not at all like the Siamese of my youth. These cats had extremely pinched faces, huge pointy ears, and skinny, elongated bodies. At the opposite extreme, there were several short-nosed breeds, like the Persians, whose faces have become smushed to the point that the bridge of the nose actually curves *inward.*

Based on my observations, it was plain to see that the same tendency to breed for extremes that characterizes dog show breeding has also taken hold among cat fanciers. One can only hope that they will have the sense to pull these cat breeds back from the excesses that have negatively impacted a number of breeds of dogs.

Finally, it's time for Venus to make her appearance. As advertised, she is magnificent.

Her owner tells us that Venus was born a barn cat on a North Carolina dairy farm. Like nearly all cats, she was the product of a random mating between cats of no determinate breeding. Now, Christina tells us, she makes the rounds of talk shows and events like the Denver County Fair, using Venus' celebrity to share the message to adopt shelter cats.

"It's a wonderful thing to be able to use all the attention Venus has received to do good for all the cats in need of homes," she says. Later, I visit her booth, which is strategically placed next to a cat adoption organization where tamed feral cats are on display. The purebred cat organization that sponsored the show had relatively few visitors looking at its brochures.

Today, people acquire about 5 percent of their cats from pet stores and purebred cat breeders, like the ones at the Denver County Fair. About 20 percent come from friends or relatives. But the vast majority, nearly three-quarters of all new cats in homes, come from animal shelters and rescues or find their own way to a friendly home from the streets.

COWS

*And I will send grass in thy fields for thy cattle,
that thou mayest eat and be full.*
                              —Deuteronomy 11:15

FIFTEEN

THE CHEESEBURGER: A NATURAL HISTORY

*Man who invented the hamburger was smart; the
man who invented the cheeseburger was genius.*
—Actor Matthew McConaughey.

A t the hungry age of sixteen, Lionel Sternberger placed a slice of
American cheese on a sizzling hamburger patty while working
the grill at his family's restaurant in Pasadena, California. And so
was born America's most iconic food, the cheeseburger.

It was 1926. Road workers had just completed Route 66, the
legendary highway that winds from Chicago to L.A. Before termi-
nating at the Santa Monica Pier, "America's Main Street" passed
the Sternberger's aptly named diner, The Rite Spot. For many

weary travelers, it was the last meal stop before they dipped their feet in the Pacific Ocean.

The groundwork for the cheeseburger had been laid in 1845 by a German inventor with the extraordinary name of Baron Karl Friedrich Christian Ludwig Freiherr Drais von Sauerbronn. In addition to inventing the typewriter and an early form of bicycle known as the Velocipede, Drais designed the world's first mechanical meat grinder. Germans were already fond of the "Hamburg steak," a minced meat patty, and Drais' meat grinder made it easy to prepare. Migrating Germans introduced the hamburger to Americans, who hungrily welcomed it.

Someone had the bright idea of adding sliced bread or split rolls (buns would come later) so customers could eat their hamburgers on the go. By the turn of the twentieth century, hamburgers were popular in diners, at fairs, and especially near industrial factories where workers could grab a quick, cheap meal from mobile lunch carts.

Americans' taste for ground meat, however, spoiled in the wake of the 1906 release of Upton Sinclair's novel *The Jungle*. Prior to writing the book, Sinclair spent seven weeks working in the Chicago stockyards amid brutal conditions. His experiences in "Packingtown" resulted in his book's gruesome depictions of unsanitary practices and health violations in the meat business.

In 1921, two Kansas restaurateurs, fry cook Walt Anderson and his business partner, Billy Ingram, set out to rehabilitate the hamburger's public image. The men made sure everything about their hamburger restaurants projected an air of wholesomeness. The interiors featured stainless steel cabinets and counters, shiny tile floors, and employees in spotless white uniforms. Even the restaurant chain's name conjured up thoughts of purity, even grandeur: White Castle.

To drive home their message about their hamburgers' wholesomeness, they hired a distinguished biochemist to devise a novel experiment. One of the professor's students, Bernard Flesche, ate a diet of nothing but White Castle burgers and water for thirteen weeks. Though he grew weary of the sandwiches, he suffered no ill effects. (In 2004, Morgan Spurlock conducted a similar experiment for his documentary *Super Size Me*, with startlingly different results).

When Flesche's story broke, White Castle's sales skyrocketed. Dozens of imitators with names like White Manna (in New Jersey) and Royal Castle (Florida) shamelessly copied the White Castle formula of cleanliness, standardization, and rapid service, creating the first wave of fast-food restaurants.

Fast-food burger joints entered their golden age following the Second World War. A burst of new restaurant chains, most originating in California, swept across the nation. Among them was a Modesto restaurant owned by two brothers: the McDonalds. The world would never be the same.

Each day, roughly 1 percent of the world's population eats at one of more than 36,500 McDonald's restaurants, devouring seventy-five McDonald's hamburgers each second. As the world's biggest restaurant chain, McDonald's symbolizes the globalization of American food culture. According to the International Franchise Association, today's fast-food industry generates revenue of more than 570 *billion* dollars per year. That's more money than the gross domestic product of 82 percent of the world's nations.

The worldwide growth of the fast-food industry nourishes the demand for highly-processed, highly standardized western foods exemplified by a typical McDonald's meal of a hamburger, fries, and a soft drink or milkshake. Its evidence can be seen in the growing per capita consumption of the principal ingredients of the fast-food cheeseburger: beef and dairy cheese.

While the world's human population has doubled since the early 1960s, its population of cattle has quadrupled. Across the globe, people's diets today include twice as much beef as they did in 1961. Global demand for milk (the largest percentage of which is sold as cheese) is set to surge by 36 percent by 2050. Most of that demand will result from growing prosperity in Latin America and Asia.

Much has been written about the impact of the fast food industry on the global production of beef cattle. Both Eric Schlosser, author of *Fast Food Nation* and Michael Pollan, who wrote *The Omnivore's Dilemma*, focused attention on the conditions under which beef cattle are raised, fed, fattened and slaughtered. As they showed, the fast-food industry's worldwide growth has dramatically altered the landscape in the domestic and global meat packing industries, encouraging concentration, cost-cutting, and what is regarded by many as inhumane conditions for both employees and livestock.

What's been seldom remarked upon is the contribution of the dairy business to industrial meat production. Most people do not realize that the dairy industry is the single biggest contributor to the hamburgers and cheeseburgers sold at the big three burger restaurants, McDonald's, Burger King, and Wendy's. Dairy beef also makes up the majority of ground beef sold by leading international food retailers Costco and Walmart, the two largest buyers in the ground beef marketplace. Regardless of where you buy it, nearly all commercial and restaurant ground beef contains some percentage of dairy meat.

During my years spent working as a cowboy, I naively assumed that the hamburgers sold by fast-food outlets and retail grocers came entirely from beef cattle (those purposefully raised for meat), like the ones I tended in the mountains of Colorado. But in fact, only about 40 percent of hamburger meat comes from "fed beef trimmings," the leftovers you get when you butcher cattle for steaks. The remaining 60 percent comes from dairy cows.

Unless you raise cattle, "culled cow" is a term that probably doesn't enter into your dinner table conversation. Due to the pressure to maintain peak production, American dairy farmers remove roughly one-quarter of the cows from their herds each year. This amounts to about 2.3 million former milkers going straight to meat processing plants. About 80 percent are culled cows, those whose milking performance or health has fallen off after a lifespan of between four and six years. Sales of culled cows for meat make up anywhere from 5 to 15 percent of a dairy's gross income.

In addition to the culled cows, dairy calves are weaned off their mothers' teats immediately so that the milk can be diverted for human consumption. Most of the young females, called "heifers," are kept or sold to other dairies to replace the spent milk cows, while their less fortunate baby brothers end up on the dinner table as veal or low-grade steaks. Regardless of when, virtually all dairy cows end up being slaughtered for the dinner plate.

Lean, tough and unsuitable for steaks, dairy cow meat is mixed with fattier, tastier beef cattle meat to make ground beef for fast-food hamburgers and supermarket retail. Aged and spent dairy cows bring the lowest prices on the beef market, which helps keep fast-food prices low.

The ability of the fast-food industry to hold down costs and increase profit margins depends on these favorable prices for ground meat, along with cheese, butter, and milk. What's made those ever-lower prices possible is the dairy industry's ability over the past several decades to literally squeeze greater and greater productivity from the star of this section of the book: the Holstein dairy cow.

SIXTEEN

SEX AND
THE SINGLE COW

*I'm sorry for the cows who have to boast of affairs
they've had by parcel post.*
                              —Author E. B. White.

P icture a dairy cow. I'd wager a hundred dollars that in your
mind's eye, she's black and white.

Of the six most popular dairy breeds in North America—
Ayrshire, Brown Swiss, Guernsey, Holstein, Jersey and Milking
Shorthorn—all but one comes is some shade of brown. The lone
exception is the Holstein. Although a small number of Holsteins
are reddish brown and white, the vast majority are black with white
splotches (or vice-versa).

Holsteins are the poster girls of the modern dairy industry, appearing in advertisements, on dairy containers, as Halloween costumes—even on fast-food chicken chain Chick-fil-A's billboards, where Holsteins armed with paint brushes implore us to "Eat mor chikin." Symbolically, all one need do to represent anything having to do with dairy is to add black splotches to a white background. Everyone gets the message.

The largest of the dairy cattle breeds and by far the most productive, Holsteins form the backbone of global dairy farming. In North America, Holsteins account for 86 percent of all milk cattle. In Australia, a key supplier to Asia, Holsteins likewise make up 82 percent of the national herd. Holsteins can be found on every continent and in almost every milk-producing country.

The Holstein breed originated in northwestern Holland in the wet, perennially green grasslands bordering the North Sea. Known as Friesland, it was the home of the Frisii, pastoralists who inhabited the land before the birth of Christ. About one hundred B.C., a second group, the Batavia, migrated into the area. Black Batavian cattle interbred with the Frisiis' white or tan-colored cattle, resulting in a distinctive black-and-white breed.

Beginning in the thirteenth century, the Netherlands became Europe's primary source of butter and cheese. To keep up with demand, Dutch breeders needed cows that produced as much milk and meat as possible. They turned to the Holstein-Friesian cow, already renowned across Holland for its milk production. By selecting especially large and productive breeding stock, the Dutch increased both the size of Holstein cattle and the quantity of milk the cows provided.

In 1852, a Massachusetts man named Winthrop Chenery bought a Holstein cow from a Dutch shipmaster. The cow had been aboard the Dutch vessel to supply fresh milk for the crew. Chenery quickly recognized the merits of the Dutch cows as compared to the British Shorthorn cattle then favored by New Englanders.

In the dusty prose of his day, Chenery wrote: "For the dairy, the qualities of the Holsteins must be acknowledged as remarkable . . . [they] have been long bred and cultivated with a view to develop their lacteal production to the utmost . . ."

After importing his own herd, Chenery enticed dairymen to switch to the overachieving milk cows. Holstein breeders imported close to 8,800 Dutch cattle, stock which became the foundation of today's American Holstein breed.

In 1919, Carl Gockerell took a job milking cows at the Carnation Test Farm in Washington State. On his first day, he noticed that a particular Holstein cow produced twice as much milk as the others. When he returned to milk the cows six hours later, she did it again. This was repeated the following day. And the next. Gockerell took an immediate liking to the cow, who always lifted her head and looked for him around milking time. Her name was Segis Pietertje Prospect, but her keeper affectionately nicknamed her Possum Sweetheart.

On Dec. 19, 1919, Carl began to carefully measure the amount of milk Possum Sweetheart produced. He put her on an intensive schedule, milking the cow six times each day. In a year's time, she produced 37,361 pounds of milk—two tons more than the previous record. (Milk is measured in pounds because of tradition and in the interest of honesty—when milk was wholesaled in large cans it was easier to tamper with the volume than the weight).

Newsmen around the world told Possum Sweetheart's story, and she became an international celebrity on par with Pauline Wayne, a Holstein that had served as President William Howard Taft's White House pet. Heavyweight boxing champ Jack Dempsey, among the most famous athletes of the 1920s, came to see Possum Sweetheart and drank a glass of her milk.

In 1929, Carnation proudly erected a statue of Segis Pietertje Prospect at the test farm's entrance. Only a few years later, the Holstein surpassed the Jersey cow as the most popular dairy breed in America. In the coming decades, Holsteins grew to dominate the global dairy business. Like Possum Sweetheart and the Dutch cows from centuries past, today's Holsteins are the key subjects in an experiment to find out how far we can push cows to produce ever greater quantities of milk.

Nowadays, Possum Sweetheart's once spectacular feat of "lacteal production," as Winthrop Chenery would say, would go unnoticed. According to Nigel Cook, a dairy expert at the University of Wisconsin's School of Veterinary Medicine, today's dairy cows produce an average of twenty-three thousand pounds of milk per year. But Cook can already point to especially productive herds that yield more than thirty thousand pounds per cow. And he often finds exceptional individuals that can produce more than fifty thousand pounds annually.

"I never thought I'd see cows producing two hundred pounds of milk a day. That was beyond my ability to imagine twenty years ago," said Cook with a measure of awe. "There doesn't appear to be a cap yet on the projections."

No cap, indeed. In 2010, a Holstein named Ever-Green-View My 1326-ET, owned by Wisconsin dairy couple Gin and Tom Kestell, pumped a whopping 72,168 pounds of milk through an udder the size of an inflatable beach ball. To help put that into perspective, that's enough to top 115,472 cheeseburgers with a one-ounce slice of American cheese or to provide 365 schools kids with an eight-ounce glass of milk every day for a year. It's nearly double Possum Sweetheart's record and, based on an admittedly sketchy account of a nineteenth century Dutch dairyman, about four times what a top cow in Holland yielded in Winthrop Chenery's day.

While certainly an outlier, 1326-ET is indicative of the vast increase in dairy cow productivity that's occurred since 1990, when the average yield per cow was eight thousand pounds less than today.

Some of the credit for 1326-ET's massive production goes to Monsanto, the giant multinational agrochemical and agricultural biotechnology corporation. The company that brought us DDT and

Agent Orange also introduced recombinant bovine somatotropin (rBST) to the dairy industry. The controversial synthetic hormone, now marketed by Eli Lilly & Co under the brand name Posilac, increases a cow's milk output by 11 to 16 percent.

Despite a consumer revolt in the late 1990s that led milk bottlers and dairy retailers to label and market dairy products that are rBST-free, dairymen still use it to boost production in about one in six US dairy cows, and it's used in 42 percent of dairies with more than 500 cows—the fastest growing segment of the dairy industry.

There's been no definitive proof that the milk or cheese produced from rBST cows is harmful to humans. Nor, for that matter, any that it's not. Studies, so far, are inconclusive. Nonetheless, many countries have banned its use due to humane concerns.

One influential European Union report concluded that the use of rBST in dairy cows often results in "severe and unnecessary pain, suffering and distress" associated with mastitis (an acute inflammation of the mammary glands and/or udder tissue), foot disorders, and reproductive problems. Its use is banned in Canada, Australia, New Zealand, Japan, Israel, Argentina, and the European Union—but not on the farm that produced 1326-ET.

In the recent history of milk, however, greater productivity through biochemistry takes a back seat to advances in the cows themselves. Compared to her twentieth century ancestors, today's twenty-first century cow is a genetically superior dairy producer. That's largely because reproductive technology and the Internet have revolutionized dairy breeding by allowing dairymen to select top-producing bulls and cows from anywhere FedEx picks up and delivers.

1326–ET, for instance, was sired by a particularly prolific bull named Stouder Morty-ET. She has sixty-seven thousand half-sisters in more than fifteen thousand dairy herds around the world. Their dad, Morty, achieved his startling feat of bovine fertility not by mating with actual cows, of course, but instead by having his semen shipped by courier to a multinational harem of ovulating mistresses. What this technologically advanced approach lacks in romance it more than compensates for in efficiency and safety, as dairy bulls like Morty can be ferocious beasts when they get turned on.

🐂

Most dairy farms don't have their own bulls, so about three-quarters of all Holstein cows bred in the United States are artificially inseminated. The first step in the process involves collecting the semen. There are two methods used: the first is "electrojaculation," in which the technician inserts an electronic device into the bull's rectum. This device—perhaps coming to an adult toy store near you—stimulates ejaculation via a powerful electric shock. But this method is not common.

In most instances, the modern bovine sex act most closely resembles a strip tease. First, the bull is aroused by a sexy cow or, more commonly, by a docile, castrated male steer who is in fact called a "tease." If the bull is not feeling sufficiently turned on, the bull semen collectors may perfume the air with an aerosol spray containing cow hormones.

Properly sexed up, the bull mounts his not-necessarily-willing partner in a metal stock rack meant to protect both participants. But before the act of lovemaking is consummated, a reproduction tech rushes in to catch the bull's semen in a rubber tube filled with liquid and lined with latex. The romantic interlude—more like a hand job—is over in about ninety seconds.

Following collection, the semen is tested for motility, mixed with a stabilizing "semen extender" and antibiotics to protect it from bacteria, apportioned into plastic tubes resembling drinking straws, flash frozen in liquid nitrogen, and stored in a warehouse to await dairymen's orders.

Buyers can specify "sexed" semen, which has been separated to (almost) exclusively include only female-producing gametes. Sexed semen is more expensive and less fertile than regular semen but cuts down on the birth of unproductive and undesired male calves. Many dairy farmers reserve it for their best cows to produce a high proportion of high-quality heifers to replace their spent, aging mothers.

The price of a bull's semen depends on his "proof," the proven ability to sire cows with high milk yields and other desirable traits. A single straw from a top producer like Morty may fetch fifty dollars and more while a lesser bull's may bring only five dollars. Each ejaculation can yield as few as fifty straws or as many as five hundred.

An especially sex-crazed bull may perform every day while a so-called "lazy bull" (perhaps one that's grown tired of the ol' bait-and-switch routine) may only produce once a week. In the supply and demand world of elite bull breeding, semen from a lazy bull with a high proof can be worth its weight in gold.

Bulls with the highest proofs are as famous in the international dairy community as Hollywood movie stars. Jocko, a particularly prized French bull, "donated" 1.7 million straws and sired between three and four hundred thousand offspring over a seventeen-year career as a taurine gigolo. His obituary from the *Reuters* news service was headlined, "Cows worldwide to mourn superstud Jocko the bull."

But both Morty and Jocko pale in comparison to Toystory, a Wisconsin bull with a ravenous libido (he reliably donated sperm nine times a week) whose fame among dairymen was equivalent to, say, George Clooney's.

Over a ten-year span, Toystory sired five hundred thousand daughters in fifty countries while also shattering all records for semen produced. The bull managed to fill more than 2.4 million straws, a total of about six hundred gallons of sperm. When he passed away on Thanksgiving Day 2014, fans snapped up mementos that included Toystory hats, t-shirts, and commemorative semen straws.

Toystory got his start at Mystic Valley Farm in Central Wisconsin. Owner Mitch Breunig named the fast-growing bull calf after one of his daughter's favorite animated Pixar movies. At six months, Breunig sold the promising calf for four thousand dollars to a leading bull semen producer, a dairy farmer cooperative named Genex. There, Toystory went on to become a sensation in the dairy world, earning tens of millions of dollars for the firm.

Toystory's popularity boomed because he passed down a peerless mix of fertility, genetics, and looks to his offspring. His semen reliably resulted in a high percentage of pregnancies among the cows, ensuring a steady flow of milk. His daughters were easy to birth, prolific milk producers and reliably strong. In a show of esteem, the bull's handlers at Genex buried Toystory not far from a new breeding campus named in his honor. A memorial service was held in the spring for the company's most famous bull.

Genex Cooperative Inc. is one of five companies that control 95 percent of the $225 million annual bull semen business in the United States. Company websites allow semen shoppers to scan spreadsheets listing prospects with names like Wolfgang (as in Mozart), LeBron (as in James), and even McNuggets (as in, well, McNuggets). A quick click reveals a prospective bull in a posed cheesecake picture plus a mind-boggling array of statistics and indexes to help decide if he fits one's needs.

For instance, a farmer who produces milk used for butter or cheese can select bulls whose offspring predictably yield more butterfat or protein. Another might want to put sturdier legs underneath his cows to better equip them for the burden of their gargantuan milk bags, so he'll look for sires with outstanding physiques.

Annually, the three leading US companies sell more than twenty-one million straws of frozen bull semen to the global cattle industry. Semen from a top bull like Toystory or Jocko can bring in as much as three million dollars a year. That's a lot of money—and a lot of hand jobs.

But the days of these movie star bulls are numbered, if not already past. Anxious to produce ever higher yields and "super cows" that have the bone structure and strength to support massive milk loads, the semen companies now heavily market young, unproven bulls based purely on genetic markers that indicate a variety of desirable traits.

John Beckman, whose Applenotch Farm in Minster, Ohio, once led the nation in top-producing dairy "seed" bulls, told me that today's bulls will likely never achieve the grandfatherly age and famed stature of Jocko, Morty and Toystory.

In the late 1990s, scientists began mapping the bovine genome, Beckman explained. As the science advanced, they were able to target specific gene combinations found in bulls and cows with economically desirable traits.

"The first genes they identified controlled things like the percent of milk proteins. Pretty quickly, they mapped out the whole genome. Today, genomics are the name of the game," Beckman told me. "Nowadays, you don't even have to wait for a bull to prove himself because you can identify the desired traits genetically."

In just this decade, it's become possible to genetically test a recently born bull calf or heifer and predict such things as milk yield, butterfat content, physique (conformation), and even whether future offspring will or won't have horns. (A "polled" or hornless cow is typically easier to handle, as the horns won't snag on fences, machinery, or human handlers). This allows progressive dairymen to make selection decisions without waiting for offspring to mature and actually produce milk.

Today's dairyman is, in effect, a geneticist who can select the DNA-coded characteristics he wants in his herd. As a result, Beckman tells me, fewer bulls will live to enjoy the long, leisurely life of a dairy stud.

"The thing is, you can collect a huge amount of semen from a young bull and, at three years of age, you can send him to slaughter because you've already collected more than you can sell. He's already yesterday's news," he concluded.

In short, before they even reach their prime, the bulls are being replaced by young guns that already benefit from another generation of lab-proven genetic advances. Few are the semen companies willing to hold on to a promising bull for the six years or so it takes to prove his value by the traditional method of inseminating a test herd of a few thousand cows then measuring their production.

What impact will the demise of movie star-bulls have? Contrary to the *Reuters* headline, it's doubtful that cows will mourn the loss of super bulls like Jocko, Morty and Toystory. Like most, 1326-ET's mom and the tens of thousands of other cows in Morty's harem never saw the super bull in person. And increasingly, their babies don't spend much time with their biological moms, either.

That's because fewer and fewer top moms bear the majority of their own offspring. The "ET" designation in a registered dairy cow's name signifies that a cow or bull was the product of embryo transfer. Early in her embryonic development, 1326-ET was flushed from the uterus of her genetically superior mother and placed inside an inferior surrogate cow.

Dairy farmers that want to rapidly improve their herds increasingly use embryo transfer. Under normal conditions, a cow produces only one offspring each year. But during breeding season she will come into heat every twenty-one days. If you inject her with hormones to stimulate the egg follicles, she'll produce not one egg per cycle, but ten or more. These can then be artificially inseminated with the sperm of a top bull, like Morty.

A week later, the breeder flushes her uterus with a saline solution, catches the embryos in a fine stainless steel sieve, and re-implants them in a herd of surrogate cows. Typically, a cow produces about six viable embryos per flushing, making it possible to produce dozens of calves from her each year.

Another option to extend the genetic influence of a particularly outstanding cow is in vitro fertilization, the production of embryos in petri dishes. The advantage of this laboratory procedure is that eggs can be taken from promising cows with reproductive problems, heifers as young as ten months, and even cows already carrying calves.

But Internet semen studs and super cows flush with babies are hardly the outer limits of what is possible in the high-tech world of twenty-first century cattle breeding. The technology also exists to clone cattle. Which means that, theoretically at least, it's possible to not only create dairy herds consisting entirely of 1326-ET's sisters—it's possible to build a herd consisting entirely of, well, 1326-ET herself.

SEVENTEEN

FRANKENCATTLE?

Red meat is not bad for you. Now blue-green
meat, that's bad for you!
                    —Comedian Tommy Smothers

America's first cloned cow, whimsically named "Gene," hit
the ground in 1998. Since then, scientists have produced
hundreds—perhaps thousands—of cloned beef and dairy cattle.

I took a trip to the Texas Panhandle to see a new twist on the
practice and, well, to satisfy my curiosity about what a cloned
animal looks and even feels like. How the cows I went to see came
to be copied turns out to be one of the oddest and most fascinating
stories in this book, and one I never hesitate to share over cocktails.

The clones started out in a slaughterhouse near Amarillo as a
twinkle in the eye of scientist Ty Lawrence, director of the meat

science program at West Texas A&M University. Lawrence grew up in a cattle-raising family and is an expert when it comes to evaluating a side of beef. He's inspected tens of thousands of them.

In his office, Lawrence keeps a fiberglass model of a beef carcass cut open at the twelfth rib to reveal a cross section of rib eye. It's here that USDA meat inspectors look when grading meat quality and meat "yield"—the percentage of meat that can be sold as steaks. The pinnacle of success in the American beef business is a ribeye steak marbled with tendrils of fat that give the meat tenderness, juiciness, and flavor, but whose cut lacks the thick outer layer of fat that nobody wants.

"It's the taste fat without the waste fat," quips Lawrence.

In the USDA's grading system, this meat is both "prime" and "yield grade number one," and it's as rare as a five-foot three-inch pro basketball player. That's because it's a marriage of opposites. Lean cattle seldom produce prime meat, the kind you'll find almost nowhere else but white tablecloth steakhouses.

Prime beef is rare enough—only about 2 percent of the country's beef makes the grade. But, according to Lawrence, you might have to look through ten thousand carcasses or so to find one or two that are prime, yield grade one. And when you do, you've already lost that animal's breeding potential. Its outstanding genes end up on someone's plate at a Morton's or Delmonico's Steakhouse. And that's what got Lawrence excited about the possibilities of cloning.

"With cloning, our thinking was to recapture those genetics before they went into someone's stomach," he told me.

A chance occurrence convinced Lawrence it was time to put his ideas into action. One evening, Lawrence was at an Amarillo meat plant when two prime, yield grade one carcasses passed by him in less than ten minutes.

"It was like being struck twice by lightening, but in a good way," he said. Lawrence pulled out his cell phone and called his boss, Dean Hawkins, and told him, "We have to try cloning these." Hawkins heartily agreed.

Lawrence's team extracted DNA from the nuclei of the muscle cells and inserted it into de-nucleated egg cells from donor cows, then fused the two with a jolt of electricity. About a week later, they placed the resulting embryos in recipient cows who gestated the calves just as they would their own.

The project began bearing fruit the following summer when a bull they named "Alpha" was born. He turned out to be a handsome black calf with the conformation of an Angus and the meat qualities of a Wagyu, the slow-growing Japanese cattle renowned for their heavily-marbled meat. The following winter, three black heifers from a different cut of meat walked on wobbly legs for the first time. The team named them Gamma 1, Gamma 2, and Gamma 3.

"People who came to visit the heifers were often surprised that they're as alike as sheets from a Xerox copier," Ty Lawrence said. "But they should be; they are identical triplets."

News of animals whose parents were a rib eye and a filet mignon caused a stir. *National Geographic* sent science writer Robert Kunzig to get a first-hand look. While visiting the animals in the pasture, he and caretaker Kelly Jones had to flee in a feed truck because the triplets followed them like eager puppy dogs. Bottle-fed and hand raised, the heifers had bonded to Kelly, a PhD student at WTAMU who had cared for the clones since birth.

Publicity about the cloned cows coincided with allegations that two bulls from a cow cloned in the United States but unrelated to the WTAMU experiment had entered the British food system. The international media attention resulting from the clone offspring reinvigorated the debate about the ethics and safety of cloning food animals. Anti-cloning sentiment in the European press and public overwhelmed food scientists and biologists whose informed opinions were that meat and milk derived from clones and their descendants were no different from the products of naturally raised animals.

An example of the public's alarmist tone was struck by Wayne Pacelle, president of the Humane Society of the United States

(HSUS). In an editorial he wrote for SFGate, a progressive news-paper and website for residents of the San Francisco Bay Area, Pacelle wrote:

> It won't be long before biotech companies in the hire of agribusiness announce plans to sell commercial clones as food. Cloned ham, steak, and even drumsticks may be served at retail operations in the future, and there's no law to forbid the sale of meat or milk from clones produced in a laboratory.

I asked Ty Lawrence if he thought meat from cloned animals would ever enter the food system. His answer was unequivocal: "No."

"It's simply too costly and inefficient to clone animals for meat. You'd go bankrupt trying to do that," he said.

Cloning a cow costs fifteen thousand dollars or more, and though the price will undoubtedly go down over time, Lawrence argues that, for the cattle raiser, cloning will never compete favorably with raising farm animals naturally. The same goes for dairy animals—it will likely always remain more cost-effective to improve herds with conventional breeding.

So why clone in the first place? A partial answer can be found at WTAMU's Nance Ranch, the property on the outskirts of Canyon, Texas, where Lawrence and his team are carrying out the second part of their cloning experiment. Having cloned the first genera-tion of animals, the researchers cross-bred Alpha with the Gamma cows using artificial insemination. Lawrence believes it was the first clone-to-clone mating ever done.

In the spring, thirteen calves were born on the ranch, all of them full Alpha-Gamma siblings. Though they are the *product* of cloned parents, their genes were randomly mixed in the same way that the genes of your parents were mixed to create—you. It's normal sexual reproduction, and it's been going on for billions of years.

Of the thirteen Nance Ranch calves, nine were bulls and four were heifers. Lawrence has kept two of the bulls and the four heifers for breeding. But seven of the bulls were castrated and raised as steers. After reaching weights of between thirteen and fourteen hundred pounds, the steers were slaughtered at the WTAMU meat lab. The results were, to be a bit indelicate, delicious.

One steer graded prime, three were high choice and three were average choice—the industry average is low choice. The steaks had 16 percent less trim fat, 9 percent more rib eye, and a whopping 45 percent more marbling than the industry standard.

"Our long-term goal in the research is to see if we can move the needle in the percentage of genetically superior, prime, YG1 carcasses that are produced in the commercial cattle system in the United States," Lawrence says. "And how far can we move it? We don't know what that answer is. But we hope to in the next few years."

Lawrence and his team are well on their way to creating a new breed of cattle, one capable of producing both better quality beef and leaner animals that yield more product. These improved cattle will likely become seed stock to improve the overall value of cattlemen's herds and the quality of meat in restaurants and grocery stores. This is a highly desired outcome for cattlemen, who have been losing meat locker space to pork and chicken raisers for decades.

But public opinion could put the brakes on the commercialization of cloned animal offspring. Gallup polls over a twelve-year period have consistently shown that about three in five Americans disapprove of animal cloning. Sixty percent of the public objects to cloning being used even to prevent the extinction of endangered wild animals.

It appears most people form their negative opinions at gut level. In a review of seventeen public surveys conducted between 2000 and 2006, the Food Policy Institute at Rutgers University concluded that while Americans, Canadians, and Europeans express strong opposition to cloning animals, "Most also have limited knowledge about the basics of genetics, and little familiarity of biotechnology and conventional animal breeding practices."

Wealthy, college-educated residents of a New Jersey suburb who were surveyed in another Rutgers study likewise held negative opinions about cloned animals. Yet they knew next to nothing about the science underlying the animals' creation. Most were even confused about the differences between cloned and genetically modified (GM) animals.

To clarify, a clone is genetically identical to the animal from which it was cloned. Or, in the words of veterinarian and equine cloning expert Gregg Veneklassan, "it is a twin, only separated from its other twin by time."

Genetically modified organisms, whether plants or animals, result from artificially inserting new genes into DNA. A common term for this is *transgenics*, a contraction of the words *transferred* and *genes*. Though these genes can come from the same species, most people use it to refer to genes combined from two different, ones.

To illustrate, think of DNA as a song, like the Beatles classic "Let It Be." Now, change a word so that it becomes, say, "Let It Bleed," or "Let It Free." Or change a single note, or a chord. It's still the same tune, but with a new and different expression. That's a GM. A clone, on the other hand, would be another identical copy, like another pressing of a vinyl record.

The first commercially available transgenic food was a tomato called the "FlavrSavr." It used genes already found in some tomato varieties to yield a GM product that ripened on the vine, tasted better than the bland store fruit, and stayed plump and firm much longer, too. After initial public success, FlavrSavrs languished in produce aisles due to a blizzard of bad publicity. Media witheringly labeled it "Frankenfood."

Critics of genetically modified organisms sometimes confuse the FlavrSavr with the "fish tomato," another long-lasting GM tomato containing a flounder gene, which never made it to market.

Coincidentally, the first GM animal approved by the FDA for the dinner table is a fast-growing fish, the AquaAdvantage Salmon.

Americans are not completely opposed to GMOs. Many readily adopted the "GloFish," a genetically engineered Zebrafish that fluoresces in all the colors of the rainbow thanks to a gene transferred from other marine species. But, in the minds of most, having a genetically modified fish in your home aquarium is one thing; having fish genes in your salad tomatoes is quite another.

The first transgenic bull, Herman, was bioengineered in 1991. Early in his embryological development, scientists spliced Herman's DNA with a human gene coding for a milk protein important to human infant growth. Researchers hoped that the experiment would result in Herman's daughters producing a more complete and nutritional human baby formula.

News of Herman's birth caused an uproar among Europeans concerned with the safety of GM foods. Despite this, the Dutch parliament allowed the scientists to artificially inseminate cows with Herman's sperm, producing fifty-five calves. And the cows did produce milk with the desired human milk protein, though it was never commercially marketed. Ironically, Dutch law called for Herman to be destroyed at the end of the experiment, but the public protested against that, too, and Herman's life was spared. He lived to the ripe old age of thirteen, about average for bulls.

Scientists involved in transgenic research offer compelling reasons why genetically modified plants and animals should be allowed to enter the food system. For example, let's suppose you're a pediatrician in a Third World country. Poor parents in your practice who cannot afford vaccines could be given bananas genetically modified to include vaccines. Simply eating bananas could save children's lives.

Equally compelling arguments exist for GM animals. In South Dakota, a biotech firm is genetically engineering cattle to produce large quantities of human antibodies—proteins that help remove potentially lethal pathogens from the body. By vaccinating the cows, the scientists can compel them to produce antibodies that can later be harvested for use as human drugs. The end result could help produce a rapid response to infectious diseases, such as Ebola.

And there are instances of GMs that can benefit cows and humans alike. Researchers, for instance, have made GM cows that are immune to Mad Cow disease, the terrifying neural cell wasting disorder that's infected both cows and humans.

Scientists are also at work transferring polled genes from cattle breeds to dairy breeds. The goal here is to produce hornless dairy cows, thus saving cattle from the painful dehorning process and also making them safer for humans to handle.

In one more example, consider Africa. Nearly one-third of Africa is cattle free because of the Tsetse fly. The fly carries a lethal infectious cattle disease. Using a baboon gene, scientists believe they can genetically alter cows so that they can survive this disease. This would significantly reduce malnutrition and starvation in sub-Saharan Africa, says molecular geneticist Steve Kemp, and not for reasons you might suppose.

"Western people don't understand the role of livestock in developing world agriculture," he said. "[Westerners] think of steak and milk. But livestock are fundamental. If someone's main business is growing maize, but he's got a bullock that can pull a plow in the field and pull a cart to market, that's huge."

Livestock have been estimated to provide power for tillage of as much as half of the world's cropland. Where there are no cattle or water buffalo, poor farmers must plow by hand.

Common foods can also be made safer using GMs. Scientists in New Zealand have developed transgenic dairy cows whose milk won't trigger milk allergies, the second most common food allergies after peanuts. For millions of children worldwide, such allergic reactions, which can occur as a result of unwittingly consuming milk products found in a huge variety of processed foods, are potentially life-threatening.

Despite many positives that could result from GM crops and animals, Americans overwhelmingly distrust GM foods. In a poll of US consumers, 92 percent said that the government should require labels on genetically engineered foods. And in response, in 2016, the US Congress passed legislation to mandate some form of GMO labeling for foods.

It's hard to argue against this. As consumers, we do deserve to know what's in our food and make informed decisions. However, we've already been eating in the dark for decades now. The reality is, about 70 percent of all processed supermarket foods already contain GM crops. Should we be concerned?

Currently, the United States produces almost half of all GM plant crops grown worldwide. Ninety-four percent of soybeans and 93 percent of corn grown in the United States is genetically engineered, according to the USDA.

Genetically modified corn is used to make corn syrup and dextrose sugar, which are incorporated into sweetened cereals, soft drinks, cakes, cookies, and even ketchup and cough syrups. Other corn-based food additives include corn starch (sauce thickeners), corn meal, caramel and other flavorings, preservatives, and anti-caking agents. Soy-derived additives like soybean oil and texturized vegetable protein are even more common ingredients.

GMO corn and soy also make up nearly all the grains fed to cattle not certified as organic. Counter intuitively, this fact might actually be the best proof that, at this point at least, GMOs appear to not pose a threat to ours or our animals' health.

In the most comprehensive study of GM food ever conducted, geneticist Alison Van Eenennaam of the University of California at Davis reviewed nearly thirty years of data on livestock health and productivity dating before and after the introduction of GM crops. All told, the data considered more than a hundred billion animals.

The researchers found nothing unusual in the health of animals consuming GM crops since 1996, when GM seeds were first introduced. It's estimated that the animals fed GM crops had devoured more than *one trillion* meals. And yet, the impact on their health was exactly . . . zero. One can reasonably conclude that, though the public debate rages on, the scientific debate is closed.

Whether we realize it or not, we've all been unwitting participants in a GM experiment for decades. If you were born in the late 1980s or later, the first time you bit into a juicy cheeseburger, it's highly likely that you were consuming a GMO byproduct. That byproduct is cheese.

In cheese production, cheese makers use a coagulant called *rennet*. Rennet contains an enzyme, *chymosin*, which acts on milk proteins, causing them to ball up and form curds. Traditionally, rennet comes from the stomach lining of unweaned calves that use it to break down and digest mother's milk. But in the 1970s, Americans' growing appetite for cheese collided with a growing distaste for killing baby calves.

In the 1980s, geneticists figured out a way to transfer cattle's chymosin coding gene into single-cell microbes, tricking them into becoming chymosin micro-factories that churned out a product genetically identical to the real thing. In 1990, the Food and Drug Administration classified the fermentation-produced rennet as "generally regarded as safe," meaning the consensus of expert scientists was that it posed no human health hazards. Today, 90 percent of hard cheeses made in America are made with this GMO-derived rennet.

If knowing that your cheese is a GMO byproduct makes you queasy, you can opt for cheese certified as organic, which cannot be made with fermentation-produced chymosin. Then again, if you're an animal lover like me, it might bother you that the rennet used in your organic cheese came from the stomachs of unweaned baby calves slaughtered within weeks of birth.

Most bioscientists consider GM foods to be extremely safe. To find out why, I met with microbiologist Mark Johnston, editor of GENETICS, the journal of the Genetics Society of America. Mark's area of study is yeast cells. His team's groundbreaking discoveries about nutrient transfer in yeast may one day help us conquer diabetes. Fittingly, I met the yeast expert in a microbrewery steeped in the smell of robust, yeasty beers. Mark loves the stuff and often stops in for a brew after work.

Mark's argument went like this: the moment man first planted a seed, he began altering the genetic balance of nature. Selecting for desirable traits (greater yields, distinctive flavors, or resistance to disease or drought) in plants and animals was our first form of genetic modification. Genetic traits that proved beneficial to a being's health and survival (or that simply made it more desirable to us) got passed on to later generations.

Favorable genes typically come from natural variation in the animals' gene pool, but not always. New genes may also arise from mutations, natural changes in gene alleles that bring something new to a plant or animal species' genetic blueprint. Some mutations are beneficial; some are not.

But genes can also transfer from one species to another. The process is known as horizontal gene transfer, and its recent discovery undermines arguments against genetically modified organisms, according to Johnston.

Scientists now know that humans harbor at least 145 genes transferred from other species. These genes, which jumped or wedged their way into our DNA sequences from bacteria, fungi, other micro-organisms, and plants, now play roles in human metabolism, immune response, and basic biochemistry. Nature, it seems, has been engineering GMOs for eons.

"There are lots of ways that genes transfer between species," Johnson said as we finished our beers. "So, engineering organisms' DNA is nothing new or unnatural; it's the same as the tinkering we've done since the dawn of agriculture, when our labs were the crop fields. Now, we're simply doing it more efficiently."

When it comes to clones and cloning, scientists and food safety experts in government and in the academic community are even more reassuring. Even if cloned animal products—meat, cheese and the like—enter the human food system, science assures us that they are perfectly harmless. Well, no more harmful, at least, than the food we're already eating.

Anticipating the commercialization of cloned animals in the livestock industry, the National Academy of Sciences conducted a comprehensive study of cloned animals and their offspring, including nearly all of the cattle cloned up to that time. In 2007, the NAS researchers concluded that there are no differences between the offspring of cloned animals when compared to the offspring of animals produced through normal sexual reproduction.

Furthermore, scientists with the US Food and Drug Administration looked extensively at cloned animals' health records and bloodwork, a process similar to what you'd get at your annual check-up. Clones, they found, walk, grow, mature and behave like conventionally bred animals. Similar conclusions were reached by panels of scientists in Japan, Great Britain, and the European Union.

Hugh Pennington, emeritus professor of microbiology at the University of Aberdeen, wholeheartedly endorses the food safety of products derived from cloned animals or their offspring. "They are just the same as their parents from the genetic point of view, so there's no problem there. It's perfectly safe."

But the idea of cloned livestock in the food system is not to everyone's taste. Since 2006, the leading natural food chain in the United States, Whole Foods Market, has banned the sale of products from cloned animals. According to its global vice-president of quality standards, Margaret Wittenberg, most Americans remain unaware that cloned animal products may already be entering the food system.

"A lot of customers in the United States are oblivious to it," she said. "You don't hear about it in the media. And when you do tell people about it. they look at you and say, 'You're kidding! They're not doing that, are they? Why would they?'"

Presently, the FDA has asked meat and dairy producers to voluntarily withhold cloned animal products from the marketplace.

But it is all but impossible to keep them out without legislation to mandate cloning bans. And even if there were the means and wherewithal to pay for government inspections, cloning is virtually undetectable.

Despite assurances from people like Ty Lawrence that the primary purpose of cloned animals is for breeding, a cloned dairy cow used for breeding can still produce milk that will likely be sold. And cloned beef and dairy cattle used for breeding will grow old and be slaughtered. Presently, in the United States there is nothing to prevent a dairyman or rancher from selling his cloned cattle for food—other than his conscience and the awareness that, at least for now, the majority of North Americans don't want clones on their dinner plates.

As for products from the offspring of cloned animals, that cow has already left the barn. There are no food safety requirements or restrictions in the United States or the European Union for food produced from the offspring of clones. Furthermore, it would be impossible to keep track of parentage information about the billions of food producing animals in the international food system. To do so, you'd have to track not only the offspring of clones, but their offspring and their offsprings' offspring *ad infinitum*.

Technologically-advanced breeding practices only compound the problems of accountability. Imagine if, rather than mourning the great dairy bull Toystory, the folks at Semex had chosen instead to clone the great taurine gigolo. Now, imagine that rather than make an exact copy of Toystory, they decide to make a transgenic, genetically modified sequel, Toystory 2. Say, a version of the bull that coded for non-allergenic milk.

Frozen semen would allow the cloned, transgenic Toystory 2 to sire hundreds of thousands of offspring with the new or introduced genetic mutation. It's easy to imagine that, in the interest of avoiding milk allergy lawsuits or to simply offer a product with a marketing advantage, the processed food industry would rapidly adopt Toystory 2 milk.

GM animals are already making inroads into the beef cattle industry. In 2011, a heat wave resulted in the deaths of thousands of cattle across America's Midwest. This got cattlemen thinking about raising cattle in an age of global warming. One challenge these cattlemen face is fortifying their herds against rising temperatures. Traditional cross-breeding may not achieve the desired combination of high productivity and greater heat tolerance fast enough to keep pace with a rapidly heating planet.

So, two researchers, one at Vanderbilt University and another at Middle Tennessee State University, put their heads together and came up with the idea of producing a living oxymoron—the white Black Angus.

By transferring color-determining genes from another breed, the rare Silver Galloway, they plan to reengineer the highly productive Angus beef cow with a white-colored coat better suited to rising temperatures. The fact that that white color genes exist in other cattle makes the whole thing seem more natural. But the scientists could just as easily have taken the color genes from a white chicken—something they considered, before acknowledging that using such poultry genes would probably freak people out too much for the offspring to gain mainstream acceptance.

If the experiment proves successful and the white Angus tolerate heat better than their black ancestors, the researchers will clone the cows to replicate the genome and create a foundation breeding pool. In the face of a growing human population, changing climate, water shortages, and shrinking farmlands, genetically driven solutions like this will become increasingly commonplace in both animal and crop agriculture.

In the brave new world of twenty-first century livestock breeding, anything seems possible. Artificial reproduction technology now allows us to rapidly advance domestic animal productivity and even change the characteristics of the products we derive from them.

Scientists have, for the greatest part, come to the conclusion that GMOs and cloned animals are safe. From their perspective, gene variation and mutations within species and even across species has been going on as long as sexual reproduction. It's just that now, with the help of scientific advances, we can do both in the lab much more efficiently than we did over many thousands of years using traditional selective breeding.

Genetic science utilizing animals holds the potential to solve vexing human diseases, like cancer. It could yield animals, like those immune to diseases carried by Tsetse flies, that could help feed millions. It could help to alleviate some of the difficulties presented by global warming by making cows that are more efficient producers of meat and milk—thus reducing the environmental impacts of the billions of cattle walking planet earth.

Barring a worldwide effort to ban GMOs and clones, these things will happen. Many already have—not only to cows, but to chickens, sheep, pigs, and all other farm animals. The question that remains to be answered in the minds of many is at what cost to the animals . . . and to our own peace of mind.

EIGHTEEN

THREE DAIRIES, ACT ONE: THE RAW DEAL

The cow is the foster mother of the human race. From the time of the ancient Hindoo to this time have the thoughts of men turned to this kindly and beneficent creature as one of the chief sustaining forces of the human race.
—*Hoard's Dairyman* publisher W. D. Hoard

On a gloriously warm, sunny day in January, I set off from Denver for my first of several dairy farm tours. For the first visit, I'd chosen a small, diversified raw milk "micro dairy" in the foothills of the Colorado Rockies. I'd later visit a 240-cow organic dairy in Oregon, and a large Colorado confinement dairy. The three farms represent the spectrum of approaches to dairy management and marketing. As such, they also represent the divergent consumer attitudes toward the relative health benefits, animal welfare concerns, and costs of dairy products in today's America.

Eagle Canyon Farm is a small acreage located on the outskirts of Lyons, Colorado. For more than a century, Lyons' stonecutters have quarried a particularly hard variety of red sandstone that figures prominently into the Tuscan revival architecture of the University of Colorado, Boulder, just twenty miles to the south.

As I drive up to the white two-story farmhouse, a group of curious pigs rush up to an electric fence enclosure, grunting mightily as they inspect my truck. Across the way from them, heirloom chickens cluck-cluck-cluck in a makeshift hen house cobbled together from building scraps. Pinyon pines and juniper bushes dot the hills surrounding another makeshift corral of electric fencing that, on this day, encloses three Jersey cows—half of farmer Jake Takiff's herd.

I knock on the front door, expecting to be greeted by a middle-aged hippie farmer in sandals, ponytail, and an unkempt beard. Instead, I spy through the door glass a couple—Jake and his girlfriend, Alexis Mahon—still young and in love enough to be caught kissing in the kitchen.

Jake, who turns out to be in his late twenties, has been considerate enough to wait until my arrival to milk his cows. After pulling black rubber muck boots over brown Carhartt work pants and grabbing a stainless steel pail and two stainless steel milk cans, Jake leads me through a corral covered in fresh tree mulch into a small milking shed. He measures out a pint bucket of feed containing millet, sunflower seeds, apple cider vinegar, and sea kelp. To this he adds a dollop of organic molasses.

"It's a good breakfast for the cows," he tells me. "Lots of good energy and minerals. The rest of the day, they eat nothing but good grass hay."

One of the cows nudges open the gate, spots me, and stops. She looks at me with her big, soft, curious brown eyes. Jake assures her that I'm okay. Whether or not his soothing words work, her anxiety is quickly overcome by habit and hunger. She pushes her way into the shed, sticking her face into the steel head gate so that she can get to the grain trough. Jake clamps the head gate shut around her neck to hold her in place while milking.

"Meet Mabel," he says as I watch the tan-faced cow contentedly stuff her mouth like a kid eating candy on Halloween. He stoops down and begins washing Mabel's udders with warm, soapy water. Over his shoulder he says, "She's from New Zealand dairy stock. New Zealanders don't feed grain because they have so much grass. So the cows there are better adapted to grazing. It's becoming common [among raw milk farmers] to get bull semen from New Zealand, where they've preserved the old grass-fed genetics."

Holsteins produce the largest quantity of milk, but Jersey milk is richer in butterfat and protein, making it superior for producing butter, cream, and cheese. Jake's particular cows also produce a type of milk protein that may be healthier than that of other cows. He calls them "A2 A2" cows, and when I ask what that means he tells me "it's complicated." Days later, I find myself enmeshed in research materials.

It *is* complicated, involving detailed factors of various milk proteins and dairy genetics, but I'll try to make it as simple as I can. Originally, all cow's milk was of the A2 variety. But about five thousand years ago, a natural mutation in European dairy cattle created a variant type, A1. A single genetic mutation in the A1 variety allows a digestive enzyme in humans to snip out an amino acid known as beta-casomorphin-7, often abbreviated BCM-7.

This amino acid became the subject of an influential book called *Devil in the Milk* by Keith Woodford, a professor of farm management at Lincoln University in New Zealand. BCM-7 is a natural opioid. We've long used opioids to relieve pain and, well, get high. Common opioids include heroin, codeine, morphine, and opium itself.

One theory as to why BCM-7 exists in milk is that it helps make cows more docile. But that makes little sense because cows drink water, not milk. It's possible, however, that A1 milk's calming effect might lessen a calf's trauma when separated from her mother. It may also be why a warm glass of milk helps you fall asleep at night, or why some people are seemingly addicted to milk shakes. Who can say?

However, Woodford claims that BCM-7, when consumed by humans, contributes to an increased risk for certain diseases such as autism in children, schizophrenia, cardiovascular diseases, and type one diabetes.

For this reason, Jake's Jersey cows have A2 genetics, meaning they produce only milk protein that doesn't fragment into BCM-7. This implies a significant health benefit to his cows' milk that is important to his health-conscious customers.

Whether or not the health risks of A1 milk are valid is a hot topic in the health food community and dairy world, particularly in Australia and New Zealand, where several companies are heavily marketing A2-branded milk products. A2 milk, I noticed, is also finding its way into American grocery stores. It's boosters have taken to demonizing A1 milk in print, online, and in YouTube videos that call it "the new gluten" and "mutant milk."

However, in 2009, the European Food Safety Authority reviewed the science and found no justification for claims about the A1 milk's health risks. But that hasn't stopped people from paying premium prices for A2 milk.

Jake's mobile phone rings and he takes the call. He milks Mabel with his free hand while chatting with someone interested in buying one of his cows. Mabel's an easy milker and some of the milk squirts from her teats in a thin stream without Jake having to squeeze them. In less than ten minutes, he's pulled enough milk to about half fill one of the two-and-a-half gallon milk cans.

Released from the stocks, Mabel ambles out the door and another cow, Abigail, noses her way into the milking shed to take her place.

When the milking is done, we head back to the kitchen. Jake pulls six half-gallon glass milk jars from the shelf, then carefully filters milk into the containers. Afterward, he labels the milk jars with customers' names and deposits them in a refrigerator in the garage for later pickup.

Jake maintains six cows, two of which are in milk at any given time. At their peak, the cows produce about fifty pounds (six gallons) of milk per day, but on the day I visit, Abigail and Mabel are down to about five gallons. Jake is anxious for another cow, Dandelion, to deliver her calf so he can dry off one of the others. I ask Jake what he does with the calves.

"I keep the best heifers and sell the others. There's a lot of demand for the A2 cows with grass-fed genetics," he says. "People new to keeping dairy cows who've read about these types of cows will pay top dollar for them."

He'll pick the grumpiest of his cows and put all the season's calves on her for about six months so that he can keep the other mothers in daily production. The milk from two cows will feed about thirty families. Jake says he's sold out every month, despite a share cost that works out to about twenty dollars per gallon—more than five times the price for standard whole milk sold in local supermarkets, and about three times the price of store-bought organic milk.

"Some people give me crap about the prices, but I just tell them to go get their own cow," Jake says.

"It's what I need to make this worth my time. I don't cut corners. When you milk two cows a day instead of two thousand, you can pay a lot more attention to detail. They get the best feed, the best care. I produce milk that makes me feel good, and it makes the people who drink it feel good, too."

But milk is just part of Eagle Canyon Farm's income stream. He feeds milk's whey and waste hay to the pigs, who turn it into bacon, pork, and piglets. He uses some of the pig lard to grease the cows' udders and prevent chapping. He also sells shares in the pigs and butchers them for customers, but prefers to market the meat through his popular home butchering classes.

"I can actually charge a lot more when I do it that way," he says.

His chickens are responsible for picking through the cow manure and eating the hay seeds, as well as dispersing the cow, pig, and chicken manure so that it fertilizes the pasture and the couple's vegetable garden. The chickens and barn cats eat the pig entrails and provide much-appreciated fly and pest control by eating insect eggs and rodents. In summer, Jake and Alexis sell eggs and Jake butchers chickens for them and their customers. There's almost zero waste in the system. I am impressed with its synchronicity.

Eagle Canyon Farm benefits from being close to Boulder, a predominantly liberal city whose median family income exceeds $113,000 and where the median home price is $548,000. Perennially ranked among the top cities in the nation for education, health, and quality of life, Boulder is the kind of place where people appreciate things like heirloom chickens and organically-raised pork chops—and have the money to afford a twenty-dollar gallon of milk.

But Jake believes that his model of farming can benefit others besides wealthy, health-obsessed baby boomers, Gen X tech warriors, and trust fund millennials. He points out that a century ago, a majority of Americans lived on small, diversified farms that grew vegetables, fruits, and grains and raised livestock for themselves, their neighbors, and their communities. Rather than being an anachronism, the small, diversified farm is the wave of the future, he says.

"The current system can't last. It doesn't really make sense—all those acres of corn grown to feed cows who stand all day on concrete. Why bring the corn to the cows when you can convert the land to pasture? You wouldn't have to spray all those chemical pesticides and herbicides, and manure would fertilize the grass."

"You don't need an actual farm to farm," Alexis chimes in. "Just throw a couple of animals in the backyard and go."

As we sit at the table discussing the economics of small, diversified dairy farming, Alexis toasts some bread and puts a billiard ball–sized lump of plated butter on the table. The butter is a deep yellow and it melts enticingly smoothed on the warm, homemade bread. Jake hands me a glass of raw milk, which less than ten minutes ago was inside a cow. I hesitate.

I am not naive regarding the risks of food-borne pathogens. While living in Mexico, I was severely sickened by food on several occasions. I do not wish to repeat the stomach cramps, vomiting, and diarrhea that resulted from a greasy street taco or a fruit smoothie made with contaminated water. Food poisoning is not only not fun, it can be deadly.

Milk fosters bacteria on par with a petri dish, which is why it spoils so quickly when left unrefrigerated. Pasteurization, a process of rapid heating and cooling, kills off microbes that cause the milk to spoil or cause disease. But certain bacterial strains survive this heat shock as spores. It is these spores, which become active bacteria, which cause even pasteurized milk to eventually curdle and spoil.

Raw milk, however, is more susceptible to microbial contamination because disease-causing microbes introduced during milking (on an errant flake of feces, growing on the udders, or the hands of an incautious bottler) are not subjected to pasteurization.

Although modern medicine has effectively controlled diseases like typhoid that were linked to unpasteurized milk a century ago, the threat of food-borne pathogens in raw milk today remains real. For decades, both the Centers for Disease Control (CDC) and the US Food and Drug Administration (FDA) have warned consumers not to drink raw milk.

Raw milk, they warn, can harbor a variety of nasty bacteria that include salmonella, campylobacter, listeria, and a virulent form of E. coli (E. coli O157:H7), a potentially lethal variant which didn't exist a mere thirty-five years ago.

In the United States, whether or not you can legally purchase raw milk depends on where you live. In nine states plus the District of Columbia, raw milk simply cannot be bought. In sixteen states, raw milk can be purchased only directly on the farm where it is produced. Only ten states allow raw milk sales in grocery stores.

However, in a majority of states, including Colorado, it's not illegal to drink the raw milk of cows you own. So, like many raw milk producers, Jake skirts the illegality of selling raw milk to consumers by selling shares in his cows instead. He is not a scofflaw; he's just exploiting a loophole that states knowingly allow. Outlawing raw milk sales but allowing herd shares helps states to restrict raw milk's distribution and increase the traceability of a product widely regarded as a public health risk.

When raw milk from a cow-share dairy sickened twenty people in Pueblo County, Colorado, a two-hour drive south of Jake's, other people who bought the milk were easily identified and contacted. That would not be the case if the milk were sold in a store.

Raw milk's risks provoke fervent debate, with commercial dairy producers and the government pitted against health food advocates, natural grocers, artisan cheese makers, and farmers like Jake.

"I think there are a lot of people [who are part of] this back-to-nature movement, wanting to support local farms and eat organically. I think the raw milk movement has emerged from that," said CDC epidemiologist Hannah Gould. In spite of the perceived health benefits, her organization routinely cautions people that raw milk and raw milk cheeses are not always benign, and that contamination can lead to severe outcomes including renal failure resulting in death.

Raw milk advocates, or whole milk advocates, as they like to call themselves, say that pasteurization diminishes the nutritional content of milk and spoils its taste. Because of its rich flavor, high vitamin content and digestive enzymes, raw milk has developed a devoted following of people willing to fight for the right to buy it. The debate over raw milk safety has been raging for well over a century.

At the dawn of the twentieth century, meat was not the only food that became discredited in the public mind. Urbanization in the mid to late nineteenth century created a number of public health crises, among them high rates of infant mortality. High death rates among children under five were a sad fact of city life. In New York, for instance, the city inspector reported that in 1840, the rate of mortality for that age group was 50 percent. And despite improving conditions in the cities, "it was clear to statisticians that . . . infant mortality was actually rising in the latter decades of the nineteenth century," noted historian Deborah Valenze of Barnard College.

Health officials fingered milk as a primary murder suspect. Physicians knew that the greatest number of infant deaths occurred in the hottest months. They even had a name for the seasonal affliction: summer diarrhea. Bottle-fed babies were known to contract summer diarrhea at much higher rates than breast-fed infants. One health officer in Birmingham, England, estimated the mortality of "artificially fed" infants to be "at least *thirty times* as great as among those who are nursed at the breast." It was a short intellectual jump to recognize that contaminated milk was its cause.

Cow's milk was not only implicated in summer diarrhea epidemics, but in the transmission of such diseases as tuberculosis, brucellosis, scarlet fever, diphtheria and typhoid. The problem, however, was usually not the milk itself but the often careless and unsanitary manner in which it was collected, bottled, stored, shipped, and otherwise handled. A single unhealthy milkman with tuberculosis, for instance, could pass his disease on to hundreds of families.

In the 1890s, milk reform began as a private venture of Nathan Straus, a successful New York retailer (he co-owned Macy's, as well as Abraham & Straus). The German-born Jewish immigrant recognized the need for sanitary fresh milk to help mothers, especially the poor. In 1893, the philanthropist created the "Nathan Straus Pasteurized Milk Station" on the waterfront at the Third Street Pier. The milk came from regularly inspected dairy farms and disease-free cows, and was processed in a sterile facility made just for that task.

As a result of Straus's efforts, in the first months of July 1864, infant deaths in New York City fell by 7 percent. By August, they were down 34 percent. Straus expanded the number of milk stations in New York to twelve, distributing hundreds of thousands of bottles of pasteurized milk per year. By the turn of the century, pasteurized milk stations like Straus's had been set up in major cities including Chicago, Philadelphia, and Boston. Most were run by charities. Meanwhile, influential backers and pediatric health experts helped to spread Straus' clean milk campaign.

Finally, in 1913, an outbreak of typhoid fever stuck New York State, claiming thousands of lives. A *New York Times* article pinned the epidemic on contaminated milk. By now, it was well established that milk could carry the typhoid bacillus and that the germs could be killed with pasteurization. In the typhoid outbreak's wake, New York City began to take milk safety seriously. By 1914, 95 percent of its milk supply was pasteurized.

Adoption of pasteurization in the United States was spurred on by dire warnings about raw milk safety published in magazines including *Ladies Home Journal, The Progressive,* and *Reader's Digest.* One article in *Coronet* written by Dr. Robert Harris M.D. included an especially lurid description of an outbreak of undulant fever (brucellosis) in a Midwestern town called Crossroads. The epidemic, he wrote, "struck one out of every four persons in Crossroads. Despite the efforts of the two doctors and the state health department, one of every four patients died."

The account, it turned out, was entirely fictional. In a subsequent interview with J. Howard Brown of Johns Hopkins University, Harris admitted that no actual outbreak had occurred. There was no Crossroads, nor any Crossroads citizens to be sickened. But magazines and newspaper reporters continued to write alarming articles about raw milk's risks, which were read by tens of millions of Americans.

By 1917, nearly all of the fifty largest cities in America had passed ordinances requiring milk pasteurization. By the early 1940s, the entire country was blanketed with safe milk statutes.

Today, stories about raw milk's dangers continue to stoke the fires of fear. *Time* magazine's Alexandra Sifferlin, for instance, wrote a dire report about the rise of raw milk outbreaks in the United States. In it, she referred to a CDC report which stated that nearly one thousand people had been sickened from raw milk between 2007 and 2012, and that 73 percent went to the hospital.

But even though raw milk causes more food poisoning out-breaks than pasteurized milk, the actual incidence of dairy-related food poisonings of any kind is small. Since 1998, only two people in the United States have died as a direct result of drinking raw milk, and two more from consuming raw milk cheese. Compare that to the average of fifteen deaths per year resulting from raw oyster consumption. Notably, three big food poisoning outbreaks involving peanuts, eggs, and cantaloupe accounted for thirty-nine deaths from 2009 to 2011—yet the CDC is not cautioning Americans not to eat those foods.

Of course, the seemingly infinitesimally small risk of getting sick from contaminated raw milk is no consolation for Jill Brown and Jason Young, the parents of then two-year-old Kylee, who con-tracted an E. coli O157:H7 infection from raw milk. The infant was among nineteen people (fifteen of them under age nineteen) who fell ill from raw milk produced at Foundation Farm in Wilsonville, Oregon, in 2012. Four of the sickened children were hospitalized with kidney failure. Kylee survived only because of a kidney trans-plant from her mom. The child suffered a stroke and heart failure, spending close to two hundred days in the hospital, all told.

Jill Brown says that her choice to feed her child raw milk came from a heartfelt belief that buying raw milk from a local farmer was healthier than buying milk from giant dairy corporations. On health grounds, she had rejected the corporate model of agriculture and turned instead to the local food movement to which many of her friends ascribed.

"I wanted to know where the milk I was buying was coming from," she said. "My research led me to believe that raw milk from a local farm would be healthier than the milk I brought from the store.

"If I had known what I know now, I would never have fed it to my daughter."

Sitting at the table at Jake's farmhouse, knowing the milk in my glass came out of the cow only minutes ago, having watched how carefully Jake handled each step of the process and the care he gives to his cows, I don't agonize over my choice. I take a bite of the toast, rhapsodizing at the sweet taste of the home-churned farm butter, and wash it down with the cup of raw milk. The taste is smooth, full, creamy and . . . sublime.

Would I buy my milk from Jake? Perhaps. The cost is extravagant, but you're paying for Jake's exceedingly good care of his cows and the premium quality of his products. His cows seem truly happy. The milk is delicious. Does the risk bother me? Not really. Anything you put in your mouth puts you at risk, and there are many foods far riskier than raw dairy milk.

But, myself, I might just choose to pasteurize it.

NINETEEN

THREE DAIRIES, ACT TWO: COWS IN THE MACHINE

The cow is nothing but a machine which makes grass fit for us people to eat.

—Journalist John McNulty

When was the last time you saw a herd of dairy cows out grazing on pasture? Over the last several decades, they seem to have vanished from the landscape. Their absence caused me to wonder, "Where have all the milk cows gone?"

On a three-day drive from Denver to Seattle, I spotted the answer. There, alongside a highway in southern Idaho, was an open-sided shed the length of two football fields with a concrete feed trough and gray steel bars running its entire length. Behind the manure-spattered bars were Holsteins. Thousands of 'em.

Over the last forty years, the dairy industry has been going through a dramatic transformation. The nature of the changes are threefold. Small farms are failing at the expense of huge "megadairies" that stock anywhere from one thousand to thirty thousand animals apiece. Traditional dairy states in the Northeast and Great Lakes regions are losing ground to western states, where megadairies are flourishing. And thanks to huge gains in dairy cow productivity, the nation is producing more milk than ever despite historically low numbers of dairy cows.

Today, half of the nation's milk and cheese is produced by a mere 3 percent of the nation's dairy farms—those with more than a thousand cows, according to the USDA. Super megadairies, like Fair Oaks Farm in Illinois and Threemile Canyon Farms in eastern Oregon, have more than thirty thousand cows. That's enough to slake the thirst of everyone in the city of Chicago, or in the states of North Dakota, South Dakota, and Montana combined.

Conversely, small dairy farms have become a quaint anachronism, like quilting bees and horse-drawn plows. In 1970, there were 470,000 dairy farms in the United States. That figure has nose-dived to fewer than 65,000 today. Over the past forty years, New York and Wisconsin combined have seen their herds decrease by nearly one million cows.

But out West, it's another story. In that same time span, California's dairyman added nearly a million cows to their herds, bringing the state's current inventory to 1.8 million head. While doing so, they created a new type of dairy farming known throughout the global dairy industry as "the Californian model."

Leslie Butler, a dairy economist at the University of California at Davis, explains it this way. "The Californian model is simply that you don't have to grow all your grass and raise your own feed crops, you can import feed and water and all your input and house a thousand head of dairy cattle on just forty acres of land."

"CAFO," short for Concentrated Animal Feeding Operation, is a commonly used acronym for this method of farming, in which large numbers of animals are effectively warehoused in a small amount of space. Animal rights activists have their own term for this practice: factory farming.

Of course, I'd read and heard a great deal about cruelty at factory dairy farms. I'd watched undercover YouTube videos depicting unspeakable abuses of cows by confinement diary workers. I'd spoken at length with a Mercy For Animals investigator named Cody, whose videos documented workers cutting off cows' tails without benefit of anesthetic, and a dairy boss striking a cow with a pipe wrench. But I felt I needed to see a large confinement dairy myself and form my own opinions.

So I contacted the Western Dairy Association, a group composed mainly of dairy-owning families in Colorado, Wyoming, and Montana. Finding a large farm to visit proved to be a teeth-pulling process. Bill Keating, the WDA's senior director of producer relations, was understandably concerned that I was about to do a hit-job on the dairy industry.

Based on my early conversations with Mr. Keating, it was clear that the WDA had become extremely sensitive to recent negative attention rained down on dairy farming by groups like Mercy For Animals, the Humane Society of the United States, Farm Sanctuary, and others. After weeks of back-and-forth emails, phone interviews, and discussions with the WDA board of directors, I finally wrangled a farm visit with a Colorado dairy couple.

On the phone, I asked the owners if I could come for the morning milking. He assured me that any time of day was fine. With 1,500 cows to milk twice daily, he said, milking goes on round-the-clock. I arrived at dawn anyway and waited outside a small office attached to the milking barn.

Out of the dim morning light, a man approached me cradling a rifle. He didn't appear menacing. In fact, his face and hairstyle bore a passing resemblance to former president George W. Bush. As with Bush, he looked like the kind of guy you'd enjoy talking to over beers.

"Sorry, but I had to shoot a cow that's been sick. Not how I wanted to start my day," he said, extending a hand and introducing himself as Jon Slutsky. He ushered me into his small, windowless office and rested the rifle in its rack. He slumped in his chair for a few moments. I remained quiet, sensing that the day's first chore still weighed on him. After a respectful moment of silence, we began our talk.

Jon and his wife, Susan Moore, operate La Luna Dairy, in Wellington, a small town midway between Denver and Fort Collins. The Rocky Mountains provide a dramatic backdrop to the historic sixty-acre farm, which has been in continuous use as a dairy since the early 1900s.

When they met at University of California at Riverside in the early 1970s, Jon and Susan were self-avowed hippies. Though neither had an agricultural upbringing, they both shared an interest in animals. Not unlike raw dairy producers Jake Takiff and Alexis Mahon, they rented a place in the Colorado countryside where they could raise farm animals—chickens, rabbits, some pigs, at first, and then sheep and goats. It was the goats that most interested them. They began breeding and showing the animals, along with milking them and making cheese.

"We were spending a lot on our hobby, so we decided to go into business," said Jon.

But no bank was willing to finance two hippies with a goatherd. The bankers reasoned that there simply wasn't much of a market for the milk. And though Jon had earned an advanced degree in animal science at Colorado State University and Susan had worked testing milk at the Dairy Herd Improvement Association, they lacked know-how in the day-to-day operations of the business. So, Jon took a job at a local dairy.

Eventually, they met another dairy couple who were moving back home to Wisconsin. In 1981, Jon and Susan bought the herd of sixty-four cows, plus two tractors, keeping the name "La Luna" from their goat milking days. (Susan says the name, Spanish for moon, originated with a children's book about a goat that jumped over the moon).

"It was hard, even then, to enter the business," says Jon of those early days. "We did all the work ourselves. We'd literally put in twenty-four hours of work every day between the two of us."

From day one, they took a progressive approach to dairying. They brought in a nutritionist to improve their cows' productivity and health and they steadily improved their herd to increase individual milk production. One day, for the first time, the cows produced enough milk to overflow the holding tank of their antique milking parlor.

"We thought that was pretty cool, until we realized that it was money going down the drain," Jon recalls.

By 1985, they'd outgrown their property. So, they secured a farm loan, bought the historic dairy farm where Jon had worked while learning the trade, increased their herd to two hundred cows, and began hiring employees. Over the next two decades, they continued expanding the herd to five hundred, then fifteen hundred (plus offspring), following economic pressures in the dairy industry that pushed them in the direction of ever larger herds.

Large dairy farms, like La Luna, have significant advantages over small producers. According to USDA studies, as herd size increases, the cost of production per hundred pounds of milk drops sharply. Big farms with at least a thousand cows have 15 percent lower production costs than farms with between five hundred and a thousand cows. The smallest farms, those with fewer than a hundred cows, are even more disadvantaged, paying out as much as 35 percent more in production costs per milk unit sold than the large-scale dairies.

A big part of those savings comes from capital utilization: if you install a state-of-the-art milking parlor, it's the most cost-effective to use it round the clock, as they do at La Luna. Banks typically offer the large farms better loan rates, and suppliers give them breaks on supplies and bulk feed. According to Jon, economies of scale also make it easy for the large farmer to increase herd size.

"Once you've invested in the land and all the equipment, it's not hard to add another hundred or two hundred cows," Jon tells me.

After our talk, Jon takes me on a tour of the dairy barn. The milking parlor has a checkerboard floor made of colorful rubber mats that provide cushioning and traction for the workers. Two elevated decks on either side of the aisle place the cow's udders at eye level, saving the back-aching labor of bending over all day. Three workers, two men and a woman, chat in Spanish as they clean the upper deck floors, moving mounds of manure toward the drains with pressurized water and brooms. A gate opens and a pen of Holstein cows shuffles in, aligning themselves in the herringbone milking stalls, twenty on either side.

Quickly and efficiently, the workers move down the rows, washing the cows' udders with disinfectant before attaching vacuum-suction milking cups. Immediately, milk begins to flow into clear plastic tubes as the pumps rhythmically pulse. By the time the workers reach the far end of the line, the milk from the cows at the near end is already beginning to sputter. So, the workers start again, removing the cups with a "pop" and a hiss of air and cleaning them with disinfectant, which they also reapply to the udders.

When the last cow is done, a pneumatic gate opener makes a "whoosh" sound, the gates open, and the milk-depleted cows amble off through a door at the far end. Another group enters from the near end, and the process begins once more.

About 200 cows are milked each hour, and every cow is milked twice a day. It takes two tanker trucks, each capable of sucking 6,000 gallons of milk into its stainless steel belly, to haul the day's milk to a Dairy Farmers of America processing plant in Greeley.

Back in his office, Jon uses a computer to monitor his cows. An ear tag transponder permanently attached to each cow records the number of pounds of milk she produces and how quickly she milks. A program aggregates a cow's output on a spreadsheet so Jon can evaluate her productivity over time. Jon can also tell at a glance if a cow has a high somatic cell count in her milk, an indication that she may be developing mastitis. As a result, he tells me, he can often determine if a cow is sick before his milkers spot the problem in the milking parlor. Data also helps Jon make culling decisions.

Jon says that each of his cows averages about twenty-eight thousand pounds of milk annually, which indicates an exceptionally well-managed and productive herd. La Luna's monthly milk production is about three million pounds, which, depending on the volatile commodity price for milk, brings in anywhere from $430,000 to $770,000. But, as Jon points out, most of the money goes to overhead—feed, bedding, utilities, equipment, and salaries for his twenty-eight full-time employees and several part-timers.

"These days, you pretty much have to go big in order to pay the bills," Jon says. "If it takes twelve hundred cows to cover your expenses and you're milking thirteen hundred cows, all the profit comes from those last one hundred cows."

In other words, margins for a dairyman like Jon are tight. Profitability can be hugely impacted by swings in the prices that milk and cheese processors pay. Two years before I visited La Luna, milk hit a record high of twenty-four dollars per hundred weight; feed prices also were low and La Luna was swimming in black ink. But sixteen months later, milk prices had plummeted to just sixteen dollars per hundredweight, about what producers paid when Jon and Susan began dairy farming in the early 1980s.

When I meet Susan later that day, she tells me there have been years when the couple was a million dollars in debt, hoping for prices to go up. Boom and bust cycles are endemic in the dairy industry, and that can put an almost unbearable strain on farmers. Even the largest dairies tend to be owned by families, many of whom have been in the business for generations.

Dairy farm incomes are seldom stable and can be affected by downturns in commodity prices, high feed costs, high loan rates, droughts, floods, overproduction of milk across the entire industry, and a dozen more variables. It's not unusual for farmers to pay more to produce the milk then they can sell it for.

Prolonged periods of financial distress often lead to despair among food producers. Suicide rates among American farmers are twice that of people in the general population, and dairy farmers are more vulnerable than most. One of the problems that all dairymen face, Jon tells me, is that there is no way to shut off the spigots when the milk price drops below the cost of doing business; dairy farmers are forced to keep spending even when they are losing money.

"There's no way to dial down production or lay off workers when the price goes down, because when prices recover, you've sold the animals and you're understaffed," Jon says. "It's not like most businesses. You can't just close down the pizza oven."

In early 2009, during the height of the recession, one Maine dairy farmer hanged himself in his barn and two others shot themselves. Two more dairy farmers in California also committed suicide. In 2010, New York farmer Dean Pierson, who raised a hundred head of cattle, went into his barn and shot fifty-one dairy cows that he'd been milking twice each day, then turned the .22 caliber rifle he'd used on himself.

Michael Marsh, former CEO of Western United Dairymen in Modesto, California, explains that farm family tradition and a strong ethic of self-sufficiency within the farming community place tremendous burdens on today's generation of dairymen, even when they have no control over external economic challenges.

"Let's say your farm operation started in your family in the 1880s and stayed in the family all these years," he said. "Your parents, grandparents, great-grandparents built it. And here you have the business and all these beautiful animals and barns and milking parlors and employees. And then, one day, it's gone. It's pretty easy to see how depressing that can be."

Feed is the dairyman's biggest expense—an animal nutritionist told me that about 60 percent of a farmer's overhead goes toward buying feed. Even when milk prices are good, profits can be wiped out by high feed prices. Controlling feed costs, therefore, is critical to La Luna's bottom line. Jon is always chasing the best feed buys.

Following milking, the cows return to their pens for feeding. La Luna cows eat a diet that's fairly standard, but which varies in response to local feed availability. While I am there, a semi truck arrives and dumps a load of feed material on the ground. It has the alarmingly bright color of curry, the consistency of corn meal, and it's unlike anything I've ever seen cattle eat. Even when mixed into their feed ration, it sticks to the cows' faces like pollen on a bee.

Turns out, it's dried corn distillery waste from an ethanol plant in Windsor. Jon says La Luna also sometimes buys wet brewer's grain, a distillery by-product of the Budweiser brewing plant in Fort Collins. Though these initially strike me as nutritionally suspect foods, it turns out that distillery grains are energy-dense, low in starch, rich in fats and protein, and can increase dairy cow productivity. As factory byproducts, they're also cheap and the cows seem to enjoy them.

When they're not being milked or eating from troughs, the cows spend most of their day resting on sand—a great bedding because it doesn't breed bacteria, is cool, and keeps cows clean and comfortable. Open stall barns allow the cows to roam a bit while protecting them from the summer sun and winter cold.

Animal rights organizations criticize containment farms for not giving animals access to "natural" environments. It's a perplexing assertion, as domesticated animals, by definition, don't live in a state of nature. In India, which leads the world in cattle population, millions of cows live in congested cities like Mumbai and Kolkata, feeding off human trash and dodging traffic. For them, this is natural. But it's hard to argue against the fact that cows evolved to feed on pasture grass, not to eat corn and distillery grains in containment pens.

Still, despite not spending time in green grass pastures, La Luna's cows seem pretty contented. They move easily from place to place; they know the routine and are used to their human handlers. Jon's workers don't use electric cattle prods as the cows are trained to be led by their halters. Jon even politely asks me to leave Onda, my Aussie Shepherd, in the car because the animals aren't used to seeing dogs and might get upset. Jon sees animal abuse as counterproductive. He doesn't understand why any dairy farmer would allow it.

"When we train employees, we teach them not to run the cows. We don't want the cows to be beaten or hit or kicked—the very things that hurt them also lower their productivity. A cow that's full of adrenalin won't produce. Or if she does, she won't let her milk down.

"And from a humane perspective, we just don't tolerate abuse. We like our animals. This is our lifestyle," he continues. "When I walk among my cows, the first thing I think is how beautiful they are."

After spending the morning with the cows, including visiting the "hospital," a quarantine area where workers tend to the sick or injured, I don't see signs of open sores, prolapsed uteruses, dried feces caked on the legs, or the other horrors documented by undercover YouTube videos.

As someone who's worked with large farm animals, I'm impressed with the care at La Luna. Because La Luna serves as a teaching center for Colorado State University vet students and its dairy program, top-quality veterinary attention is nearly constant.

So I am curious to know what Jon thinks about the video exposés done by Mercy for Animals and others.

"What can anyone say? Those of us in the industry initially thought they were staged. Nobody thinks that anymore. And nobody wants to see that . . . it's just so disturbing and disappointing," he says.

Jon has work to attend to, so I'm given the opportunity to tour the farm on my own. As I am en route to see the calf pens and nursery, Susan Moore and the couple's adult daughter, Raisa, join me. They take me to see the antique milking parlor, dusty from disuse, that the couple slaved in when they bought the place. We walk outdoors to a pen where the pregnant cows are kept and, to everyone's surprise, one of them begins to deliver her baby.

"Oh, it's been a long time since I've seen one give birth," says Susan, who is apparently no longer hands-on when it comes to the daily dairy chores. As the cow strains to push the baby out, I take the opportunity to talk to Raisa. I ask if she has any desire to take over the family dairy business.

"No" she says. "I work in civil rights as an anti-racial activist. Growing up here among mostly Hispanic workers, I developed an awareness that people, especially minorities in this country, had it rough. Mom passed that along to me at a very early age."

Susan tells me that she'd like to retire someday, but admits that Jon prefers to persevere. Besides, she says, "I'd miss the people and the bi-cultural experience."

Aware that the major critique of factory farms comes from environmentalists and animal rights activists who fall mainly on the left side of the political spectrum, I ask liberal-minded Raisa about her take on large farms and on the issue of rBST in dairy cattle.

"Honestly, I'm not sure how I feel about large farms. I guess there's good and bad. It comes down to how much the people care about the animals. That's far more important than size.

"And although I'm not opposed to hormones, Monsanto has done some really screwed up things in parts of the world. It does bother me that my parents do business with them."

Earlier, Jon had said that he likes the improved productivity of his cows that comes with rBST and doesn't feel that it's inhumane. Sound management practices and veterinary attention have helped him counteract mastitis, a common side effect of rBST. But in the same breath, he said that using rBST "is a pain in the ass. It's another list to make, another day's work for somebody."

I ask if he has considered going organic, but he says that he can't. "To be certified organic, your cows have to spend at least 120 days of the year on pasture. That's impossible for us because we don't have the land. And in Colorado, the growing season is only four months long. You'd be pushing the limits."

Back at the calving shed, the cow is groaning with exertion and two legs protrude from her birth canal. It's been a slow and arduous delivery, and a longtime employee Enrique comes to see if she needs help. But just as he arrives, the wet calf comes squirting out and lands gently on the ground. Another cow noses over to take a look, sniffing at the newborn.

After a few minutes, the mother gets up and begins licking the calf dry. This helps to stimulate circulation, too. When she's almost done, Enrique enters the pen pushing an oversized wheelbarrow. He picks up the calf and places her in the wheelbarrow to be carted to the nursery.

"We take them right away," says Susan. "It's easier on the cows if they don't have time to form a bond."

And indeed, the cow doesn't seem to miss her calf at all. She doesn't even look over her shoulder to watch Enrique leave, but instead walks over to a trough and begins eating hay alongside the other cow. After all the horror stories I'd heard about the agony of separation, her nonchalance takes me by surprise. But I can't help but feel a sadness at the act. It's a part of dairying that, I guess, you get used to, but seeing it drives home the reality that milk intended for baby calves is instead diverted to nourish us.

Before I leave, Susan takes me to the dairy's entrance to show me something. It's an old, weathered sign with the dairy's name and a hand-drawn goat jumping over a moon. There's wistfulness in Susan's voice as she tells me about their earliest days as goat farmers. Deep down, I sense that she misses those simpler times and perhaps regrets some of the compromises they've made to build their business up from a small herd of goats to a huge herd of dairy cattle.

She tells me it was their dream to be prosperous and to share that prosperity with their Mexican immigrant employees, and ultimately to put the employees' kids through college. But with the relentless drive for greater cost control in the dairy industry, the dream never came to pass. The tight margins, the up and down milk and feed prices, and the relentless pressure to (as President Nixon's Secretary of Agriculture Earl Butz famously said) "get big or get out" made their dreams of social equality and a middle class living for their farm workers an impossibility.

Jon told me that he pays his workers on salary, but it works out to be about ten dollars an hour plus performance bonuses. Despite the low wages, most of the workers stay on. The pay is better than the minimum wage they'd make working in restaurant kitchens or as hotel maids, and the work is steady. To a dairy cow, there are no weekends or holidays; every day is a workday.

TWENTY

THREE DAIRIES, ACT THREE: EMERALD PASTURES

Man's attitude toward nature is today critically important simply because we have now acquired a fateful power to alter and destroy nature. But man is a part of nature, and his war against nature is inevitably a war against himself.
— Rachel Carson.

Organic is a grocery store term that means "twice as expensive."
— Comedian Jim Gaffigan

I f you wanted to take a relaxing Sunday drive through an idyllic rural landscape, you couldn't find a much better locale than Yamhill County, Oregon.

As you drive south from Portland, beige houses and suburban strip malls give way to hillsides covered in evergreen fir trees. Making your way down the Willamette Valley, you find cultivated fields broken up by streams and groves of big leaf maples.

Century-old wooden barns and grain elevators—most still in use—testify to the area's longstanding agricultural tradition. So too does "Turkey Rama," a three-day turkey barbecue held in McMinnville, the county seat. Yamhill turkey farmers founded the festival in 1938, back when a booming turkey market made the birds Yamhill's main source of wealth.

Nowadays the turkeys are gone, but in their place is a thriving wine industry. Yamhill County is at the center, both geographically and economically, of Oregon's $3.35 billion dollar wine business. More acres are planted in grape vines in Yamhill County than in any other county in the state.

One other thing you'll see is dairy cows. Lots of 'em. Milk is Yamhill County's third most-important farm commodity, bringing in $22.5 million annually—about a tenth of overall farm sales. Among the county's dairymen is Bob Bansen, owner of Emerald Veil Jerseys.

New York Times' Pulitzer Prize winning columnist Nicholas Kristof, who grew up on a cherry farm here, was one of Bob's classmates. He described Bob as "a self-deprecating man with an easy laugh" and a third-generation dairy farmer "who has figured out how to make a good living running a farm that is efficient but also has soul." Bob seemed like just the guy for me to see about organic dairying.

Around 2004, Bob converted Emerald Veil from conventional dairy farming to organic. Or rather, he converted *back* to organic dairy farming. Most of today's farming advances didn't exist a century ago when his grandfather, Peter Bansen, emigrated from Denmark to California and started a dairy farm. But around mid-century, the nature of farming changed.

In 1939, Swiss chemist Paul Muller discovered the insect-killing ability of dichlorodiphenyltrichloroethane, which you almost surely know as DDT. Its virtues were that it was toxic to a wide range of insects, it was easy to apply, and it was cheap. Hailed as an agricultural miracle, DDT quickly spread across the planet.

DDT helped launch "the Green Revolution," a new way of farming that relied heavily upon synthetic chemical inputs. By controlling insects, weeds, and other crop-damaging species, post-war innovations in farming methods helped the world's farmers steadily chip away at mass starvation and hunger. Ever-higher crop yields resulted in ever lower food prices.

DDT was also directly responsible for saving millions of lives from insect-born diseases including malaria, typhus, and dengue fever. In 1948, Paul Muller received a Nobel Prize in Medicine for discovering DDT's insecticidal power.

A decade later, author and environmentalist Rachel Carson received an angry letter from her closest friend, Olga Huckins, regarding the deadly effect of DDT spraying on her two-acre bird sanctuary in Massachusetts. Soon after, Carson was visiting the Huckins when a plane flew over, spraying DDT to control mosquitos. That next day, she was sickened to see dead and dying fish, along with crabs and crayfish struggling drunkenly as the poison intoxicated their systems.

These experiences compelled the best-selling author and biologist to spend the next four years investigating environmental and human health problems related to pesticides, with a particular focus on DDT. In 1962, her landmark book *Silent Spring* debuted.

Silent Spring showed that the widespread use of pesticides and herbicides was causing injury to animal populations (especially birds and fish), damaging ecosystems, and potentially harming human health through long-term exposure.

Just as Upton Sinclair's novel *The Jungle* had caused a public outcry against the meat packing industry, *Silent Spring* aroused widespread concern about the misuse and overuse of pesticides. Joni Mitchell poignantly expressed American's misgivings about the chemical fog in her 1970 hit song *Big Yellow Taxi*: "Hey, farmer,

farmer, put away the DDT now. Give me spots on my apples, but leave me the birds and the bees. Please!"

Silent Spring catalyzed the modern environmental movement, sparking grassroots activism that led directly to the creation of organizations such as the Environmental Defense Fund and Friends of the Earth—organizations which expanded the meaning of environmental protection beyond merely conserving land to limiting the environmental impacts of chemical pollution and nuclear proliferation.

Silent Spring also demanded a response from government, beginning with the Democratic administration of John Kennedy, who met with Carson and commissioned studies on DDT, and extending into the term of Republican Richard Nixon.

In 1970, President Nixon proposed an agency to write and enforce environmental regulations. The US Environmental Protection Agency was approved with bi-partisan support from Congress. One of its first acts was to ban the use of DDT, along with placing stricter controls on the registration and use of all pesticides.

In a reversal a decade later, pro-business president Ronald Reagan relaxed EPA restrictions on pesticides written during the Nixon era. In good times and bad, agrochemical companies have aggressively promoted the use of pesticides, herbicides, and synthetic fertilizers. Today, the list of toxic chemicals (including herbicides, rodenticides, insecticides, fungicides, and microbicides) registered with the US government exceeds twenty-one thousand.

On average, farmers today spend more than 5 percent of their total operating budget on pesticides, most of it to control weeds and insects. In many states, the use of pesticides on commercial crops like corn and soybeans (both commonly used as animal feeds) varies from 92 to 100 percent. GMO varieties of these two crops were actually developed to tolerate the herbicide, glyphosate (aka "Roundup"), and while the crops themselves are considered safe, scientists have raised concerns about the pesticide.

Pesticide residues are found everywhere in the American food system. They turn up in 30 to 40 percent of the food sampled by the FDA. Many of them are known carcinogens, endocrine disruptors, and neurotoxins, which are all dangerous at some level. One of the FDA's tasks is to set limits on the amounts of these chemicals present in crops, but nobody knows whether those levels of exposure are truly safe. As with DDT, the long-term health risks simply cannot be determined. So, the FDA sets its standards based on weighing the costs versus the benefits—and the benefits are not to you and me, but to agricultural product producers like Roundup's manufacturer, Monsanto.

In February of 1989, an event raised fresh doubts as to the safety of America's chemical-dependent food system. The CBS network news program *60 Minutes* featured a segment on twenty-three agrochemicals found in common fruits and vegetables. Among them was Alar, a synthetic chemical sprayed on apples that penetrated to the core. Alar regulated fruit growth, preventing ripened fruit from falling off the trees. This reduced windfall losses and kept the apples red and appealing during storage.

Based upon a report from the National Resources Defense Council, the program exposed Alar as a potent carcinogen. Forty million viewers tuned in. Upon realizing that baby Sally's apple juice and the shiny apple placed each day in little Johnny's lunch bag might harbor cancer-causing chemicals, parents sought swift action. Within a year, the EPA banned Alar's use and the USDA initiated a program to test foods for pesticides and other agrochemical residues.

But following the *60 Minutes* agrochemical exposé, a growing number of consumers and farmers proved no longer willing to place their faith in the assurances of chemical firms, big agriculture, and the federal government agencies charged with food safety. Organic foods, hitherto mainly the province of back-to-the-land hippies, went mainstream.

Today, organic food accounts for roughly fifty billion dollars in United States sales and is experiencing double-digit annual growth, going from a less than 1 percent share of the grocery market in 1997 to a 5 percent share today. Dairy ranks as the organic market leader, running neck-and-neck with baby food.

At Whole Foods market, which is a bellwether for health food trends in North America, three of the twenty best-selling items are organic dairy products—whole milk, reduced-fat (2 percent) milk, and unsalted butter. Industry trade magazine *Hoard's Dairyman* calls organic dairy products "the gateway for organic marketers" because milk is usually the first product consumers switch to on their journey down the organic farm road.

Bob Bansen had already begun thinking about organic farming long in advance of this trend. One of Bansen's college projects in the 1980s was to design a business; he chose an organic nursery. But even as the market for organic dairy grew, Bansen wasn't sure he could take the risk; it takes at least three years to transition from a conventional to an organic dairy, and the changeover costs are usually measured in the hundreds of thousands of dollars.

But he began to cautiously dip his toes into organic farming practices. The first thing he did was to withhold antibiotics. The way conventional dairymen routinely use antibiotics, he told me, is to inject them directly into the udders. Pharmaceutical salesmen claim this helps prevent bacterial infections while the cows dry up. But he soon saw that there were no adverse effects when he stopped using them.

"I discovered I had not been getting any benefit from antibiotics," he told me. "I'd been wasting money for years."

Not only this, but Bob noticed his cows were actually healthier. He realized that by injecting the udders, he'd been creating a pathway for pathogens. So long as the cows were kept clean and on pasture, he says, there seemed to be no need to routinely use antibiotics and other pharmaceuticals.

"Nature has a way of dealing with things, and has long before the chemical companies got involved," he said.

Once Bansen found a supplier willing to commit to selling him organic feed grains, going organic was not a difficult decision.

He'd never had to spray pesticides or fertilizer in his pasture. A rotational grazing system, healthy soil, and decades of grazing had kept the fields relatively weed-free. The cows' manure kept the grass well fertilized. Furthermore, Bob had always resisted using rBST on his herd.

"Monsanto would come around every three months and offer free samples. I turned them down. My big objection was, I didn't want to jab my cows all the time," he said. "Besides, people were already skeptical of rBST—it was like steroid use in baseball players. Nobody trusted it."

Under pressure from consumers and farmers, the USDA updated its organic standards to include a rule that organic dairy cows had to remain on pasture for at least 120 days each year, and that the cows' diets must contain no less than 30 percent pasture grass during the mandatory grazing season. With 600 acres of prime grazing land sufficient to feed his herd, Bob was already meeting this requirement when this new rule went into effect.

"My cows have been out on pasture every year since we went organic," he says. "It's not only good for the cows' health, it's good for my own sanity. I turn them out between milkings, and they take care of themselves."

During winter, Emerald Veil cows go indoors or get corralled. Bob says that when he turns them out in the springtime, "it's like Christmas, Easter, and the Fourth of July all put together. The cows play and buck and run . . . until they realize there's sweet grass at their feet."

The USDA's pasture requirement is one of the key tenets of the organic dairy farming movement, whose original proponents believed not only that food should be safer but that animals should be better cared for and should live more naturally. But not everyone adheres to that ethic like Bob Bansen.

In 2009, the organic watchdog group Cornucopia Institute filed a class action suit against Aurora Organic Dairy of Boulder, Colorado, the nation's largest organic dairy producer. The lawsuit alleged that

Aurora's High Plains Dairy was failing to graze its dairy cattle as required by federal organic standards and was therefore fraudulently representing their product to consumers.

Though the court ruled that Aurora's milk met organic standards, it allowed that Aurora had "misrepresented the manner in which dairy cows were raised and fed." Without admitting guilt, Aurora settled the class action suit for $7.5 million.

It was not the first time that Aurora, which packages private-label milk for big box grocery stores Costco, Safeway, Walmart, and others, was taken to task over its organic bonafides. In 2006, the USDA found Aurora in violation of fourteen of the organic regulations, including confining their cattle to feedlots instead of grazing and bringing thousands of "conventional" (non-organically certified) cows into their organic operation.

Critics complain that Aurora and other large-scale producers have been capitalizing on the organic dairy boom while diluting the ethos that gave rise to organic in the first place. Contrary to the practices at small organic dairies like Bob's, critics like the Cornucopia Institute allege that Aurora, its rival Horizon Organic, and a handful of others source their milk from Concentrated Animal Feeding Operations (CAFOs) indiscernible from conventional factory farms.

Aurora, for instance, keeps forty thousand cows on six farms, four in Colorado and two in Texas. Their High Plains Dairy near Gill, Colorado, has more than fourteen thousand cows. In Texas, there are another twenty-four hundred. Though the cows are given an organic diet of hay, proteins, and grains and produce milk that's rBST-free, it can be argued that the consumer is being duped into believing that the milk comes from small family farms, like Emerald Veil.

"People are paying more for organic products because they think the farmers are doing it right, that they're treating animals humanely and that the quality of the product is different," said Ronnie Cummins, executive director of the Organic Consumers

Association. "There have never been farms like Horizon or Aurora in the history of organics. Intensive confinement is a no-no. This is Grade B organics."

🐄

And Mark Kastel of the small-farm advocacy group the Cornu-copia Institute says that big ag appears to be intruding more and more on organic dairying. "Since the new grazing requirements were enacted [in 2010], we've seen [organic] confinement dairies grow from two to twenty," he said. "And the bad actors still aren't complying."

Kastel tells me that "real" organic farms have made great financial investments in converting to pasture-based production—enhancing the nutritional properties of the milk and safeguarding animal health.

"These large corporate-dominated enterprises are happy to just pay lip service to required organic ethics," he concludes.

The Cornucopia Institute evaluates and rates organic producers, based largely on a self-reporting system along with field research conducted by its staff. In the case of dairy, they use a cute five-cow scale, with five cows being outstanding and zero cows being "ethi-cally deficient." More than forty organic dairy producers received zero cow grades, including Aurora and Horizon.

Bob Bansen and his two brothers all operate organic dairy farms. Bob and younger brother, Jon, sell their milk through the farmer-owned cooperative, Organic Valley, which Cornucopia rates four cows, meaning "excellent."

Organic Valley began in 1988 when seven like-minded organic dairy farmers in Wisconsin joined together to market their milk. In the 1990s, it expanded to become the first nationwide, commer-cial organic dairy producer. Still made up almost entirely of small family farms with fewer than three hundred cows, Organic Valley employs strict standards for co-op members (such as a stocking limit of just three cows per acre) and enforces them with regular farm visits.

My own visit to Bob's Emerald Veil dairy started hours before dawn, when I drove down from Seattle to arrive in time for the 7 A.M. milking. The cows needed no coercion to line up for their turn in the milking parlor. Their heavily laden milk bags swayed and their voices mooed in complaint as they jostled for position, eager to relieve the weight of their milk and receive a reward of a few pounds of grain.

Sixteen at a time, they lumbered into the herringbone milk parlor, burying their faces in the troughs as Bob and his Latino helper swabbed their udders and attached the suction cups. As they devoured their measured, organically grown rations, several cows began banging the stainless steel feed bins. Bob tells me they learned the trick so they could dislodge a few loose grains, which they lap up with their enormous pink tongues.

One of the cow's udders hung just inches above the concrete floor. Bob considered her objectively, telling me, "I'll have to sell her off soon." It was a decision, I knew, that pained him in the same way that Jon Slutsky was pained to have to put a cow down on the morning I visited.

Contrary to the way farmers are frequently portrayed by animal rights organizations like Mercy For Animals or PETA, most with skin in the game who still interact with their animals daily really do form attachments to them and care about their welfare.

Bob, for one, knows every one of his cows by name, a tradition that goes back to his grandfather's day, when a name placard hung above each cow's stanchion in the milk barn. Bob's father, Lloyd, tried to number the cattle one year, but he grew frustrated, saying "I hate this! I can't remember who's who!" So the naming tradition continued and was passed along to Bob and his two brothers.

"Giving them names makes me feel closer to my cows," Bob told me.

In most ways, the milking itself was like the one I'd seen at La Luna in Colorado. But unlike at La Luna, when the men finished with each new set of cows, the gates would open and the cows would walk out an open barn door onto a lush, green pasture. After visiting confinement dairies in Texas, New Mexico, Idaho, and Colorado, I'd come to expect that the farms I visited would not compare to the milk cartons, dairy labels, ads, and websites upon which cows grazed contentedly on green pastures. But that's precisely what I was seeing at Emerald Veil.

As the men attached a new string of cows to the hydra-headed milk machine, Bob asked me over his shoulder, "So, how many calves did you get out of a cow on the ranch where you worked?" I strained to remember, but thought the number was six, maybe eight.

"Six or so," I said.

Bob grunted. Then he told me something I found frankly shocking. "Ours'll go through ten or eleven calving cycles."

That meant Bob was keeping some of his cows, at least, well past the age of twelve—something unheard of in the confinement dairy world. He said the *average* age of his milk cows was about six years.

What that means is, Bob keeps his cows well beyond the age at which commercial cattle usually succumb to the colossal biological demands of milk production and either become too lame, too worn out, or too underproductive to keep using. Bob attributes his herd's longevity to a number of factors. He says that grass is more nutritious than silage (green fodder stored in airtight conditions for use as winter feed) and other grass hay substitutes. Bob doesn't use corn, either, which he says "isn't what a cow is designed for."

Daily grazing helps keep his cows in shape, he says, which cuts down on lameness, and pasture keeping helps reduce respiratory and communicative diseases. Bob's cows also get a long dry off following lactation, so that they have plenty of time to rejuvenate udder tissue.

"We won't work these cows to death. We give them a long rest period," he adds.

And finally, he doesn't demand peak production. Emerald Veil cows produce anywhere from five to eleven gallons of milk per day, but the average is closer to six. He says that's about 20 percent less than a normal, commercial dairy. Lower production puts much less stress on his Jerseys—a breed whose productivity is already just two-thirds that of Holsteins. Whereas commercial dairyman Jon Slutsky was pushing close to 28,000 pounds of milk annually per cow, Bob Bansen's Jerseys put out about half that.

Bob says that despite this, his farm is as financially healthy as it has ever been. High demand and premium prices characterize today's organic dairy market. (While I was writing this, the nationwide price for organic butter was double that of non-organic, a gallon of organic milk was 70 percent higher, and an eight-ounce package of natural cheese cost 76 percent more).

Bob benefits directly from these premium prices. At the beginning of the year, Organic Valley sets producer prices for milk and contracts with its farmers to sell milk at those prices. So, Bob knows roughly what he'll make based on his production estimates, making financial planning reasonably reliable.

Meanwhile, a conventional dairyman like Jon Slutsky is at the mercy of the commodity market. In the year I spent researching dairy farming, the "mailbox" price of milk (the average size check a farmer receives for his milk) plunged by nine dollars, from a near-record high of about twenty-five to about sixteen dollars per hundred pounds. Meanwhile, the mailbox price paid for the equivalent quantity of organic milk stayed consistent at thirty-five dollars per hundredweight and thirty-nine for "grass milk," which is produced by cows fed solely on organic grass.

Because demand in the organic market exceeds supply, organic dairy processors must compete to secure milk contracts and gain the allegiance of farmers who've committed to organic. This has given Organic Valley, which has more member farmers than any other organic dairy producer, the power to set the market price for organic milk. More than half of all organic dairy farmers in the

United States belong to Organic Valley, while only one-quarter sell to Horizon. (Aurora, the third big player, produces its own milk). In order to hold on to its share of producers, Horizon therefore can't offer sellers less for their milk without losing the dairymen to competitors.

Consequently, Organic Valley has become the de facto protector of small, independent dairy farmers like the Bansens. The typical Organic Valley dairy farm milks approximately sixty-five to seventy cows.

Even if an organic dairy farmer chooses not to sell his milk to Organic Valley, he or she still receives roughly the same premium price for milk set by the member co-op. This has enabled many small, conventional dairy farmers willing and able to convert to organic to stay in business, says Regina Beidler, whose family owns an organic dairy farm in Vermont.

"Organic farming often provides a fair and sustained price for farmers, which allows farms like ours to continue to thrive while offering opportunities to other farms across the country," she said.

But the presence of large-scale organic farms modeled upon the confinement dairy plan has raised concerns about organic's future, particularly among small-scale, pasture-based dairy farmers. In 2008, it became public knowledge that Organic Valley had been purchasing milk from a ten-thousand-cow confinement-style dairy in Texas. This led to an uprising among the rank-and-file co-op members, who forced Organic Valley's board to cancel the dairy's contract.

Their action underscored a schism that persists in the organic farming movement. On the one hand are those who believe that organic should support small, family-owned farms where the animals benefit from the natural system of pasture raising. On the other are those who argue that in order to meet public demand for a healthy alternative to conventional dairy products, organic dairying needs to adopt large-scale production methods that will help lower prices and make organic more affordable to the masses.

"There's a certain idealistic appreciation for a farm with ten cows grazing on a hill at sunset," said a former Horizon executive. "But there are 280 million people in the United States. If moms and consumers care about avoiding hormones and antibiotics, then it's our job to fill that need as much as possible. And if profits are rooted in noble causes and honorable intentions, then honesty pays. Long ago they said small was beautiful; they forgot to tell you, it's not profitable."

Bob Bansen begs to differ. And he'd say that's beside the point.

"For productivity, it's important to have happy cows," he said. "If a cow is at her maximum health and her maximum contentedness, she's profitable. I don't even really manage my farm so much from a fiscal standpoint as from a cow standpoint, because I know that if I take care of those cows, the bottom line will take care of itself."

As organic gained momentum at the turn of the twenty-first century, noted author Michael Pollan, whom many credit as the driving force behind the "local" direct-from-farm food movement, identified a schism in the organic-buying public that has long-term implications for farmers like Bob Bansen. A minority of consumers are the old school "true naturals," whom Pollan describes as "outwardly directed, socially conscious consumers devoted to the proposition of 'better food for a better planet.'" These were the people who created and fostered the organic market in the first place.

But growth in the industry is increasingly driven by a larger group of consumers called "health seekers," who Pollan claims make up about 20 percent of the public. These individuals are inwardly focused in their motives and interested primarily in their own health rather than the health of the planet, or in the case of dairy, the health of the cows.

The environmental reforms that resulted in cleaner air and water in the 1970s might not have happened had it not been for middle class and upper class Americans turning up the pressure on government to take action. But that interest could not be separated from the public good, as we all drink the same water and breathe the same air.

With organics, however, it's easy to take the position of "I've got mine . . . you're on your own." When a large proportion of the more influential consumers are no longer concerned with the healthfulness of the entire food system (since they can afford to eat organic foods), the pressure to make reforms to that system evaporates.

This is one of the arguments for industrial scale organic agriculture, which aims to lower the price of organic dairy, produce, fruits, meats, etc. so that it can be accessible to "the masses." It may not achieve the aims of organic purists who started the movement, its proponents argue, but it provides for the most general good for the most people by making organic more affordable.

I try not to take positions on what's best for society, but in this case, I would make a stand for the cows *and* the wholesomeness of the product. A Washington State University study of regular and organic milk concluded that there are significant health benefits to organic, which has measurably higher levels of the beneficial protein linolaic acid and omega-3 fatty acid, along with other nutrients. This enhanced nutrient quality is attributed to the higher fresh forage intake of organic cows. Furthermore, the National Institutes of Health concluded that consumption of predominantly organic dairy products may improve public health by decreasing omega-6 to omega-3 ratios from today's unhealthy levels.

A majority of small organic dairy farms (about two-thirds) use pasture to provide more than half of their cows' nutrition throughout the growing season. But in the attempt to scale up in size, it becomes less feasible for the dairy farm to rely to such an extent on pasture grazing. So, their feed system incorporates more grains (which also increase a cow's productivity), albeit organic ones. This change diminishes the nutritional benefits that more grass in the diet appears to deliver. Consequently, the organic milk from confinement-style organic dairies might well be an inferior product, as advocates of small farm organics have long claimed.

If, in the end, large-scale organic dairies deliver a product only slightly better than commercial milk without also providing a better environment for the cows, is it worth it? Though consumers say that the health benefits of organic are the most important reason they purchase it, about one-third also say that they support organic because it improves the overall welfare of the animals themselves.

While visiting Bob Bansen's farm, I feel satisfied that I'm getting my money's worth when it comes to his cows' organic milk. For decades, the dairy industry has sold us the pastoral image of cows grazing on verdant pastures on farms owned by happy families who care about their animals. Through its own advertising and promotion, the dairy industry implicitly admits that this is the most natural life of a cow, and the life that we as consumers expect them to have. But for decades, the conventional dairy industry has steadily moved in the direction of an entirely different model in which cows are ever-more productive units in milk factories masquerading as farms.

I don't think it's unrealistic to believe that we can have healthy, nutritional, organic dairy products for the masses without resorting to the huge confinement-type operations that have already forced tens of thousands of families to abandon their conventional dairy businesses. After all, one of the substantive reasons people are willing to pay more for organic is the belief that it affords the cows and the farmers who care for them better lives.

To my mind, knowing that that glass of milk or that slice of cheddar cheese comes from a cow that has a name seems worth a price we should all be willing to pay.

TWENTY-ONE

THE MOO-NIVERSE

*An alien ecologist observing earth might conclude
that cattle is the dominant species in our biosphere.*
—David Wright Hamilton, biologist.

In 1992, more than forty thousand people lined up behind twenty-nine cash registers for the grand opening of the first McDonald's in China. For years, the Beijing restaurant would hold the distinction of being the busiest McDonald's on earth.

Since the arrival of Ronald McDonald and Colonel Sanders (who'd come to Beijing five years earlier), fast-food restaurants have multiplied like bunnies across China: more western fast-food restaurants operate there than in Canada, Russia, and India combined. Today, urban Chinese diners visit fast-food restaurants more frequently than Americans do.

Fast food's explosive growth, combined with the arrival of western-style supermarkets like Walmart and Costco, have given the Chinese, a population with no prior dairy tradition, an unprecedented taste for beef and dairy goods. As a result, China's dairy industry is growing exponentially, having gone from just half a million cows in 1967 (the year McDonald's opened its first outlets outside the United States) to more than 12.6 million today. China is now the world's third largest dairy producer, behind the United States and India, as well as the world's largest dairy importer.

China's booming dairy industry represents the final stage of cattle's global takeover. From the cow's early domestication in Turkey close to 8,500 years ago, it has spread across the globe to become the animal kingdom's most dominant species, at least when measured by mass. There are now about 1.4 billion cattle on earth, about one-fifth of them used exclusively for dairy. Their combined weight is more than two-and-a-half times that of the second most massive species, humans. And if current trends continue, another billion will be added by 2050.

One of the biggest challenges of the twenty-first century will be to figure out what to do with all those cows. It's not an exaggeration to say that cattle and other farm animals present a mortal threat to humankind. Ample scientific evidence indicates that our taste for meat and dairy is already having calamitous environmental consequences.

Cows gobble up one-third of all our grains and guzzle down 5 percent of our fresh water. Residues from pesticides, herbicides, and fertilizers used to raise feed crops, plus manure runoff generated by hundreds of millions of cows, are poisoning water supplies and oceans and draining underground water resources.

Cow burps, farts, and manure contribute to global warming—according to one highly cited United Nation's report, cattle produce nearly 10 percent of human-caused greenhouse gasses. When you add in emissions from goats, sheep, pigs, and other farm animals, our livestock's contribution to global warming exceeds that of planes, trains, ships, and automobiles.

Dairy scientists and commercial dairymen, for the most part, believe we can breed our way out of these environmental disasters. The strategy, they argue, is to continue improving dairy cattle output to reduce overall cow numbers, or at least keep them in check. Chad Dechow, an associate professor of dairy genetics at Penn State University, made this case in a single, easy-to-digest sentence.

"One high-producing cow eliminates the need for a lot of lousy cows," he said.

It's logic that's hard to deny. In Dechow's vision, the dairy cow of the future will perform more and more like Ever-Green-View My 1326-ET and the new record holder, a cow named Bur Walleye Gigi, who added another two tons to the milk production record as I was completing this book.

In the 1940s, America had four times as many dairy cows as we do today. But, thanks to all the progress farmers have made in improving dairy cow efficiency, the national herd produces almost twice the milk that it did back in my father's youth. Let me repeat that: we now make twice the milk, with one-quarter the number of cows.

That's obviously good for the planet; fewer cows producing more milk means fewer emissions, less feed, less water, etc. And there's more. According to Cornell University researchers, today's highly efficient cows generate only one-quarter the manure per gallon of milk to be produced. They produce only half the methane per gallon, too. Those are significant figures. Especially when you multiply them by hundreds of millions of large farm animals.

As long as we humans continue to insist on enjoying Lionel Sternberger's culinary masterpiece, the cheeseburger, and all the other delicious foods that dairy provides for us, we're going to need more efficient cows across the entire global cattle industry.

But what impact do ever-higher production demands have on cows? Is it possible we're already reaching the upper limits of what's biologically desirable, or feasible? According to Dechow, the science of genomics and advances in reproductive technology have enabled the dairy industry to make cows not only more productive, but sturdier. Evaluators of Ever-Green-View My 1326-ET, for example, scored her conformation as "excellent" in overall shape and fitness, a mark of exceptional health that fewer than 1 percent of the nation's cows attain.

Likewise, her super-producing competitor, Gigi, earned third place in a national Holstein show for the quality of her udders—a measure of grave importance to dairy farmers. "We're really sure that she's a complete cow—her width and length, her feet and legs and udders are out of this world, and she really likes to milk," said her owner, Bob Behnke.

Dechow and others in the field of dairy improvement make the case that one doesn't have to sacrifice a cow's health to achieve extremely high production. But there's a counter-argument that says breeding cows with the physiques and stamina of world-class athletes may be stretching their biological and physiological limitations to the max.

It takes an almost unfathomable amount of metabolic energy to produce large volumes of milk while simultaneously carrying a calf (most milk cows are re-impregnated within four months of giving birth, and carry the calf for nine months). In human terms, Nigel Cook, dairy expert at the University of Wisconsin's School of Veterinary Medicine, put it this way: "They have a metabolic rate that's their equivalent of Lance Armstrong doing the Tour de France."

But at the conclusion of the Tour de France, Armstrong could get off his bike and go sightseeing. Modern dairy cows, on the other hand, maintain this pace over a milking season that typically lasts ten months. A cow gets a break only when she is allowed to dry out then rest for the two-month period preceding her next birth. But rest is a relative term as she's still on the hook for the gestation of her calf, whose birth weight (if she's a Holstein) will be around ninety pounds.

Does it sound like making vast quantities of milk is utterly exhausting? To me it did. And my thoughts were confirmed by John Webster, Emeritus Professor of Animal Husbandry at England's University of Bristol, who told me, "The dairy cow is exposed to more abnormal physiological demands than any other class of farm animal, making her a supreme example of an overworked mother."

Reproductive technology—which includes shipped semen, embryo transfer, in vitro fertilization, cloning, and genomics—is allowing us to make cows of incredible bio-productivity. And if the global demand for dairy and dairy beef continues to grow, we're going to need to replace a lot more "lousy cows," to borrow Dr. Dechow's words, with efficient ones.

But the question I had to ask myself was, should we be doing this? Four decades ago, dairy cows usually lived into double digits. Today's commercial cow seldom surpasses the age of five. Most dairy cows in this system are spent, lame, or dropping in productivity after just three productive milking cycles.

As the cliché saying goes, "There ain't no such thing as a free lunch." Nor, I might add, a free glass of milk to go along with it. A price must be paid for the modern milk cow's enormous biological productivity, and that bill is mainly being picked up by the cows.

A small but growing group of bioscience researchers and technology entrepreneurs believe there's a better solution. They'd like to do away with cows (and chickens, and other farm animals) altogether, yet still harvest their biological gifts in the form of lab-raised meats and dairy products. If the dreams of these futuristic thinkers come to pass, the world may be dining on artificial cheeseburgers (and hot dogs and milk shakes and chicken nuggets and more) in the not-too-distant future.

In 2013, researchers in London made a big splash by cooking the first artificial hamburger grown from muscle stem cells cultured in a lab. At a large gathering attended by international press, Josh Schonwald, a food writer and author of the book *Taste of Tomorrow*, sampled the bio-cultured beef patty. He gave it high marks for eye-appeal and "mouth feel." But he also remarked that it lacked the juiciness and flavor of the real thing.

Google founder Sergey Brin provided the funding behind Mosa Meats, the Dutch company responsible for the man-made meat patty, whose estimated cost was $330,000. He acknowledged that the team was still a long ways from bringing the product to market. But the publicity the burger garnered, he felt, made the debut a success. With the burger, the Internet entrepreneur and billionaire was making a statement: if we are going to improve animal welfare, we need to find ways to create animal proteins . . . without the animals.

"When you see how these cows are treated, it's certainly something I'm not comfortable with," said Brin.

While many people can empathize with that statement, the hard truth is that unless and until the lab-cultured meat is at least as tasty, if not more so, than conventionally-raised meat, people aren't likely to switch at any price. But already, scientists and entrepreneurs backing cultured meats seem to be edging closer toward satisfying man's blood lust for toothsome meat without the attendant environmental and animal welfare costs.

In 2016, entrepreneurs at the San Francisco Bay Area startup Memphis Meats debuted a lab-grown meatball prepared with Italian herbs and sautéed before an eager audience made up of employees, invited guests, and the media. When an independent taste tester failed to show for the meatball's serving, a random guest stepped up to the plate.

"Tastes like a meatball," said the woman identified by *Newsweek* only as Stephanie, a friend of a friend of a Memphis Meats employee. "Can I have more?"

At eighteen thousand dollars a pound, there weren't a lot of free samples to go around. But the race to bring down costs and get products to market is on among investors, from Silicon Valley venture capitalists to meat industry giant Tyson Foods, who recently pledged $120 million to fund the efforts of lab-based meat and dairy researchers.

These goals are not entirely altruistic. Though the investors believe bio-cultured foods will provide solutions to some of animal agriculture's most vexing environmental and animal welfare problems, they also foresee a global industry in new products worth billions of dollars.

Similar goals motivate a group of biotech entrepreneurs who are at work perfecting bio-engineered dairy products. At Counter Culture Labs, a bioscience incubator housed in a former heavy metal nightclub in Oakland, scientists have "bio hacked" yeast to produce milk proteins. Their end goal is Real Vegan Cheese, a synthetic product that will look and taste like the real thing.

It's not a new technology they're using, but rather a modern twist on an ancient one. Since the dawn of agriculture, humans have fed carbohydrates to yeast, which converted them to beloved end products like wine and beer. The only difference is, instead of producing alcohol, the bio-engineered yeast at Counter Culture labs produces milk proteins. That's accomplished by taking genes that code for milk in cows and inserting them into the yeast's DNA—a "biohack" that's actually a GMO.

Another California company, Perfect Day, has also bioengineered yeast cells to produce milk proteins. Combined with vegetable fats and sugars, the proteins yield milk that's hard to discern from the real thing and has the further advantage of being lactose free, hormone free, and antibiotic free, according to its inventors.

When I shared news of the bio-engineered dairy milk with microbiologist and yeast expert Mark Johnston, he was both skeptical of the results and amused by the possibilities. But after deciding that it was feasible to make milk proteins from genetically modified yeast (and that other components like fats and sugars could be obtained from vegetable sources), he conceded that it was probably a great idea.

"It's easier to feed a flask of yeast cells than a barn full of cows, that's for sure!" he said.

Yet the bio-cultural hurdles of creating lab-based meats and dairy products may prove easier to surmount than the cultural hurdles. Bio-cultured facsimiles could greatly reduce animal suffering and the environmental problems associated with the global cattle industry. They could also provide better food security for the world's seven and a half billion people—and the billions more that will be added in decades to come.

But are people ready for these alternatives? As we've already seen, consumers tend to be skeptical of the claims that these new bioscience technologies are safe. Although genetic modification is not strictly necessary for the production of lab meats, it is for the creation of lab-based dairy goods, which are much more likely to make it to the grocery store in the near-term.

So far, the media has been very kind to these bio-cultured meat and dairy ideas. But once the products reach grocery store shelves, will critics turn on them as they did on the Flavr-Savr Tomato? Only time will tell.

In the meantime, what are we to do with all these cows? I thought that visiting with dairy experts, scientists, food ethicists, and especially dairy farmers would help me sort through the answers. But I came away feeling less certain than when I began.

During my tour of dairy farms, I spent a few hours with Dr. Juan Velez, a Columbian-born veterinarian who directs the animal management program for Aurora Organic dairy. He made a comment that surprised me. He said it's his belief that we will all likely look back on the present as a time when animal protein was plentiful and affordable to the vast majority of humans.

In the meantime, he says, one of the biggest myths that the dairy world needs to address is that big is always bad, and small is always better.

"It's one of the greatest challenges we face, the distance between perception and reality," he told me. "I speak with animal activists who tell me that it is important for them to target the large farms. That you don't get the same traction targeting small farms.

"But the truth is, you will find outstanding cow wellbeing and welfare in large and small farms, in organic and conventional. And you can find horrible welfare in all four systems. It's all about individual management."

And that's exactly what I found.

Before I met Jake Takiff and saw his delightful micro-dairy, Eagle Canyon Farm, I stopped off to visit another raw milk farmer in Langley, Washington. This dairyman kept his two cows in a small, dilapidated barn on the edge of a roadway. I'd gone there to pick up raw milk for my landlord, a naturopathic physician who is a devotee of the stuff.

As I retrieved the jars from a rusty, mildewed fridge in the barn, I was appalled not only at the unsanitary conditions of the stalls, where the cows stood hock-deep in feces, but also at the bony, undernourished condition of the cattle themselves. Though my doctor friend told me I could have a gallon of the milk, I wouldn't have taken a drop of it from those grimy bottles for all the tea in China.

Similarly, after visiting the cloned beef cattle in the Texas Panhandle, I made a swing west to visit Curry County, home to one-fifth of New Mexico's 322,000 dairy cows.

I'd called ahead to try and schedule a commercial farm tour at one of the dozen dairies there, but each one turned me down. Similarly, calls and emails to New Mexico's dairy association proved fruitless. The stonewalling was understandable and expected; in 2014, Mercy For Animals had gone undercover at the Winchester Dairy in Chaves County, New Mexico, and the results hadn't been pretty.

The video showed workers hitting, kicking, and beating cattle with chains, "hot shotting" downer cattle with electric prods, and dragging sick cows chained to a front-end loader. Denver-based Leprino Foods, makers of the mozzarella cheese used by Pizza Hut, Domino's, Papa Johns, and many others, severed its contract with Winchester dairy, which in turn fired its employees and dispersed its cattle to other Chaves County dairies.

Absent an invitation, the best I could do was to drive out to one of the dairies and see what I could see. And what I could see astounded me. Traveling down a paved county road, I came upon a complex of dairy farms stretching across 640 acres of land, every acre jam-packed with Holsteins. Further north, another square mile was taken up by a massive cattle feedlot. If La Luna Dairy could be compared to a 7-Eleven, this concentrated cattle compound was a Walmart Super Center. In the entire two square miles, I saw not a single green blade of grass.

Along the Curry County road where I was driving, there were actually three separate dairy businesses. All were owned by different entities, but they coordinated like a man's three-piece suit. One end of the row was a proper dairy whose cows produced milk. On the other end of the row was a dairy feedlot where culled cows and dairy steers were being fed high-energy grain diets to fatten them for sale to meat packers. And sandwiched between was what's known as a "custom calf" or "heifer grower" operation, which produces replacement heifers—young cows—for other dairies. It was the latter that affected me most.

As I drove along, I passed row after row after row of decrepit hutches little bigger than doghouses. Each squalid hut was surrounded by a small pig fence that left the baby calf barely enough room to turn around. There was no hay for bedding, as there had been at La Luna; the calves had to lie down in their own runny manure.

In one row, I spotted a group of Hispanic workers in a farm truck filled with baby bottles. One drove as the other three hustled to the hutches, placing a bottle in a holder and hurrying to the next. The young men all wore handkerchiefs around their mouths to block out the swirling cloud of manure dust kicked up by the truck. There was no interaction between the men and the calves and not a single adult cow to be seen. Yet the sight of the vehicle caused the hungry calves to bawl, as though calling out for their mother's udders.

Later, I located satellite images of the custom calf operation on Google Earth and counted the dilapidated hutches by rows. There were seven thousand of them.

My experiences have shown me that farm size is not the determining factor in the quality of a cow's life. Nor, for that matter, whether the cows are raised using raw, organic, or conventional practices. Raisa Slutsky, the daughter of two former goat-milking hippies was right. What matters most is compassion. And that's a hard thing to put a label on.

HORSES

A horse is a thing of beauty . . . none will tire of looking at him as long as he displays himself in his splendor.

—Greek historian Xenophon

TWENTY-TWO

LIFE ON A HORSE RANCH

No hour of life is wasted that is spent in the saddle.
—Winston Churchill

It all began with a horse named Peanut.

Thirty-five years ago, I was a freshman at Colorado College. My Dutch roommate, Hennie, invited me to join him on a school-supported horseback riding adventure. It sounded like fun, so I signed up.

One Saturday morning in May, we arrived at Bear Basin Ranch, a ramshackle old place owned by a fellow alumnus. As we gathered our equipment from the van, we were greeted by the ranch's manager, Amy Finger. She ushered us into "the bunkhouse," a century old farm residence made of weather-bleached logs and concrete chinking. We threw our suitcases and backpacks onto the rough-hewn triple-decker bunk beds, then shuffled into the pinewood-floored dining room, where a large wood stove was still radiating heat from the morning meal.

"There's no running water, but you can wash up after the ride in the sink. The water is in these jugs," said Amy, indicating ten-gallon containers on the floor, "but be sparing. We have to haul the water up from the water trough.

"Also, there's no electricity. We have oil lamps for light, but please don't adjust the wicks. They smoke and get soot on their glass chimneys if they're not done right."

In short, Bear Basin had yet to emerge from the nineteenth century. Which, to me, made the horse adventure even better—it was like a trip back in time, to when the horse was still a necessary part of the landscape.

After our orientation, we walked down to the corral made of rough-sawn wood where a group of horses stood saddled. Dressed in a straw cowboy hat shading a cascade of blonde curls, faded blue overalls, and Converse All-Stars, head wrangler Dan Weiss gave us a ten-minute riding lesson which covered the barest rudiments of mounting, steering, sitting the trot and canter and, most importantly, stopping. The New Age horseman divided us into groups by riding ability. I took my place among the beginners while Dan began handing out horses. Eventually, he brought out a buckskin gelding and handed me the reins.

"Your horse's name is Peanut," he said.

"Hi Peanut," I said, looking him in the near eye and stroking my hand along his neck. After tightening the cinch, Dan flipped the stirrup toward me. I took hold of the saddle horn and clambered up into the seat. Dan adjusted my stirrups then moved on. I stroked Peanut's neck some more while the remaining riders were readied. Once everyone was on horseback, Dan deftly mounted his horse and led us out the corral gate and onto the trail.

It was the kind of day in the mountains when the voices of song-birds carry on the breeze for miles. The sun was perfect—warm, not hot. Our view of the Sangre de Cristo Range deserved to be on the cover of a National Geographic magazine.

We rode the trails for five hours, mostly at a walk, although Dan also gave us opportunities to trot and canter. He didn't believe in nose-to-tail riding, the staple of most dude ranches, but instead encouraged us to spread out and get our horses to respond to our reins. Peanut, however, resisted straying far from his pal Alfred Packer, a mouse-gray horse named for the famous Colorado cannibal. Since Alfred was carrying a pretty co-ed who liked talking, Peanut's sticky behavior bothered me not in the least.

The experience was thrilling and I was immediately smitten with horses. I liked the connection with the animal, so different from riding a mountain bike or a trail motorcycle. There was also something wonderful about being up so high. It felt powerful, even regal. I was no longer one of those poor, miserable souls on foot.

By day's end, I'd bonded with Peanut. I loved the feel of his hide, the earthy smell of his sweat, and the warmth in his kind brown eyes. I remember wanting to thank him for carrying me over many miles, but didn't know quite how to do that. When we got back to the corral, I dismounted but lingered there, petting Peanut for a while before handing his reins to Dan.

The next day when they were handing out horses, I asked for my pal Peanut. And my love affair with the horse continued. At day's end, I wrapped my arms around his big neck, inhaled his horsey scent, and rubbed his velvety nose. I left the ranch feeling the tiniest bit of sadness that I wouldn't be there to ride him the next day and the next.

But as fate turned out, I'd see Peanut again. On a signboard at school was an announcement that Bear Basin needed summer horse wranglers. I called Amy and applied for the job. Although I had no practical horse experience, my background as a wilderness guide and my first aid training got me a position. When the school semester ended, I moved to the ranch and took up residence in a small, dirt-floor cabin called "the Hobbit Hole." It was as cave-like as it sounds but fortunately, nobody thought to nickname me "Frodo." At night, mice scurried over my sleeping bag and cold wind whistled through the gaps in the chinking. But I was happy.

I worked at the ranch for four summers, using the money I earned to help put myself through college. Eventually, I would move up from the Hobbit Hole to the Corral House to the Main House, the plushest home on the place. I would go from junior to senior wrangler, and graduate from a know-nothing "green" rider to a fledgling horse trainer. It was an education, one vastly different but just as valuable to my future career as my formal studies.

"Total immersion" best describes that education. I was often in the saddle for ten hours a day, six days a week, riding several different horses each day. One of the first things I learned was that Peanut was not "all that." As my skills quickly progressed, I realized he was pokey and not terribly responsive. After my first month, our love affair had cooled. I moved on to better and more willing horses, following a pattern that's familiar to most horse riders. We're always on the lookout for the next, better horse.

Fortunately, there were many from which to choose. Bear Basin had sixty-five horses, and I came to know them as a schoolteacher knows her class. Each had his or her own virtues and vices.

Santa Fe, for instance, was a handsome chestnut Quarter horse with a white blaze. He looked good standing in the corral but was as lazy as a professional bed tester. Rosita was an all-white half-Arab, clever in her ways; she liked to hide in the woods during morning roundup so that she could stay out on pasture and have the day off.

Then there was Barney, a big old Roman-nosed gelding with a graying muzzle who knew how to open gates and who kept his own harem of mares, like a stallion. I admired his smarts but not his rough, pile-driving trot or his tendency to bully the other horses, especially Peanut's pal Alfred Packer.

Some I considered my "teacher's pets." Among my favorites was Skeeter, a fast-galloping blue dun with a black stripe down her back. She never liked to be passed or outrun, and was the horse to pick for a race. Misty was a chestnut Quarter horse mare with a kind eye, a willing attitude and smooth at any gait. She was ideal for long days on the trail, and always my preference while guiding.

My favorite activity was rounding up the herd at dawn. It was a job most of the wranglers loathed because it meant getting up before the coffee was made and saddling up in the dark and the cold. But I loved the absolute stillness of the land and the warm blasts of steam coming from the big, dilated nostrils of my "catch" horse. It was quiet and peaceful trotting out in dew-soaked, knee-high pasture grass just as the sun hit the snow-covered mountains, blasting the gray world like a shotgun load of color.

Watching Whammo, my herding dog, gather all the horses into a big bunch often inspired awe. I reveled in the power of the herd's steel-clad hoofs as they shook the ground.

My work at the ranch and a subsequent job tending cattle and riding colts further south led me to the offices of *Western Horseman*, where I spent eighteen years as a columnist and freelance feature writer. Those assignments helped put me on the backs of some of the finest horses in the world—athletic cutting horses and reining horses worth hundreds of thousands of dollars; Arabian show horses, racing Quarter horses, an imported European dressage horse, several roping horses used at the National Finals Rodeo, and even a Thoroughbred jumping horse. I got so spoiled I could hardly stand to get on a horse that wasn't distinguished in some way. After you've driven a Ferrari, it's hard to go back to a Hyundai.

But despite having amazing experiences on some of the most refined and well-trained horses on earth, I still recall most clearly that first ride on Peanut, a plodder at best. The experience stands out as one of my favorite riding memories. I think I've been chasing that feeling ever since.

Horses are an addiction. Nearly every horse person I know can recall a moment, usually early in life, when they became hooked. We keep at it so that we can recapture that exquisite moment of being one with this powerful, sentient creature as it carried us, god-like, across a golden pasture.

TWENTY-THREE

IN THE BEGINNING

*If God made anything more beautiful than horses,
he kept it to himself.*

—Anonymous

I t's a neat coincidence that my horse education began in Colorado,
because that's where horses began, too.

Just as the Rockies finished pushing up from the plains fifty-
five million years ago, the earliest horses emerged on what are
now the Great Plains. They were about the size of my Australian
shepherds, and as many of you will recall from biology texts, their
name was *eohippus.*

Eohippus didn't look much like a horse, and it didn't live much
like one either. In fact, if you happened upon one, you'd probably
mistake it for a very odd-looking dog. It had an arched back, a short

face (compared to modern horses) that tapered into a rounded nose, and it walked on foot pads, not hoofs. It was adapted to life in the shadowy woods and ate mainly fruits and leaves.

At the time, the world was a considerably warmer and more luscious place than it is today, and was almost entirely covered in forests. North America had a subtropical climate, with palm trees and fig trees growing as far north as Alaska. Camels, rhinos, and alligators flourished alongside little eohippus, who lived with few changes in form for close to twenty million years.

But over the course of thirty-eight million years, the climate changed from a sauna to an ice box. Sheets of glacial ice covered the poles, the subtropical forests ebbed south, and across much of North America and Eurasia, vast prairie grasslands took their place. Eohippus was forced to evolve.

Fortunately, equids (of which eohippus is considered the first) were primed to exploit the new conditions. As their descendants moved out onto the grasslands, they evolved spatula-shaped front teeth to crop the grass and coarse, ridged molars to grind it. These teeth grew continuously and had a tough cement outer layer to counter the abrasive effect of prairie sand.

In order to outrun predators in the open, their legs grew longer, their respiratory systems more efficient, and their bodies bigger and stronger. Their leg bones fused together to form powerful columns and, along with their muscles, became specialized for efficient, powerful back-and-forward strides. Most significantly, the ancestral horse began to stand on tiptoe (another adaptation for speed), with the toes eventually uniting into one central digit with a hard, wedge-shaped nail: the hoof.

The reason we know so much about equine evolution is because the bones of these ancestral horses have been found throughout the American West. In the 1870s, a paleo-archaeologist named Othniel Charles Marsh amassed a large collection of equid fossils spanning millions of years of evolution. He arranged them to show a steady progression beginning with little eohippus and ending with the relatively gargantuan modern horse, *Equus*. The result made tangible the principle of Darwinian evolution. Thomas Huxley, an English biologist known as "Darwin's bulldog" due to his zealous advocacy of evolutionary theory, seized upon the model to promote Darwin's theory.

The American Museum of Natural History featured the exhibit, helping educate millions of people about evolution. As one of the best examples of descent with modification, Marsh's exhibit was also featured in nearly every twentieth century high school biology textbook.

Scientists continued to unearth new types of fossil horses, leading them to conclude that things were generally messier than Marsh and Huxley had supposed, with plenty of false starts and dead ends. As recently as five million years ago, there were up to a dozen distinct varieties of horses in North America—some big, some small, some with hoofs, some with toes, some dwelling in the forests, and others roaming the Great Plains. But for some reason (probably having to do with changes in climate), all but one eventually became extinct.

The sole survivor, *Equus*, dates from about four million years ago. It is all that remains of equids in modern times, much as we are all that remain of upright-walking hominids.

When the beginning of the ice age descended on the Northern Hemisphere about 2.6 million years ago, early *Equus* began migrating out of North America, crossing over the Bering Land Bridge from what is now Alaska to Siberia. Some spread south into Asia, the Middle East, and North Africa to become onagers and wild asses. Others went deeper into African to evolve as zebras.

But a group of them continued moving west, spreading across Asia, the Middle East, and Europe to evolve as the "true horse," *Equus ferus caballus*. About forty to fifty thousand years ago, modern humans moved into Eurasia and encountered their first "true" horses. In time, of course, the two would become intertwined in ways that would shape the course of human and equine history.

Paleolithic people hunted the large Pleistocene mammals of the open grasslands. However, they were tied to the edges of forests, where they could obtain firewood and windbreaks. From these forest margins, the animals migrating across the open grasslands were the most fascinating and arresting objects in Stone Age man's visual world—the prehistoric equivalent of the television.

From Paleolithic cave art, we know that horses played an oversized role in the thoughts and imaginations of Stone Age hunters. For tens of thousands of years, Paleolithic artists copiously and prominently painted horses in their galleries.

Nowhere is this more true than in the Lascaux cave in the Dordogne region of Southern France. Inside is a collection of more than six hundred paintings that decorate the walls and ceilings. Of those, 364 are of horses. Radiocarbon dating puts their dates of creation around seventeen thousand years ago. But similar drawings have been found in much older cave art, such as the 33,500-year-old paintings in France's Chauvet cave. Which is to say, horses were on people's minds for a long, long time.

Many art historians and some archaeologists have speculated that the animal paintings were created by shamans and were important as religious symbols. But for natural historian and sculptor R. Dale Guthrie, the search for religious meaning in the art obscures something more obvious and organic: primitive humans knew and understood horses in a very comprehensive and intimate way. The artists' amazingly accurate depictions, not only of horses but all other animals, reflect the keen observation and understanding of the animals' observers.

"Paleolithic art shows the grittiness of reality, but also the sensitivity of sophisticated animal watchers, hunters, trackers, and admirers. In the art, we see how the animals fed, drank, nursed, knelt, slept, rested, defecated, thought, moved, groomed, courted, copulated . . ." Guthrie wrote in his book *The Nature of Paleolithic Art.*

"These hunter-artists of Eurasia documented mammalian behaviors that were not studied or illustrated so well again until the twentieth century, when natural historians refined observations of animal behavior in the wild into the evolutionary discipline of ethology," he concludes.

When they picked up a piece of charcoal or pigment they'd prepared and began to draw, prehistoric artists didn't just imagine a vague idea of a horse. They pictured the horses' lives in very minute detail. They knew how horses moved at the walk, trot, and gallop, how a stallion behaved among mares, how a horse's muscles and tendons moved in motion, how its mane swayed in the breeze, the length of its coat in winter, the curl of the stallion's lip when courting, the intention of a horse's gestures. Lifetimes of observation and accumulated knowledge were shared in camps and on hunts, and passed down from generation to generation over tens of thousands of years.

Looking at these ancient stone-age cave paintings, we can appreciate them as masterpieces of both art and natural history. Stone age humans shared a deep and intimate relationship with horses, knowing them in ways inconceivable to us in modern times.

TWENTY-FOUR

HORSES AND HUMANS

If a horse misses its herd, it stamps its back hooves. If a man misses company, he harnesses his horse.

—Kazak saying.

I t's a long way from Colorado to Kazakhstan, but the ancestors of the saddle horses at Bear Basin Ranch began their journey toward domestication in the wilds of that faraway place.

After nearly fifty million years of evolution in the Americas, horses died out here. Based on the latest evidence, the last remaining ones perished just 7,600 years ago. Most scientists believe that a combination of climate change and human hunting caused the horses' extinction. Whatever the case, they would not return to the American continent for five thousand years, with the arrival of Spanish explorers in 1519.

So, from North America, the story of the horse and its domestication moves to the Eurasian Steppe. Stretching from the Pacific coast of Asia to the plains of Hungary, the Great Steppe is a series of vast grasslands devoid of trees and woody shrubs. When the horse migrated out of North America, these grasslands provided an ideal environment, as they closely matched the conditions of western North America. Only the Eurasian steppe is immensely larger, reaching almost one-fifth of the way around the Earth.

Some five thousand years ago, tribes of hunters called the Botai people inhabited the northern region of the Kazakstan portion of the Steppe. It was the heartland of the wild European horse's native range.

Life for nomadic hunter-gatherers of the Steppe consisted of following herds of large wild animals, much as the Inuit and Sami people followed reindeer in more recent times. They travelled in small bands and were constantly on the move, remaining in encampments for short periods before packing up and moving on.

But for a time, at least, the Botai lived differently. Instead of constantly moving, they formed small, semi-permanent settlements in homes that they dug in the sod. In 2006, a group of Botai village sites became the subject of intense study by a team of researchers headed by Sandra Olson, an archaeologist and horse domestication specialist at Carnegie Museum of Natural History in Pittsburg.

The Botai economy relied almost entirely upon horses. Of the 300,000 bone fragments recovered there, more than 90 percent are equine. Cut marks on the bones indicate that horsemeat was the people's primary food source. More importantly, the bones at Botai were different from those of the wild horses living then on the Steppe.

According to the researchers, the horses were "appreciably more slender" than the robust native horses in the area, and more like domestic horses today. Though it's not clear if the changes were due to the Botai people practicing selective breeding, that's the most logical explanation. Horses at Botai had already passed through a period of domestication.

Researchers also found wear marks on the horses' teeth and damage to skeletal tissue in their mouths, which point toward the possibility that Botai people used bits and bridles to control the animals. Reinforcing this view, the scientists identified rawhide-working tools from the ruins. Rawhide is a common material used by horse people for millennia to create equipment such as hobbles, saddles, whips, and lariats.

Adding more to the argument were pottery shards containing fatty deposits from horse's milk. To this day, the people of the Eurasian Steppe drink fermented horse's milk as a staple beverage. Botai's villagers could not have milked free-roaming wild mares.

Surveying one of the Botai sites called Krasnyi Yar, the team used magnetic sensors to locate traces of postholes where fences once stood. The ground within the enclosures contained abnormally high levels of nitrogen and phosphates—just what one expects to find in manure-enriched soil. This and the round shape of some of the pens made it almost certain that the Botai used them as corrals.

It's impossible to say whether the Botai or some other Steppe culture domesticated the horse. Recent theories hold that the animal was domesticated at more than a dozen locations. Doubtless, once one of the Steppe peoples discovered the value of keeping horses, rather than following them, the concept swept across the Eurasian Steppe like a grassfire.

What didn't catch on were permanent settlements. According to Olson, later people of the area adopted shepherding and cattle raising. The introduction of new domesticated animals from the south required a more nomadic lifestyle, as these species couldn't survive the sub-zero winter temperatures of Northern Kazakhstan. The people sacrificed their homes for the riches of wool fiber and mutton, plus fattier milk with which to make cheeses and yogurt.

Juliet Clutton-Brock of the Department of Zoology at the National History Museum in London calls the transition from hunting to the keeping of tamed livestock "the most important change in social and cultural behavior to have occurred throughout the history of the human species."

At the root of that change was something we take for granted: food storage. With the domestication of crops and animals, it became possible for the first time to feed entire groups of people from relatively small numbers of food-sources and still have food left over for the lean winter months. Like crops, domesticated animals embodied a means to store food protein for use when it was needed. Acknowledging this, Clutton-Brock famously described livestock as "a walking larder."

For nomadic Steppe cultures, horses supplied not only meat and mare's milk, but also hides for clothing; bone and horns that became needles, awls, and body decoration; sinew and rawhide for lashing; stomach organs for carrying liquids; and fats used for candles, soap, and salves. They even burned dried horse manure for cooking and heating. (Try it sometime—you'll be surprised at the pleasant odor). The horse was more than just transportation on the Steppe—it was a Walmart on hoofs.

With the domestication of the horse, the stage was set for Eurasian Steppe tribes to play a key role in the development of civilization. Horses greatly contributed to warfare, and it is as warriors that the people of the Steppe fill more than a thousand years in history books.

A good argument can be made that nomadic, pastoral living naturally created the conditions for the development of warrior tribes and warfare itself. The reason goes to the nature of keeping herds of animals. They're easy to steal. You just come in, overpower their owners, and have the loot walk away with you under its own power.

Among pastoral horse cultures of the Steppe, status within and among tribes depended upon protecting and increasing flocks and expanding grazing territory. Unlike hunter/gatherer societies, whose strength lay in cooperation and communal sharing to maintain the health and size of the clan, pastoralism rewarded the accumulation of wealth in the form of animals, which were hoarded rather than shared. Warfare with outsiders was the most expedient way for the pastoral clans and tribes to gain wealth.

Once a tribe was rich in livestock, its people had to be constantly on guard against attacks from outside and even insurrections within. Dominating a region of the Steppe, therefore, required that the horsemen be not only livestock keepers, but also aggressive, disciplined, and loyal warriors. Once horses were domesticated, they became an absolute necessity among the Steppe tribes—they conferred such an advantage on the battlefield that to be without them was to perish. And because the nomad lifestyle depended upon constant travel on horseback, the people of the Steppe soon became the most accomplished riders on earth.

Throughout ancient and medieval times, warrior tribes of nomadic horsemen would periodically sweep down from the Steppe to invade the civilizations of Europe, the Middle East, and China. With their superior horsemanship and the ability to raise vast numbers of horses on the grasslands, they almost invariably overwhelmed and defeated their foes. The names of these tribes— the Sythians, Huns, Turks, Mongols—and their leaders still echo across time and history. The most famous of all was Genghis Khan.

TWENTY-FIVE

WHEN HORSEMEN RULED THE WORLD

A Mongol without a horse is like a bird without the wings.
                                        —Traditional saying.

I f you've ever driven across the vast emptiness of eastern Wyoming, following Interstate 80 just north of the Colorado border, you begin to have a picture of Mongolia. But to gain a more precise impression, you need to erase from your mind the roads, power lines, fences, buildings, and all other signs of civilization until nothing remains but the mountains, the prairie, and an impossibly blue sky.

In place of the Rockies are the Altai Mountains, which rise up from the plains to form the western and northern boundaries of the country. These glacial peaks, whose tallest summits reach beyond fourteen thousand feet, create a nearly impassible natural border between Mongolia and its northern neighbor, Russia. To the south is an equally formidable land barrier, the Gobi desert, which separates the country from China.

Sandwiched between the mountains and desert is the Mongolian Steppe, a vast sea of grass that stretches in all directions across an area twice the size of Texas. Since before the dawn of history, tribes of nomadic horsemen have lived here. Even today, one-third of Mongolians live on the land as herders, raising horses and other livestock, dining on little else besides meat and mare's milk, and living in portable tents they call *ger*, but that are more commonly known to us as yurts.

Nowadays, these nomadic horse people exist on the outer fringes of global society. But for a period during the Middle Ages, they assembled an immense empire led by the greatest conqueror the world has ever known: Genghis Khan. Under his leadership, the Mongols took control of more land and people in twenty-five years than the Romans did in four centuries. At its peak, the Mongol Empire stretched from Siberia to Arabia, from the Sea of Japan to the banks of the Danube River, and held under its authority more than one hundred million people.

Khan's power and the might of the Mongol Nation had entirely to do with horses.

Before Khan's rise, the Mongols were illiterate, shamanistic pastoralists no more than 700,000 in number. They lived amid other fractious tribes during a time of almost constant turmoil and warfare on the Steppe. Klans within the various tribes would form loose, treacherous, and often warring confederations. Within the confines of the steppes, the antagonistic clans, tribes, and confederations would attack and plunder each other, taking control of grazing land, stealing their rivals' trade goods and livestock, and subjugating the captured.

Khan, whose birth name was Temujin, had a particularly hard childhood, even by the Mongols' harsh standards. When he was ten, a rival Turkish clan poisoned his father, a khan or emperor of a minor tribe. Afterward, Temujin's family was shunned by his own people, who did not want to be burdened by their care. For a period, his mother dug roots and caught insects to feed her family. Temujin eventually rose up to take command over his poverty-stricken kin, killing an older brother who challenged his authority.

While still a teen, he wed a child bride named Borte. When she was kidnapped, he pursued her captors on horseback for six months, forming alliances so that he might exact revenge. He eventually reclaimed her in a daring raid, killing her abductors and their families. His allies witnessed his cunning and courage, and soon his reputation spread. He developed a following as a leader.

Through alliances, diplomacy and military force, he continued to build his following over a period of two decades, eventually uniting the perpetually warring Mongol and Turkic tribes under his rule and bringing order, stability and peace to Mongolia. In 1206, tribal rulers bestowed on him the name Genghis Khan, meaning "just leader," and supreme rule of the Mongol Nation.

Khan and the Mongols might have remained a marginal note in history, but for one thing: rain began to fall abundantly on the Mongolian steppe.

Like large swaths of the American West, Mongolia is a semi-arid desert grassland where rainfall is sporadic, intense, and typically short-lived. But for some unknown reason, a period of prolonged and steady rainfall coincided with Khan's rise and consolidation of power. In 1211, Central Mongolia entered a fifteen-year-period of uniquely warm and wet weather unprecedented in the thousand or more years preceding it.

The rains transformed the brown, parched grasslands into an oasis of green pasture nearly 500 million acres in size. The long run of unusually mild and favorable weather enabled the Mongols to rapidly multiply their population of livestock, which would soon be needed to feed their armies, as well as breed hundreds of thousands of surplus horses to carry their warriors into battle.

"Where it's arid, unusual moisture creates unusual plant productivity, and that translates into horsepower—literally. Genghis was able to ride that wave," said Amy Hessl, a tree-ring scientist whose research brought to light the unusual weather pattern.

While it's impossible to estimate how many horses the Mongolian grasslands might have sustained during those especially productive years, the comparably-sized American Great Plains were thought to have supported between thirty and sixty million bison before the animals were hunted nearly to extinction. So, it's quite conceivable that the Mongolians expanded their herds into the tens of millions, giving them an almost inexhaustible supply of war horses, along with millions more sheep, goats, and cattle to feed the warrior hoards.

In 1211, Khan's forces attacked South China's Jin dynasty. Militarily triumphant, they felled the city of Zhongdu (present-day Beijing), and took control of the Silk Road over which passed China's wealth of trade goods. Since all east-west trade flowed along this trade route, the Mongols were able to extract considerable wealth from the merchants, which served to increase their power.

In the years that followed, they would conquer nearly all of Asia, then turn south to rout foes in Persia and the Middle East, and eventually make incursions deep into Eastern and Central Europe, stopping only when they could no longer find sufficient pastureland to feed their cavalry's horses.

Born in the saddle and accustomed to hardship on the frigid Steppe, the Mongols proved to be the most formidable warriors of their day, and perhaps the greatest in all of history. Khan's conquering armies consisted almost entirely of mounted cavalry archers. These horsemen could literally gallop circles around their enemies' forces. The longbows of their adversaries were no match for their compact and jointed compound bows, which were small enough to be fired from horseback but powerful enough to pierce armor.

Never coming near the clumsy foot soldiers, the galloping warriors would shower arrows down upon them. Only when the enemy had become a panicked, wounded, and dispirited shambles would the riders exchange their bows for swords, dismount, and converge on the ground troops to end their torment.

When the Mongols took over a city, they would immediately kill the nobles and landowners who might rise up again to oppose them, installing in their places people loyal to their rule. But they would spare many of the common people, especially tradesmen and engineers. Chinese engineers were particularly valuable in future campaigns, because the Mongols used their know-how to construct siege engines needed to attack fortified cities—something no other Steppe army had ever done. The combination of mounted cavalry and the ability to lay siege to protected cities made the Mongols unstoppable.

Their biggest military assets were the tough, native ponies of the Mongol steppe. Mongols used the small but powerful horses to great advantage throughout their campaigns. Though not the fastest horses on the battlefield, the animals possessed great endurance, allowing the armies to travel distances of up to seventy miles per day.

This endurance helped the Mongol's horses outlast their foes' larger, quicker and more refined cavalry mounts in battles. They also enabled Khan to establish superior cross-country communications across widely spread out fronts, as all communications had to travel via horseback. By establishing remount stations throughout the realm, the Mongols had a "Pony Express" style system that enabled them to communicate quickly and coordinate attacks with greater precision than any foe.

Mongolian ponies needed little water and no grain rations, as many European breeds did. Accustomed to the harsh climate of the Steppe, where temperatures could fall to forty below in wintertime, the ponies were bred to survive frigid cold and would paw through snow to find forage. This made it possible to mount winter campaigns crucial to the Mongolians' defeat of Russia. Once the rivers of the North froze, Mongolian commanders used them as highways for their armies.

Reputedly, a Mongol warrior's horse could be summoned at his whistle, and would follow the cavalryman like a dog. Each warrior had his own herd, anywhere from three to twenty horses, so that he could alternate them and always be freshly mounted. This allowed the army divisions to travel distances at speeds inconceivable to their enemies.

Mongolia's mounted soldiers preferred to travel with lactating mares, which could be milked to provide them with food. Sometimes a soldier stuck without provisions would draw horse's blood from a minor neck vein, a practice that shocked their enemies and fostered their fearful reputation as "bloodthirsty" barbarians.

Khan reputedly said, "It is easy to conquer the world from the back of a horse." That's a hard statement to dispute. In terms of square miles conquered, Khan was the greatest leader of all time—his empire was four times that of Alexander the Great.

History paints a dark picture of Genghis Khan and the Mongols—a bad reputation not completely deserved. One of the problems was that the Mongols were largely illiterate, so their history has never been told through the eyes of the victors, but through the words of the vanquished. Though Khan instituted reforms, creating a writing system for the Mongol language, he didn't allow anything to be written about him during his lifetime.

After his death, someone close to Khan wrote a "secret" history of the Mongol Empire. The account, which offers great insights into Khan's upbringing and character, was lost for centuries, only to be recovered and translated in the twentieth century. By then, the world had already made up its mind about Khan, largely because of histories written by the Chinese, Persians, and Europeans who were not only defeated by his armies, but humiliated too.

Many of the claims as to Khan's barbarism were surely exaggerations; one of his tactics was to spread myths about the

Mongolians' extreme brutality to intimidate his enemies so that they would surrender instead of fight. Khan also offered every city he attacked the option of surrender, with the promise that the people would be spared.

According to historian Jack Weatherford, author of the book *Genghis Khan and the Making of the Modern World*, the claims that Khan's armies killed tens of millions of people are likely exaggerated "by a factor of about ten."

On the positive side, Khan helped to pacify much of the Old World during medieval times and put an end to medieval economic stagnation, helping to usher in the modern era. He created a strict code of law that was enforced throughout his territories. The laws were so strict and effectively enforced that it was said a woman carrying a nugget of gold on her head could wander safely anywhere in the realm.

Prior to Khan, the Old World consisted of isolated kingdoms often in conflict with one another. But under Mongol leadership, the formerly disconnected civilizations came together to form a continental trade network. Khan's control of the Silk Road, in particular, reduced the amount of tax and "tribute" gatherers, liberating traders and making their transcontinental travels safer and more lucrative. Traders like Marco Polo took advantage of this security to travel on well-maintained roads that linked Mediterranean maritime cities to China.

Among the many trade items, Silk Road caravans carried spices and silk from Asia, carpets and leather goods from Iran, and silver, cloth, linen, and other goods from Europe to the Middle and Far East.

Along with trade goods travelled ideas. From China, the Europeans adopted business practices such as bills of exchange (so that heavy coins didn't have to be carried over long distances), deposit banking, and insurance. Islamic methods of astronomy, math, and science found their way to Africa, East Asia, and Europe. Papermaking and printing, both products of Chinese civilization, likewise became widely disbursed.

Khan also practiced religious tolerance throughout the realm, ensuring that everyone—Muslims, Christians, Jews, and Buddhists—could travel without concern.

Today, Mongolia remains a country where the horse stands at the very center of life. The Mongolian horse remains largely unchanged since the time of Genghis Khan. The breed is still stocky and short-legged, with a large and unrefined head. These ponies are nothing to look at when compared to the stately horses of Europe, the so-called "Warmbloods" and the Thoroughbreds, and don't possess the exquisite beauty of the Middle Eastern Arabian. Still, they've retained the amazing stamina, strength, and ability to survive that once fueled the greatest conquering power the world has ever witnessed.

Nomads of the Mongolian Steppe continue to rear a national horse herd numbering more than three million. Traveling with their families, unencumbered by fences, the horses live outdoors all year round, surviving harsh winters and hot summers, especially near the southern desert lands. Ironically, recent droughts on the Mongolian Steppe have forced many Mongolians to leave the nomadic life and move to the country's largest urban center, Ulan Bator.

But even there, Mongolians are constantly in touch with their equestrian heritage (horse racing is the most popular sport) and the legacy of their once-great empire. Visitors to the city arrive at Genghis Khan International Airport. There is a Genghis Khan Avenue that leads to Genghis Khan Park, and outside the city is a 130-foot-tall statue of Khan, looking out over the Mongolian Steppe. Of course, he is mounted on a horse.

TWENTY-SIX

ARABIANS, FROM BREED TO GREED

If you have seen nothing but the beauty of their markings and limbs, their true beauty is hidden from you.

—Poet Al-Mutanabbi

B ack when my father Bill was still alive, one of the things we did together was attend the annual Arabian horse show in Del Mar. Back in the mid '80s, the Del Mar Arabian Horse Show was a top-drawer equine extravaganza that drew the wealthy and famous from all across southern California, including Hollywood.

As people accustomed to dusty rodeo arenas and low-budget county fairgrounds, Dad and I found the entire Arabian scene lavishly, delightfully posh. At ends of the stall rows, trainers and breeders had fashioned guest reception areas decorated like fine living rooms where they offered guests catered appetizers and champagne in crystal flutes. At night, there were private parties for the show entrants and their guests on North County horse estates and in the mansions of nearby La Jolla.

The show riders were impeccably attired. The English riders, of course, wore elegant riding jackets, boots, and tack of the finest European leather, along with velvet-covered riding helmets or always-stylish top hats. The best-dressed western riders wore boots that would have cost me two months' salary, fine beaver felt hats made of garment-quality fur, and sat atop riding saddles ornamented with sterling silver. Most impressive of all were those dressed in the highly stylized clothing of Arabia competing in native costume classes.

The horses were painstakingly bathed and conditioned, their manes and tails smooth as silk and the white ones bleached (to remove bathroom stains). Grooms scrubbed, sanded, and polished hoofs to a patent leather shine. Face whiskers were clipped and baby oil applied to make the muzzles shine like wet seal skin. The horses' coats shone like hand-waxed Mercedes, thanks to clouds of Show Sheen sprayed on their coats.

It all seemed like a fantasy, with horses conjured not from the desert sands of Arabia but from the Magical Kingdom of Walt Disney. And it turned out that that's just what it was. A fantasy. I'll pick up the story of how beauty, wealth and greed overwhelmed the Arabian horse breed soon. But first, a little historical background on this most extraordinary horse . . .

Arabian horses are an ancient breed, nearly as ancient as the Mongolian horse. But while horse people regard the Mongolian as primitive, the Arabian is widely praised as the most ethereal of all horse breeds. In terms of refinement, the one is a Jeep, the other a Jaguar.

In the beloved children's tale *Black Beauty*, author Anne Sewell described the Arabian like so:

They were small horses, even though their perfect conformation made them look larger. Their ears were small
and delicately pointed, set wide apart as were their eyes.
Their necks were slender and long, flowing nobly into
their short, wide back from which floated luxurious tails.
Even at a walk they seemed to soar, their hooves barely
touching the ground before they came down again.

Throughout history, Arabian horses have been admired, prized,
and coveted by horsemen of all nationalities, not just for their
beauty but also for their speed, agility, exceptional endurance, and
strength of bone and body. They are also renowned for their gentle
dispositions and eagerness for training. Because of all these things,
the Arab has contributed to the ancestry of nearly every riding
horse breed, from Europe's elegant "Warmbloods" to the racing
Thoroughbred and American Quarter Horse, and to Spanish breeds
such as the Andalusian. They've been used to improve Australian
bush horses, the native horses of Japan and even the Percheron
draft horse.

How did the Arabian develop its exceptional traits? Climate and
culture played significant roles in shaping the breed. The Bedouin,
nomadic herders of the Arabian Peninsula, began using the native
horses of the Middle East close to four thousand years ago. To suit
the arid desert where grass and water were scarce, they needed
light, thrifty horses that could subsist for days on scant provisions;
it's said that when grass and water were unobtainable during desert
crossings, the Bedouin would feed their horses camel's milk and
dates.

Bedouins often covered long distances under the hot sun. To
stay cool in the extreme desert heat, their horses developed thin
skins that placed blood vessels nearer the surface. Bedouin horses
not only needed great endurance, they also had to be fleet of hoof,
as warfare with competing tribes was common. These circumstances favored horses with deep chests, large, flaring nostrils, and

oversized windpipes that made it easier to breathe freely. Even the rounded dome of the Arab's forehead helped increase breathing capacity.

Harsh conditions and constant warfare weeded out any weakness in the Bedouin horses, but they didn't make the horses surly or hard to manage. Quite the opposite. The Bedouins allowed only those horses with naturally pleasant dispositions to breed. When threatened by sandstorms, predators, or raids, the Bedouins would bring their best mares inside their tents to protect them. Therefore, the horses had to be gentle and sensitive to humans. Even today, Arabs are one of the few breeds whose stallions can be exhibited by children.

Arabians likely are the world's longest line of "purebred" horses, in the sense that the Bedouins did not allow breeding with outside horses. They protected their stock's purity because they believed the horse was created by Allah, who had scooped up the southern wind and shaped it into a horse.

Though they didn't have written pedigrees (the Bedouins were illiterate), they kept track of family lines going back many generations. A Bedouin could recite a horse's ancestry as easily as his own.

Bedouins fiercely protected their horses from outsiders. They believed that a single drop of outside blood would harm the breed, and supposedly went to great lengths to preserve breed purity. One of the myths is that before attacking an enemy camp, a Bedouin would sew up his mare's nether parts, just in case an amorous stallion dared mount her. Though this seems unlikely, it shows the mentality that prevailed in the culture.

War was responsible for the early dissemination of Arabian blood. The Turks, who began on the Eurasian Steppes, invaded the Middle East, capturing the Bedouin horses. As good judges of horse quality, they abandoned their own animals and began breeding the desert horses. These Turkish horses would become a fountain from which most of the world's Arabians would spring.

During the Middle Ages, many thousands of Arabians, Turks, and Moors, swept into Europe on the fleet Arabian horses. Driven back, they left behind a swath of destruction, along with some of their horses. These became the foundation stock of the Spanish breeds used by the Conquistadors to conquer the New World. Spanish horses in turn left behind in the colonizing campaigns bred freely in the wild to become the mustangs of the American West. So that's yet another horse whose veins course with Arab blood.

Often at war with the Turks, the Polish military captured their superior Arab horses for use in their cavalry. When the wars ended in the eighteenth century, they continued combing the Ottoman Empire for stallions for cavalry horse breeding programs. A number of princely estates maintained Arabian studs to supply horses for Poland's nobles, making Poland the first important center of purebred Arabian horse breeding in Europe.

The Turks often awarded Arabians as gifts to foreign rulers and dignitaries. For instance, America's President Ulysses Grant received the first Arabian into the United States as a gift from the Turkish Sultan in 1878. Most famously, the Turks gave three horses to England in the late seventeenth and early eighteenth centuries that became the foundation for the Thoroughbred race horse for which England is famous. Since the Thoroughbred became the major contributor to the American Quarter horse, it can be said that the Arabian played a huge part in its foundation as well.

England's most famous breeder was the Crabbet Arabian Stud, a horse farm founded by Wilfred and Lady Anne Blunt in 1877. The Blunts originally sought to buy a stud for their Thoroughbred program and travelled to Arabia to find it. Enchanted with the breed, they made it their goal to find the best native horses available and preserve the horse in its purest and most authentic form. In the 1920s through the 1940s, the Crabbett Stud would become the most influential breeder of all.

Following the Second World War, America's booming economy collided with the cowboy westerns of Hollywood to create demand for recreational horseback riding. Much of that demand was fulfilled by the American Quarter Horse, a relatively young breed of horse widely used on western ranches. But for those wanting something a bit more exotic, more refined and elegant, the Arabian horse fit the bill.

Since the United States had few breeders initially, the horses were largely brought from overseas. Wealthier Americans could pay better prices than could Europeans, so Arabian breeders like the Crabbet Stud sought out buyers among Americans willing to pay high prices for quality horses; these formed the foundations of their own breeding programs.

Now, let's cue up the craziness.

In 1980, a former film actor and California governor became the president of the United States. In real life and in film, Ronald Reagan loved the cowboy image and horses, and as president he often gave foreign dignitaries cowboy hats. His favorite horse was El Alamein, a half-Arabian, half-Thoroughbred given to him as a gift from the president of Mexico.

One of Reagan's first acts in office was to stimulate the economy by creating tax incentives for a wide range of businesses. Though it was likely unintended, Reagan turned horse breeding into a fantastic tax shelter. Overnight, horse ownership became a favorite hobby of millionaires, with the Arab horse as the apple of their eyes.

Arabians were ideally suited to American tastes in the 1980s. They were ostentatious, expensive, stylish, and imported. While some of people getting involved in the breed had a sincere desire to ride, far more of them began investing in horses for the sheer thrill of speculation and the prestige that came with ownership.

"It's a bit like the art market. The appreciation is as fast as [that of] some of the French impressionist paintings," said one horse buyer. "I bought a mare in Poland for $9,000. I sold her for $450,000. I sold her daughter for $175,000. And six months later, the man to whom I sold that filly sold her at auction for $680,000."

"It was just money, money, money everywhere you looked," said Arabian horse trainer Jim Bloomfield.

Adding to the glamour was the presence of celebrities, who began investing in the horses, attending the auctions, and sometimes even riding in shows. At an auction, a buyer might sit down beside Bo Derek, Paul Simon, Stefanie Powers, or Jackie Onassis. Box office heart throb Patrick Swayze and singer Wayne Newton, who'd been involved with the breed for years, both had a deep and abiding presence in the breed.

Arabians auction sales, already notable for pizazz, became gala extravaganzas. Smoke machines, light shows, runways of sparkling sawdust and big-name entertainers like the Beach Boys and the Pointer Sisters became commonplace. At one sale, Bob Hope quipped, "Where else can you sit around and watch rich Americans buy Arabs?"

Scottsdale, Arizona, home to the largest and most prestigious horse show, became the epicenter of auction excess. One auction company, for example, constructed a street scene that evoked nineteenth century Poland in wintertime for its "Polish Ovation Sale." Acting as the official agent of the Polish government, the auction company sold nineteen horses for $10.8 million, an average of $584,000 each.

For the sake of comparison, the top sales price for an Arabian in 1968 was twenty-five thousand dollars; in 1984, a Russian stallion named Abdullah changed hands for the then-record price of $3.2 million. That same year in Scottsdale, a mare named Love Potion sold for a whopping $2.5 million—a rather astounding sum when you consider that she'd have to produce ten straight foals valued at $250,000 apiece just to recoup the investment. Ironically, the mare turned out to be sterile.

Meanwhile, the average price for top Arabians sold at Scottsdale climbed from thirty thousand dollars in 1974 to nearly half a million in 1985—a sixteen-time increase. To rope in the investors necessary to achieve these astronomical sums, people in the horse business began giving seminars on tax shelters.

The pitch went something like this: Horses, like milk cows, could be depreciated for their full value in three to five years, depending on their age. The expense of keeping the horse could be written off 100 percent. Any profit from the sale of a horse gets taxed not as income, but as a capital gain, provided you've owned the horse for at least two years.

What that meant was, if you bought a filly for $100,000, won a few ribbons at important shows, then sold her for $600,000, you could realize a capital gain of half a million dollars (less the hefty sales commission of 22 percent, a detail seminar speakers often failed to mention). Of the remainder, only 20 percent could be taxed while 80 percent of the capital gains were *tax free income.*

But here's the kicker, as explained by veteran Arabian horse trainer Mike Bloomfield.

"In order for this to work, the mares had to be in foal. A broodmare that is not in foal has no value. You can't depreciate anything. There are no capital gains there. If you sell the mare not in foal, she doesn't qualify for a capital gain," he said.

"That's why people bred everything and anything."

Because in-demand stallions could service one hundred mares a year, there was far more demand for mares. Mares, in fact, were so integral to the investment that stallion owners began offering live filly guarantees; if your horse didn't produce a filly, you'd get a second breeding to the stallion for free.

Show wins were a critical part of the equation. In order to boost the price of a horse and realize a capital gain, breeders benefited immensely when their horses won show titles, especially at the largest and most prestigious events like the Arabian Nationals or the Scottsdale show. Trainers were under enormous pressure to produce results for their masters-of-the-universe clients and were not above gaming the system.

If a horse's tail wasn't cascading like a fountain, no problem. Put a little ginger where the sun doesn't shine. Coat color a little off? There are powders that can be brushed into the coat—just don't get caught using them. And it gets worse. Although the Bedouins prided themselves on the calm, mannerly horses stalled in their tents, the show judges wanted to see fiery desert chargers bursting with energy; anything less wouldn't hold their eye. So, trainers would use anything from a fire extinguisher to a little cocaine dust blown into that big airway to make their horses prance. Owners were willing to turn a blind eye to such things—so long as the horses brought home the ribbons.

Sadly, very few of the people who got involved in the Arab industry in the early 1980s actually knew anything about horses. To them, the Arabian in their stall was like the Rolls Royce in their garage, or the multi-million dollar house that the garage was attached to—a symbol of their success and power. But because they were used to calling the shots, they often felt compelled to make breeding decisions based on scant understanding of what goes into making a really good horse.

Breeding decisions were influenced by national championship awards, fellow clueless owners, and slick marketing campaigns in the *Arabian Horse Times*. People glommed on to others' successes. Notable Arabian horse trainer Donald Webb told the tale of one particularly popular stallion, a champion at the San Francisco Cow Palace, who was known to have club feet. People bred to him anyway, simply accepting that the foals would require tendon surgery.

"Those who breed thoughtfully will be trying to get rid of that for many generations to come," Webb said.

As a result of all the breeding activity, the quantity of Arabs skyrocketed. From 1982 to 1986, the number of horses registered with the Arabian Horse Association topped 100,000—more than all the horses registered in the club's first sixty-five years. To a lesser degree, the same thing was happening to other breeds. Quarter horse registries rose from fewer than 95,000 in 1977 to more than 168,000 in 1985—an increase of 56 percent. In that same time period, Thoroughbred registrations increased by a third. But neither saw the kinds of price leaps that were occurring at the top of the Arabian market.

Writing for Sports Illustrated in 1986, sports journalist E. M. Swift compared the booming market for Arabians to the tulip mania that gripped Holland in 1634. During that market bubble, tulips became a luxury item commanding ever upwardly spiraling prices. At the peak of the market in 1637, some single tulip bulbs sold for more than ten times the annual income of a skilled craftsman. Similarly, in 1984, the then-record price of $3.2 million for the stallion Abdullah was almost 150 times the yearly wage for a registered nurse or a machinist.

Inevitably, both tulip mania and Arabian mania crashed. In 1986, the tax code was amended to close gaping loop holes, including the one pertaining to horses. Almost overnight, people pulled fortunes out of the Arabian horse breeding business.

"It was immediate. People who had horses that were bringing them a million dollars—the minute those capital gains taxes stopped, if you could get $50,000 for that same horse, you were lucky," said Mike Broomfield. "Yeah, everything collapsed."

The bottom fell out with the same dramatic thud as it had when tulip mania went bust 450 years earlier. The only difference was, the beautiful horses weren't like the beautiful tulips. They still had to be fed and cared for. Charlene Burnstein, an Arabian horse breeder who managed to ride out the turbulent times, vividly remembers the dark days of the late 1980s.

"A lot of them ended up in Mexico and France . . . and not as riding horses, unfortunately. There were trailer loads of horses that would leave from bigger farms in Scottsdale to Mexico. And if they didn't leave on the trailers, they were left starving in the fields."

In the late '80s, dispersal sales took the place of private estate auctions as Arabian horse breeders threw in the towel. One farm that had more than a thousand horses sold just eighty-three of them, leaving the remainder to be shipped off to one of the dozen horse meat processing plants flourishing at the time. I rode in a truck to a plant in Nebraska with a "killer buyer" who went to auctions to buy horses by the pound. There were several Arabians on that truck.

Though the top of the market got hit first and hardest, average people who'd been suckered into investing became victims too. One of my neighbors in Colorado was an independent truck driver. He and his wife invested half a million dollars in an Arabian stallion and three mares. When the market collapsed, he couldn't sell the horses, which he'd never even ridden. The horses ended up eating the bark off the pine trees on his property.

The Arabian Horse Association never fully recovered from the manic depression of the 1980s. Today, the registry figures still don't surpass what they were *before* Ronald Reagan's inauguration. I don't believe this decline to be a bad thing.

When the hundreds of Arabian horse owners jumped ship, they left committed horsemen behind to clean up the mess. Those who could adjust their business models and hold on survived the crash, refocused their efforts, and waited for the rebound. The smaller market and a return to realistic values for the horses allowed breeders to focus on breeding better riding horses.

The boom overshadowed a large core of Arabian horse riders who then, as now, make up the core supporters of the breed. Even at the height of Arab mania, more than 80 percent of the horses sold for less than five thousand dollars. Some for a lot less.

Today, the Arabian Horse Association (AHA) still touts the history and beauty of the desert horse. But the AHA noticeably avoids the glitz and glamor that characterized the breed's marketing in the roaring '80s. When I last looked at the AHA webpage, the first picture to pop up was of a little girl sitting on the back of a horse, her father beside her offering encouragement. The image didn't look staged, and neither of the two were models. Their clothing most likely came from a western wear store, not Neiman-Marcus.

Only a few years ago, I wrote a story about Bryna Stevenson, a fourteen-year-old who had become the youngest rider ever to win the Old Dominion endurance race, a hundred-mile contest in the Shanandoah Valley and Blue Ridge Mountains outside Orkney, Virginia. Her Arabian horse, Maddy, didn't require Show Sheen or Maybelline, and he didn't cost a fortune, either. Singled out as the best conditioned horse of the competition, Maddy had cost the Stevensons just $550.

TWENTY-SEVEN

THE ALL-AMERICAN HORSE

*The best animals in the world have always been
bred for the love of them or the love of breeding
and caring for them, rather than purely for profit.*
—Anonymous collie breeder

I f horses went to high schools, American Quarter horses would
inevitably win the yearbook competitions for "most popular"
and "most athletic."

When it comes to popularity, no breed can compete. With 2.8
million horses, the American Quarter Horse Association (AQHA)
is the biggest horse registry in the world. People ride them on trails,
ranches, and arenas throughout the United States, Western Europe,

South America, and Australia, and a few have even found stable homes in places like Israel, Japan, and Saudi Arabia.

As far as athleticism, the breed holds the record as the fastest horse in the world at distances up to a Quarter mile—hence, the name Quarter horse. It's also the most popular horse in rodeo events, including roping and barrel racing, and excels in a broad variety of western performance horse competitions.

The allure of the Quarter horse has always been its association with the American cowboy and the Old West. Although the American Quarter Horse Association didn't come into existence until the mid-twentieth century, the prototypical Quarter-type horse, also known as a "stock horse," developed out of the need for sturdy, trail-wise, cow-savvy horses during the long Texas cattle drives. Beginning in 1866, Texans began rounding up millions of feral Longhorn cattle and driving them north to rail yards in Kansas. Ranchers began breeding cow-savvy horses for use on the trail.

Though many threads were woven together to form the fabric of the Quarter horse breed, the strongest of them leads back to a Kentucky horse brought to Texas in 1845 by a man named Middleton Perry. Known as Steel Dust, the stallion saw use as a working ranch horse but earned his fame by winning short-track races. His greatest acclaim resulted from a short-distance match race in Collin County, Texas, where he defeated a highly touted adversary named Monmouth.

As a sire, Steel Dust fathered a line of horses known not only for their speed but also for their agility and "cow sense." The era of the "Steel Dust horses" coincided with the great Texas cattle drives, during which cowboys sang their praises. Many of the biggest Texas ranches based breeding programs on Steel Dust horses, along with a handful of other Quarter-type horses—Shiloh, Old Cold Deck, Traveler, and Peter McCue were some of their names.

In 1936, *Western Horseman* magazine debuted in California. Widely circulated on ranches, it quickly became a communications hub where stock horse breeders, horse trainers, and other professionals could connect with horse fanciers throughout the West. This, along with cowboy films, radio dramas, and books like *Smoky the Cow Horse*, fostered a post-war market for western stock horses. Texas Quarter horse breeders were poised for the boom.

In 1940, a group of influential and wealthy Texas ranchers met over a dining room table to form the American Quarter Horse Association. Their goal was to preserve and promote the Steel Dust strain of horses. They decided that the honor of being the first horse registered would go to the winner of the stallion class at the 1941 Fort Worth Southwestern Exposition and Fat Stock Show.

When a beautifully proportioned and muscular stallion from the King Ranch of south Texas entered the ring, judge Jim Minnick turned to judge Robert Denhardt and said, "What do you think of them pumpkins, Bob?"

When the last horse had joined the ring procession, the judges halted the parade and declared the King Ranch entry as its winner. With the blue ribbon came the honor of being the first horse registered in the AQHA. Ironically, the name of the clearly superior horse was Wimpy.

After touring the American Quarter Horse Museum in Amarillo and learning about the breed's early history, I left town to go see one of Wimpy's modern day successors. The stallion, belonging to Alvin and Becky Fults, had a name more befitting a legendary animal: Metallic Cat.

Born in 2005, the horse established himself in the sport of cutting. Cutting is a throwback to the Old West, when cows herds in open country, corrals, and feedlots needed to be sorted. While riders kept the herd grouped and settled, a cowboy and his horse would tiptoe into a group of cows and slip between a desired mark and the herd, easing her out into the open. Typically, when the cow realized she was alone and exposed, her herd instinct would kick in and she'd challenge the horse in an effort to get back with the group.

To prevent this, it took a horse with the athleticism and cow sense to anticipate and react to her every faint and dodge. It's a rare horse that has the talent, agility, instinct and inclination to cut, so a good "cutting horse" was a particularly prized possession. Naturally, a rancher with a good cutting horse wanted to show off his talents—and the arena sport of cutting was born.

In 2008, Metallic Cat won the National Cutting Horse Association (NCHA) Open Futurity Championship, the sport's most prestigious honor. Futurity events like this one test the abilities of young horses and serve as showcase events for the top breeders and trainers in the horse industry. Prize money for a victory at the NCHA Open Futurity approaches $200,000, not including rewards like a new horse trailer, trophy saddle, gold-and-silver belt buckle, and others.

After the futurity victory, Metallic Cat won a slew of competitions in 2009 that boosted his career earnings to a whopping $637,711 and also earned him the NCHA Horse of the Year title. Retired to the breeding barn at the ripe old age of four, Metallic Cat won a first-ballot selection for the organization's Hall of Fame in 2010.

The purpose of my visit to the Fults' Ranch was to chronicle the daily life of a true stud. Veterinarian Gregg Veneklassen of Timber Creek Veterinary Hospital invited me to accompany him and a few members of his equine reproduction staff on the weekly task of "collecting" the stallion.

I've seen many impressive ranch properties valued in the millions. The Fults Ranch certainly ranks among the top five. The log cabin–style residential buildings deserved a full-page picture spread in a highbrow western lifestyle magazine like *Sunset* or *Texas Monthly*. Mature shade trees lined the paved driveways, and beyond them were emerald green fields of alfalfa alternating with pastures where scores of horses grazed placidly.

Metallic Cat, whose nickname is "Denver," is the sultan of this 200-acre oasis. From sunup to sundown, life on the breeding farm revolves around his care and happiness. In the morning, breeding manager Tara Sagiere arises at seven A.M. to feed him a ration of grain and hay. On hot days, he'll stay in an air-conditioned stall, but if the weather is less sultry, Sagiere lets him free to run on a twelve-acre paddock and munch home-grown alfalfa known as "Denver hay." On either side of his ample run are paddocks for his harem of mares, usually eight to a side. When there are foals, they're kept with the mares.

"He enjoys seeing his babies, so we try to keep them close, too," says Sagliere.

On collection days, Veneklassen and his crew arrive around ten A.M. A stallion manager halters Denver and leads him to the reproduction barn where he is "teased" by a few sexy mares. Sufficiently aroused, he's led into another room, where he mounts a dummy and leaves a deposit of semen.

While that's processed, Denver goes back out to pasture to spend a leisurely afternoon with his mares. Breeding season is in late winter, with the busiest time being February and March. So, for much of the year, Denver gets put to work as a helper during arena practices or is ridden by trainer Ben Hight to gather cattle.

An eye-catching horse, Denver has a reddish coat dappled with small white spots, so that he appears to be covered in frost. His tail and mane are a contrast of dark ginger hairs mingled with white and silver strands that would be the envy of any Beverly Hills hair colorist. His face is the color of rusty steel, and centered on his forehead is a white snip in the shape of a lightening bolt.

Lightening is an apt description of his reflexes. During his arena career, the horse had moves quicker than NBA superstar Stephen Curry. Watching him face off with a cow was like watching a couple flawlessly dancing the tango. In the twelve shows in which he competed, Metallic Cat never lost a cow back into a herd—an almost unprecedented feat.

On the day I visited him, though, he just seemed like a laid-back, happy-go-lucky horse. Stallions can be handfuls, rearing up and striking with their feet, tossing their heads, and literally yanking their handlers' chains. But Denver went about the whole collecting process with workmanlike efficiency and was out the door and grazing contentedly in his pasture twenty minutes later.

Veneklassen's team quickly tested, prepared, and packaged Metallic Cat's semen for shipment. Special chilled Thermos containers were prepared to so that Fed Ex couriers could whisk the precious straws to awaiting mare farms. Optimally, these arrive at their destinations within twenty-four hours, the ideal time window for artificial insemination.

On the day I visited, Metallic Cat had sixteen clients. At $10,000 a breeding, one collection earned a cool $160,000 for Metallic Cat Ltd., the corporation set up to protect the family assets from lawsuits, which are as common as barn flies in upper-income horse breeding operations.

Since 2013, Metallic Cat has bred about three hundred mares a year, which works out to about three million dollars annually—roughly ten times what it takes to be among America's top 1 percent. Age twelve at the time I saw him, he could go on breeding for another decade. Frozen semen could extend his career years after that.

While that's certainly good for the Fults family, it may not be the best thing for Quarter horses.

People in all segments of the performance horse world are naturally attracted to the winning sires like Metallic Cat. These super sires produce hundreds, even thousands of offspring. Since there are so many more of their babies running around than those of less popular sires, there's a greater chance that some of them will also become big winners and popular sires, too. This makes for an ever-diminishing gene pool in which a greater and greater share of the horses are closely related.

Compounding the problem is the common practice of "double breeding," in which a closely related mare and stallion, perhaps brother and sister or cousins, are bred in order to double down on the desired genetics.

The University of Minnesota compared the genetic relatedness of Quarter horses from a number of disciplines including cutting, racing, and halter showing (a sort of equine beauty contest, like conformation dog shows). What the study found was that cutting horses had the lowest genetic diversity and the highest inbreeding of the bunch.

As we know from dogs, hillbillies, and European royalty, too much inbreeding can result in higher rates of unhealthy genetic mutations being passed along. We usually think of inbreeding as the paring of direct family members, such as brothers and sisters and parents, but the same effect can result when a breeding pool is highly concentrated.

Not surprisingly, that's exactly what has happened in cutting. In 2004, clinical veterinarians at the University of California at Davis coined the acronym HERDA to describe a severe skin affliction found in fifty performance-bred Quarter horses. A gene mutation in these horses caused weakened collagen fibers in the skin.

You can think of collagen as a glue that holds layers of skin together and also attaches the skin to the rest of the animal. In horses that carry both copies of the HERDA gene, the glue is inferior. They have extremely weakened and fragile skin that tears easily and heals poorly, if at all. In the worst cases, the skin becomes detached. It becomes unglued.

Symptoms of the disease often don't appear until an animal reaches the age of two and is put into training. Typically, a saddle or girth causes skin sores that never heal, or that heal poorly to create horrendous scars. New damaged areas appear continuously. There is no cure, so veterinarians have little choice but to euthanize the horses.

Researchers at UC Davis used pedigrees and genotyping to trace the HERDA mutation back to an extremely influential sire from the 1940s named Poco Bueno. Owned by E. Paul Waggoner, one of the founding fathers of the AQHA, Poco Bueno was grand champion stallion at several of the biggest livestock events, including the Denver National Western Stock Show.

After a celebrated career as a cutting horse, Poco Bueno settled down to life as a stud, fathering more than four hundred registered offspring. A number of "Poco" babies grew up to be outstanding cutting horses and acclaimed sires and dams, contributing more to the gene pool and ensuring that future generations of performance Quarter horses would carry Poco blood.

As time went by and the "popular sire" effect continued to kick in, that blood showed up in greater and greater concentrations in cutting horses. But because HERDA was a recessive trait, it revealed itself only when both parents were carriers, and then only if a baby got copies of the HERDA gene from both its mom and dad. Statistically, there was only a one-in-four chance of that happening, so many mare owners simply never saw the disease enough to suspect a genetic link.

Given Poco Bueno's prominence in cutting bloodlines, Metallic Cat is among the carriers of the HERDA gene. Poco Bueno shows up on both sides of his pedigree through the sire Smart Little Lena, an outstanding cutting horse in the 1980s and a son of Poco Bueno.

The presence of the HERDA gene isn't something Metallic Cat's owners advertise, but it's not something they would hide, either. Remember, people in the high end breeding business are a litigious bunch, and trying to mask the fact that a stallion tests positive as a carrier of the mutation would risk a costly day in court. Furthermore, HERDA is so widespread now that cutting horse breeders evaluating prospective sires know to ask about it.

Thanks to UC Davis' research, it is now possible to test dams for the recessive gene. Any owner of a mare with the HERDA gene is wise to avoid paring that horse with Metallic Cat or any of the dozens of other cutting horse sires who carry a copy of the mutation. If someone is aware of the problem and does the testing, HERDA is an easy mistake to avoid.

Still, with so many HERDA recessive animals in the Quarter horse population, the number of people who are either careless or unaware of the condition increases with each passing generation, especially now that the disease has leaked into other breeds and disciplines. Paint horses and Appaloosas are now also known to carry the HERDA gene, and it's becoming widespread in sports related to cutting, such as working cow horse and reining.

The spread of genetic diseases caused by dominant sire breeding is a pattern that, unfortunately, just seems to repeat itself.

Back in the 1970s, a Quarter horse hit the show scene with a meteor's impact. In the thirty-one halter events he entered, he won thirty-one blue ribbons, living up to his name: Impressive.

A halter horse, as the name implies, is shown in only a halter. Judges evaluate the horses based on their adherence to an ideal physique, just as at a Mister Universe competition. Impressive was like a young Arnold Schwarzenegger with a muscular body, exceptional proportions, and charisma that wouldn't quit. Judges fell all over this Platonic ideal of the Quarter horse come to life.

As a breeding stallion, Impressive proved equally deserving of his name, producing one champion after another. Many of his offspring possessed the same dramatic physique and they, too, became outstanding breeders. Of the top fifteen AQHA halter horses in 1992, thirteen were descended from Impressive. At the time, it was estimated that 55,000 Quarter horses, Paints, and Appaloosas bore his pedigree.

But what appeared to be a success story for the ages became, in the words of one prominent Quarter horse trainer, "one of the most devastating things that has ever hit the horse industry."

Within a few years of Impressive's rise to fame as a sire, people began noticing a strange muscular twitching in Impressive offspring that often left them temporarily frozen. Episodes varied in intensity and duration, from momentary and minor to prolonged and agonizing. Attacks could result in shaking, trembling, weakness, and collapse.

Sometimes, the hind muscles simply gave out, and the horses would sit like dogs, unable to lift their own weight. In other cases, the upper airway became paralyzed, causing the horses to wheeze and gasp for air. Occasionally, horses would die from heart failure or respiratory paralysis.

Since Impressive showed up in the pedigrees of every afflicted individual, it was easy to trace the problem back to its source. Though the disease was formally known as hyperkalemic periodic paralysis (HYPP), people came to call it "Impressive Syndrome."

One of the reasons Impressive and his offspring were so, well, impressive, was that their muscles were in a constant state of hyperactivity, even when not stimulated. This resulted in abnormal muscle development—the horses had the musculature of bodybuilders who never actually went to the gym. This made them easier to "fit" for competitions, and it gave them the pleasing, athletic builds that judges favored.

Although evidence strongly implicated Impressive as the disease's sole source, this could not be definitively proven. Lack of proof combined with the fact that a number of the wealthiest breeders in the industry had Impressive offspring discouraged owners from being the first to publicly implicate Impressive.

A lack of a public response meant that many people unwittingly kept on breeding Impressive offspring, despite the risk of the foals developing HYPP. And even later, when UC Davis created a test that identified the gene for HYPP in breeding animals, thus removing any doubts of its source, both the research community and the AQHA resisted pressure to reveal Impressive as its cause. Nobody wanted to open the Pandora's box and let loose the financial and legal problems that might result.

Eventually, of course, the weight of evidence and the level of damage proved too overwhelming to deny. Tests allowed breeders to find out whether their livestock had the HYPP mutation, and most used the information to breed away from the defect. Most, but not all.

"It really wasn't until people started losing money, when people didn't want horses with HYPP, that the breeding stopped," Stephen

Coleman, a professor of equine genetics at Colorado State University told me.

"It is still in the population, so there are people who are willing to take the risk, who will play with fire. They think to themselves, 'I may get a lot of defective horses, but I'll get one really outstanding performance horse.'"

In other words, there are politics involved. And genetics can't solve politics.

Just like HERDA, Impressive Syndrome remains widespread in the American stock horse population. But because it is a dominant rather than a recessive trait, it would have been easy for the AQHA to eliminate, Coleman said.

"They [the AQHA] could have solved HYPP. They knew the horses that had the condition and passed it on, because it was a dominant trait. And they could have said, 'We'll just stop registering horses with HYPP.' But that's not what happened," he concluded. And so, the band plays on . . .

The horse show businesses' emphasis on young horses contributes to the spread of genetic diseases. This is because new generations enter the breeding population so quickly. Metallic Cat, for instance, was put out to stud as a four-year-old. Therefore, a popular sire can breed hundreds and hundreds offspring before anyone catches on that there is a problem.

In performance horse competitions, the biggest prize payouts happen at "futurity" events that take place during the horse's three-year old season. Futurities are held in the United States mainly in cutting, working cow horse, reining, and barrel racing. However, they began in the Thoroughbred racing industry in England as a means of proving an animal's athletic potential and value as a breeding animal. The most famous is the Kentucky Derby, a proving ground for three-year-old racehorses.

Performance horse events—cutting, reining, working cow horse, and barrel racing—latched onto the futurity concept because they provide spectators, breeders, and participants with the excitement of seeing the up-and-coming performers. Horse owners put up money well in advance of the event on the gamble that their horse will emerge as the winner. A win at a major national futurity ensures that a horse will have a long and lucrative breeding career, even if it never competes in another event.

The National Cutting Horse Futurity, with a payout of nearly two million dollars, is one such event. Metallic Cat, one of the all-time top money earners in cutting and the sport's leading sire, launched his multi-million dollar breeding career based on his win there.

But for every Metallic Cat, there are a thousand horses entered in that same futurity that faded into obscurity the moment it ended. Some redeemed themselves at Derby events, consolation competitions in which four-year-olds through six-year-olds compete and which pay about one-third as much for a victory.

To win a major futurity, trainers typically put horses into training-under-saddle at age two. Some start riding the horses at ages as young as eighteen months. Critics think that's simply too young, that the majority of horses simply aren't physically and mentally ready for that degree of pressure. One of those is veterinarian Robert Miller DVM, a colleague from my writing days with *Western Horseman*.

"Half a century ago, when I was cowboying, 'colts' were started at four years of age or older. Once in a while, one might be started as a three-year-old. Despite some very hard work, barring accidents, those ranch horses were still sound and working in their twenties," he says.

"Today, we have all sorts of futurities—reining, cutting, barrel horse, etc. I've tried many times to get owners to postpone arduous training to give the colt a chance to mature. Most of the time, I was ignored."

Horses started young and pressured to compete can end up burned out or injured. Once, I took Simone Windeler, an English dressage trainer of German descent, to a reining futurity event.

Dressage or "schooling" is considered the highest level of horse-manship and handling in equitation.

As she watched the horses, the instructor began noting how many of the horses showed signs of lameness. She estimated as many as one-third.

"How old are these horses? You said three? That's too young for this degree of maneuver. And many of these riders are too big and too fat for these horses. They can't bear the weight of these men, who I'd guess weigh 220 pounds, at least," she said dismissively.

"It's cruel."

Reining has been called the dressage of western riding. Billy Jack Barrett, a former Quarter horse sales agent who runs the stables at the United States Air Force Academy, married his wife, Ann, an upper level dressage judge in the FEI, the international organization that oversees both reining and dressage at the Olympic level. Comparing the two disciplines, he said: "Reining is like graduating from kindergarten. Dressage is like getting a PhD"

In the FEI, dressage horses can't start their arena careers until age six and typically are not considered competition-ready before the age of nine. Most of the best horses in the upper ranks of Quarter horse performance competition—cutting and reining—are retired by age six. Metallic Cat was retired to stud at the end of his three-year-old futurity season.

With their extreme emphasis on youth, sports like cutting and reining churn through horses. Even before the big futurities have come and gone, the majority end up cast to the wayside.

One top reining horse trainer I spoke with, one with lifetime earnings of more than three million dollars, told me that he and his staff of assistant trainers typically prepare between eighty and a hundred horses for the National Reining Horse Association Futurity. He narrows the field down to just three for the big national event held each December. The rest typically get sold off to amateur riders or passed down to junior trainers. Finding buyers for these horses is always a challenge as supply typically overruns demand.

By contrast, a dressage horse must be cultivated over a decade and may have a competitive life into its early twenties. In other words, the emphasis is on quality, not quantity. In most cases, breeding decisions in dressage are made by state-run breed associations. In Germany, for example, an equestrian expert from the state stud inspects a horse to determine if it can be used for breeding. The association has the first option of buying the best horses for the state-owned stud. In this way, they are able not only to control quality, but to breed for attributes that go beyond just arena success, such as longevity, the absence of known diseases, and overall physical soundness.

Not so for American horses. Any breeder can breed, and there are minimal criteria for health. That can and has led to horses like Impressive, who negatively impact the well-being of the entire breed.

For instance, in the reining business, the second all-time leading sire was an AQHA-registered Paint horse. Though the sire is now deceased, his offspring have earned more than nine million dollars in the arena. A winner at the futurity level and a producer of futurity winners, the stallion is known to produce deaf horses.

Deafness is a common attribute of domesticated animals with a large amount of white pigmentation, especially on their faces. For instance, if you breed two Australian shepherds with the merle gene together, you'll likely get one or two puppies in the litter with excessive white pigmentation of the face and deafness. Dalmatians with white ears also often have this problem. And so do many American Paint horses, the colorful cousins of the Quarter horse. Why is not known, but it has something to do with lack of pigmentation in the inner ear.

"The pigment in the hair cells in the ear is necessary for them to work properly," said Dr. Allison Stewart, a clinical researcher at Auburn University in Alabama who developed a method for testing deafness in horses. She said that breeding two affected individuals together won't necessarily result in deafness; it all depends on the random migration of color in each horse that occurs during its development. She believes it is not likely a single gene trait but linked to a number of genes responsible for coloration.

Deafness can be an advantage in the arena because a deaf horse can't hear loud, distracting noises. At one major reining horse competition, a fire alarm went off during one of the deaf horse's performances. Even though the audience headed for the exits, the horse persisted without a flinch.

At the NRHA Futurity, I talked with Diane Bowers, who'd owned one of the deaf horses. The mare's name was An Indian Princess. Diane told me that the mare didn't react to loud noises at home in the barn, but could be spooked by things like changes of light or shadow. A barn swallow might cause her to fidget.

"It was very apparent that she was deaf. In this world, it is so common that I wasn't afraid of it at all. It's almost a trademark of that breeding," she told me.

Because a deaf horse can't hear voice cues, it requires a very experienced trainer who is deft at using his or her body alone to communicate. Even pros who spend every day in the saddle struggle to learn how to do something as simple as getting the horse to stop without the help of a "Whoa!" command.

Bowers said that few people have complained that breeding to the popular sire sometimes resulted in deafness. The deaf horses performed well and won lots of money. Which, to most of the wealthy individuals at the upper levels of the sport, was all that mattered.

But it bothered the Bowers' trainer, Dean Brown, enough to speak out.

"In general, the deaf horses have a shorter show career. And they're really not good for non-pro riders. So, I kind of agree with the people who are concerned about that trait," he told me.

"I'm glad there are a lot of non-deaf horses to cover it up. If there are too many [deaf] horses in our pool, that would harm the genetics. They're flashy and pretty, but it's not something you want to see in the gene pool," he concluded.

Nonetheless, thanks to the popular sire effect and the success of this horse's offspring, it's assured that the trait will live on in performance reining horses for generations.

While a large segment of the horse-showing public seems to think that's perfectly okay, I am less comfortable with it. I acknowledge that a deaf animal can make its way in the world nearly as well as a horse with normal hearing. Deafness certainly didn't harm a competitor or owner's chances and may have even helped them.

But still, I feel that it is wrong.

The tendency to let known health genetic problems slide seems to me to defy the mission statement upon which the AQHA was founded: to record and preserve the pedigree of the American Quarter horse *while maintaining the integrity of the breed and welfare of its horses.*

But this is America, home of freedom, democracy, and (especially) the free market economy. Let the buyer beware.

CONCLUSION

What's so unnatural about the history of dogs, cats, cows, and horses? Our part in it, of course.

For nearly four billion years, nature alone decided which organisms lived or died. When the climate grew warmer or colder, when food became more plentiful or scarce, when new predators arrived on the scene, and when pathogens evolved, there were always some lucky individuals whose traits enabled them to adapt and move forward in time. Those unable to adapt went extinct.

Twelve thousand years ago, a group of clever and highly adaptable primates altered nature's course. From the moment we first planted a seed, we began fooling with Mother Nature by picking our own winners and losers.

At first, the choices were passive. Our settlements provided a new and unnatural environment in the wilderness. For most animals, this environment was uncomfortable and unlivable, but a handful were adaptable to the human landscape. They joined us.

The arrangement proved mutually beneficial. The animals faced less competition for resources, especially food. We also protected their offspring from predators, giving them a reproductive edge over their wild counterparts. In return, we gained companionship, food, farm labor, transportation, textiles, pest control, and much more. We refined and honed these benefits through an active role in choosing which animals to mate.

In a big picture sense, this has proven to be a good deal for domesticated animals. From the dawn of agriculture to the present, the human population has multiplied more than a thousandfold, from around seven million to well over seven billion. Our animals have proliferated right along with us. According to Czech-Canadian environmental scientist Václav Smil, humans, our pets, and our livestock make up about 97 percent of the combined weight (or "zoomass") of all land-based vertebrate animals. Wild animals make up just 3 percent—and that figure is shrinking.

According to the World Wildlife Fund, each year around ten-thousand species of animals, insects and plants vanish from the planet—a rate of extinction never before seen on earth. But so far, we haven't lost a single domesticated species.

As I drove across the western United States, I only had to look out my RV windshield at the millions of acres of farmed land I passed to see that we no longer live in a natural world. Instead, we inhabit a gigantic farm filled with the plants and animals we find the most useful. More than half of the world's land is now dedicated to agriculture, and about 70 percent of that land is used to grow crops for livestock that feed ourselves and our pets.

From this standpoint, animals who left the wild made a very good choice. Their value to us has ensured their survival. But on an individual level, I see reasons to be concerned.

Overpopulation—having more animals than we can care for—is one of them. Cats, especially, face an overpopulation crisis. Feral-living cats number in the tens of millions in the United States alone. Their lives are fraught with perils that include starvation, predation, vehicle strikes, intentional abuse, neglect, exposure to weather extremes, and virulent infectious diseases such as rabies.

In addition to leading difficult lives, feral cats exert survival pressure on many species of wildlife, especially birds. While estimates of the numbers of animals they kill every year vary wildly, there is little argument that cats' extraordinary hunting abilities add to the pressure pushing some birds to the brink of extinction.

Cats fill our animal shelters to capacity, so shelter workers euthanize millions a year to make room for more. But in many communities, programs to trap, neuter, vaccinate, and release (TNR) feral cats have presented a viable alternative to mass extermination. A national survey of 208 TNR cat rescue and sterilization programs conducted in 2017 showed that the birth rate of feral kittens dropped by 72 percent following the introduction of TNR programs.

The data, collected by Alley Cat Rescue, also showed that TNR groups have sterilized more feral cats in just the past five years than in the preceding twenty. As of 2017, the study's respondents had sterilized and returned 1.3 million cats to their habitats. Efforts by other TNR programs not included in the survey likely would boost that figure beyond 3.6 million, says Merritt Clifton, editor of the shelter blog *Animals 24/7.* That's real progress.

Even more encouraging, after years of annually euthanizing millions of canines, we appear to be turning the corner on dog overpopulation in America. Experts attribute this progress to highly successful efforts by shelters, animal welfare groups, kennel clubs, and veterinarians to educate the public about the importance of pet sterilization. According to the Humane Society of the United States, 90 percent of dogs in American homes are sterilized. High sterilization rates have caused the number of dogs euthanized in shelters to plummet to only a tenth of what they were in the 1970s.

Furthermore, a greater proportion of people than ever before (especially millenials) are adopting shelter or rescue pets. That's finally creating an equilibrium between the supply of adoptable dogs and the demand for them.

Social and economic forces directly and indirectly influence animal populations. The 2007 conviction of NFL quarterback Michael Vick on dog fighting charges had the unintended consequence of increasing the popularity of pit bulls in America. Today, overbreeding of these dogs results in millions being killed in shelters each year. Public education, free spay/neuter clinics, and in some cases, breed-specific laws that mandate the sterilization of fighting dog breeds should be intensified to end this animal welfare crisis.

In the dairy industry, one of the principal causes of abuse is the free market system. When there is an oversupply of milk in the global market, prices drop to levels below that at which producers can make money. Dairy farmers often go out of business during these slack times, taking measures as desperate as suicide. As farmer Jon Slutsky pointed out, the problem with cows is that you can't turn them off as you can pizza ovens.

Volatility in the free market system has encouraged the growth of huge factory farms in the United States; some factory dairies now exceed 30,000 cows. But just across the border, in Canada, small family farms are still common. The reason is that Canada regulates its milk supply using a quota system. Farmers can produce only so much milk per quota, which helps keep supply and demand in balance.

Canadians pay more for dairy goods than Americans, but their farms provide healthier conditions for both cows and for dairy families. Similarly, the organic dairy industry in America operates in a unique market situation in which the equivalent of a milk cartel (the co-operative Organic Valley) can set prices in the market, ensuring that its members get a decent price.

In the livestock industry, an array of abuses stem from free-market systems that force producers to grow big or go home. With dairy cows, at least, Canada is demonstrating that better, more humane results are possible through supply management—a tactic the United States used to employ, but has abandoned. It's time these policies were reinstated.

But in the long run, we probably cannot sustain the world's cattle population. As one organic dairy producer pointed out to me, we're likely to reach an age when grandparents fondly recall the days when animal food products were common.

That scenario, however, may be avoided as lab-derived animal proteins become viable. Doubtless both time and marketing efforts will be required to overcome consumers' reluctance to embrace things like artificially grown lab meat and lab-cultured dairy. Early acceptance is most likely to come from Third World countries, where people cannot afford to be fussy about where their food comes from. But in time the environmental and humane benefits of not raising billions of livestock, and the benefit of dedicating greater portions of crops to human consumption, will make the transition to this brave new world of animal proteins inevitable.

As for the equine marketplace, we've seen how tax shelters in the 1980s led people to produce millions of unwanted horses. Arabians, whose values rocketed during the boom and plummeted during the bust, served as the example, but the investment craze of the Reagan years likewise fueled a boom and bust cycle in Quarter horses and racing Thoroughbreds. When tax shelters were abolished, people sold millions of unwanted horses for pennies on the dollar to slaughter horse buyers.

Distressingly, market forces that push people to overbreed horses continue today. The racing and performance horse industries, which focus on "futurity" events, create incentives for people to breed excessively. After the big futurity season ends, a few horses like cutting horse sire Metallic Cat emerge as big winners. These go on to sire hundreds and even thousands of offspring. But horses which fail to win big at crucial events can lose economic value literally overnight. Like Olympic figure skaters, these elite athletes' entire careers are made or broken during a few fleeting moments of performance.

An emphasis on young horses at these events results in rapid breeding cycles and fast turnover of animals. Because futurities reward only horses of a certain age, there is little incentive to keep older horses in competition. To absorb the glut of aging horses, performance horse associations need to continuously add new amateur riders and owners. Whenever the economy takes a downturn or marketing efforts simply fall short, surplus horses end up being carted off to slaughter.

Unfortunately, efforts to stop the horse slaughter industry in the United States haven't resulted in fewer such deaths. Instead, unwanted horses are now shipped to processing plants in Canada or Mexico, adding thousands of miles to their torturous final journeys.

On the opposite side of the coin are the "big winners." Metallic Cat, the leading sire of cutting horses, is just one example. Victory in most horse disciplines is followed by a mad rush of horse owners who want to breed their animals to the winner.

The "popular sire" effect is rampant in the animal-breeding world. When people choose to breed to only a small number of top animals, the result is a greatly diminished gene pool. Most people know that inbreeding of closely related animals, such as a son to his mother, can bring tragic consequences if genetic diseases come into play. But what many don't realize is that creating a restricted gene pool in which a popular sire appears on both sides of a pedigree is likewise a form of inbreeding.

This is exactly what happened in the Quarter horse world with Impressive, the glorious halter stallion, and Poco Bueno, the famous performance horse sire. Both of these popular studs carried defective genes known to cause severe and fatal diseases. Poco Bueno's name now shows up in the pedigree of nearly every cutting-bred Quarter horse, which has led to a widespread occurrence of a genetic skin disease for which there is no cure.

In the case of Impressive, at least, the predominant horse registry could have acted quickly to halt breeding and prevent the disease's spread. Instead, it chose to mask the problem and protect wealthy, powerful horse owners. Today, there are literally hundreds of thousands of horses carrying the gene for "Impressive syndrome."

A similar problem occurred in the Australian shepherd breed, causing my dog Kona to inherit genes for epilepsy from a particular line of show dogs. The same reluctance to name names allowed that disease to spread as well. Perhaps the people involved would have thought twice about further breeding, had they endured the heartbreak of seeing people's animals suffer. Then again, perhaps not. In many cases, money and ribbons speak more loudly than morals and conscience to people at the top of the show world.

Exacerbating the popular sire problem is modern breeding technology. Artificial insemination, shipped semen, embryo transfer, and other technologies allow people to breed animals in staggering numbers. The cutting horse stallion Metallic Cat, who potentially could sire thousands of offspring in his lifetime, and the bull Toystory, who did in fact sire close to half-a-million dairy cows in his, are just two examples. Reproduction in such numbers would have been impossible half a century ago before the Internet and overnight shipping revolutionized the animal breeding business.

It seems to me that, for their own good and that of the animals, breed associations should limit the number of offspring that any one sire can produce. I don't know what that number should be, but certainly reasonable limits need to be established. In the Thoroughbred world, this limit is maintained by requiring breeders to physically mate mares to stallions—a practice that naturally limits a sire's matings. Notably, the degree of inbreeding (called the "coefficient of inbreeding") in Thoroughbred racing horses has been shown to be much lower than that in performance-bred Quarter horses.

Despite all their problems, I am the last person to knock purebreds or the practices of purebred breeding. Purebred breeding aims to establish stable, predictable traits that are passed on to future generations. Inbreeding, outcrossing, selective mating of "the best to the best," culling, and selection for superior traits are all tools of the trade in developing animals to suit particular, specific needs.

Without purebred breeding, we would not have the Arabian horse whose exceptional qualities contributed to the dozens of horse breeds founded upon it. We would not have hard-working, highly intelligent border collies. We would not have adorable Corgis, or Siamese cats, or Jersey cows, or any number of other beguiling and special forms of domestic animals.

Nearly all of our dogs, horses, and cattle, as well as a percentage of our cats, are products of purebred parentage. Crossbred horses, cows, and so called "designer dogs" must start off with purebred parents. People who knock purebred animals may fail to grasp this reality.

Each purebred animal is a unique package of physical and behavioral traits that make it suited to some niche. In many cases, people have spent lifetimes or generations of lifetimes nurturing and developing the qualities in a breed that they deemed important. For such people, developing and maintaining a breed is a form of art.

Just as a sculptor's hands shape clay, human values shape animals. This has taken place for millennia, going back to our most ancient civilizations. When the values are good, the results tend to be, too. But when they are bad, the animals suffer.

More and more, breeders and consumers alike sense that our relationships with domestic animals needs to come back into balance. Setting things right requires that we set and maintain high ethical and moral standards for the breeding and care of the animals we keep.

A BAKER'S DOZEN
BEST PRACTICES OF
PET ANIMAL BREEDERS*

Breeders:

1. Take lifetime responsibility for the animals they breed.
2. Focus their efforts on one breed, or a small number of breeds.
3. Form relationships in the breeding community by participating in breed clubs and competitions, and seek to expand their expertise in breed history, health and inheritance.
4. Screen breeding stock for heritable diseases, remove affected animals from their breeding programs, and disclose health issues to buyers.
5. Are knowledgeable about genetics, understand the difficulties associated with inbreeding, and use this knowledge with deliberation when planning breedings.

* Adapted from the recommendations of the American Society for the Prevention of Cruelty to Animals.

6. Don't keep more animals than they can provide with high levels of care including quality nutrition, adequate space for natural movement and exercise, protection from extreme heat and cold, and regular veterinary care.
7. Limit the number of offspring that an individual produces.
8. Screen potential buyers to ensure quality lifelong homes for pets, or in the case of horses, to ensure that new owners possess the means and know-how to care for horses.
9. Remove from breeding programs aggressive individuals and individuals with behavioral issues that do not respond to training.
10. Base breeding frequency on the mother's age, health, and recuperative abilities. Avoid breeding extremely young or old animals.
11. Ensure babies are kept clean, warm, fed, receive quality veterinary care, and remain with the mother until weaned. Begin socialization of the pups and kittens at three weeks of age.
12. Ensure animals are weened before placement between the ages of eight and ten weeks.
13. Take back any animal of their breeding, at any time or for whatever reason.

ACKNOWLEDGMENTS

So many people helped with this book! I'd like to express my thanks to each and every one, and beg forgiveness in advance from those that I inadvertently left unmentioned.

I'd like to start with the people who supported this book from the beginning. Mary Fell Cheston, Wendy Ehringer, Martha Ehringer, Michael DeYoanna, Victoria Bayless, and Jarvis Owens. I truly appreciate the long conversations and encouragement when things were tough. Couldn't have done it without you!

To my editors Deb Drake and Louisa Peck for all their advice, expertise, and encouragement. Also, my agent Michelle Tessler of Tessler Literary Agency and the people at Pegasus Books.

Next, the people who dug deep and helped me finance my research and travels, especially Paul "Paul" Rosa, Patti Colbert, Carolyn Kyhl and the Ramon family.

Now, for all the scientists, journalists, animal raisers, and others who shared their insights. Merritt Clifton, your help was invaluable. Special thanks to the Hartnagle family, particularly Carol Ann, Jeanne Joy, Ernie and Elaine.

Also, Hampshire College professor Raymond Coppinger; Susan Crockford at the Royal British Columbia Museum; Ben Sacks and Kate Hurley at UC Davis; author Mark Derr; author Lorraine Chittock, Aussie breeder Laurie Thompson; C. A. Sharpe with the Australian Shepherd Health and Genetics Institute; Carol Barnes and Shari Bibich of WAIF; Tracy Reis of the American Humane Association; Elaine Ostrander of the National Human Genome Research Institute; and Jeff Borchardt of Daxton's Friends.

I can't forget to mention cat rescuers and Trap-Neuter-Release pioneers Becky Robinson, Louise Holton, and Staci LeBaron, whose activism has saved the lives of hundreds of thousands of cats, and emeritus cat show judge Pat Harding of T.I.C.A.

In the cattle world, special thanks to Bob Bansen at Emerald Veil Jerseys; Jake Takiff and Alexis Mahon, Eagle Canyon Farm; and Jon Slutsky, Susan Moore, and their daughter Raisa Slutsky at La Luna Dairy. Also, Bill Keating of the Western Dairy Association; John Beckman of Applenotch Farm; Ty Lawrence at WTAMU; veterinarian Gregg Veneklassan; Mark Johnston, researcher and editor of *Genetics*; and Mark Kastel of the Cornucopia Institute.

Horse people helped me a great deal. I'd like to especially thank John Growney for putting me up. Also, Diane Bowers of the NRHA. Plus, all the people who lent their assistance to me over the years, including: former *Western Horseman* editorial staff Patricia Close, Gary Vorhes, Fran Smith, Randy Witte, and Juli Thorson; NRHA Reiner staff Carol Trimmer, Bucky Harris, Jana Thomason and the late Cathy Swan. And all the people at the publications I've worked with over the years.

Finally, to all the people who funded the IndieGogo.com fundraising campaign: Wayne Wooden, Susan "Skye" Webber, Mary Beth Thorgren, Soraya Van Asten, Jennifer Nice, Claire Maeder, Jill Maeder, Griggs Irving, Heidi Gildersleeve, Gail Riley, Peter Heller, the McPeters family, Deirdre Sullivan, Gina Morgan, Billy Jack and Anne Barrett, Erryn Edrington, Nicole Rosa, Dave and Marilyn Schultz, Andrew Roth, Kathi Burns, Matt Derby, Suzanne Healy, Kirk Francis, Dave Arvizu, Angela Hornbrook, Anita and Bob Houk, Carl and Heather Schwarm, Jean Klein, Paul Husband, Simone Windeler, Leslie Lawrence, Cliff Sanderlin, Steve and Francesca Rother, Jean Wells, William Fisher, Leslie Wolken, Pam Collins Pruitt, Lori Passaro, Merritt Atwood, Toni Hamill, and Jan Bell.

INDEX